D1802396

Against Wilson and War, 1914-1917

AGAINST WILSON AND WAR, 1914-1917

Ernest A. McKay

KRIEGER PUBLISHING COMPANY
MALABAR, FLORIDA
1996

Original Edition 1996

Printed and Published by
**KRIEGER PUBLISHING COMPANY
KRIEGER DRIVE
MALABAR, FLORIDA 32950**

Copyright © 1996 by Krieger Publishing Company, Inc.

All rights reserved. No part of this book may be reproduced in any form or by any means, electronic or mechanical, including information storage and retrieval systems without permission in writing from the publisher.
No liability is assumed with respect to the use of the information contained herein.
Printed in the United States of America.

FROM A DECLARATION OF PRINCIPLES JOINTLY ADOPTED BY A COMMITTEE OF THE AMERICAN BAR ASSOCIATION AND A COMMITTEE OF PUBLISHERS:
This publication is designed to provide accurate and authoritative information in regard to the subject matter covered. It is sold with the understanding that the publisher is not engaged in rendering legal, accounting, or other professional service. If legal advice or other expert assistance is required, the services of a competent professional person should be sought.

Library of Congress Cataloging-In-Publication Data

McKay, Ernest A.
    Against Wilson and war, 1914–1917/Ernest A. McKay.—Original ed.
       p.   cm.
    Includes bibliographical references and index.
    ISBN 0-89464-964-7 (cloth : alk. paper)
    ISBN 1-57524-000-9 (paperback : alk. paper)
    1. World War, 1914–1918—Public opinion.   2. United States—Politics and government—1901–1953.   3. United States—Foreign relations—20th century.   4. Public opinion—United States.
I. Title.
D619.M384   1996
940.3'162'092273—dc20
                                                  95-31584
                                                     CIP

10   9   8   7   6   5   4   3   2

For Ellen

Contents

Acknowledgments	vii
1. Introduction	1
2. The Secretary of State	5
3. The Chairman	25
4. The Publisher	49
5. The War Hero	59
6. The Women at The Hague	69
7. The Tycoon	97
8. The Majority Leader	111
9. The Dissenter	129
10. The Socialist Congressman	143
11. The Progressive	157
12. Conclusion	177
Notes	185
Bibliography	199
Index	209

Acknowledgments

My special thanks are owed to the curators of manuscript collections listed in this book for their consistent courtesy and invaluable assistance. I also appreciate the keen interest of Kirk Shivell in reading parts of the manuscript. My wife, Ellen, a partner in the venture and a thoughtful critic, was always a source of encouragement.

Chapter 1

Introduction

Americans hate war, at least so they say. No subject has been denounced more bitterly on moral grounds and participated in with greater enthusiasm. When the possibility of war approaches, one set of truisms for peace is set aside, and another set of truisms for war takes its place. Usually it happens with remarkable rapidity because few things are more volatile than public opinion. The deep causes for combat, frequently misunderstood by professionals and amateurs alike, are always allied with a ready reservoir of appealing words that give the nation a sense of righteousness. Later, historians often join in the glorification of war as much as the most sensational journalists. It is easier and more exciting to write and read about the drama of war. When we won wars, or thought we did, the disease was even more prevalent. It seemed to be a matter of destiny.

Prevailing opinions have not always been right politically, economically, or morally. Since the pall cast by the Vietnam War, which was popular at the start, the United States has initiated three wars: Grenada, Panama, and Iraq. All were overwhelmingly approved even though most Americans lacked the slightest conception of the issues at stake and the gains are still debatable or nonexistent. Words about a new world order were a stale Wilsonian echo and instead of an arbiter, the United States became a battle-scarred participant. But the new world order is not doing too well, and the proper use of war as an instrument of American foreign policy remains a critical question.

More recently, the nation reached the brink of war in Haiti before last minute mediation, apparently opposed by high White House officials, avoided the needless expenditure of lives. Although the public sighed with relief that this particular invasion became bloodless, only time will tell whether or not the experience will give greater weight to the potential for mediation, a subject that runs through this book. We do know, however, that gratitude for President Carter's efforts was minimal, and his critics seemed to prefer military action to conflict resolution.

In a relatively simpler time, Woodrow Wilson, a peace-loving President who led America into a new age of internationalism, repeatedly said that the United States was a peace-loving nation. Looking backward, however, the country was involved in more than its share of wars that may have indicated a quality of impatience and bellicosity. The War of 1812 began when the cause of the war, the British orders in council, were rescinded and at the end, America merely returned to the status quo ante bellum. The Mexican War, admittedly a successful land grab, was not exactly a moral crusade, and school teachers once called it the stain on American history. The Civil War, the great American tragedy, might have been avoided if cooler heads had prevailed and eliminated romantic myths that still persist. The Spanish-American War, generally conceded to be the most unnecessary of all, was the culmination of flagrant propaganda, demagoguery, and innocence mixed with high, misguided purpose. As in the days that precede all wars, citizens were unable to separate truth from fiction, and jingoism took over. The "splendid little war" created an ominous empire with a war of suppression, the Philippine Insurrection, that cost many more lives than Cuba. There was, of course, a large segment of the population that opposed each of these wars even after they were declared. They were ignored by the same political leaders who made speeches about the influence of public opinion on foreign policy.

War is as ironic and complex as it is magnetic and mystifying and leads to endless analysis. The causes for war have been studied intensely and unremittingly. This book has a narrower scope. It is a series of personal and political sketches with a common thread, about men and women from various walks of life who opposed entry of the United States into World War I. It does not dwell on what might have happened in an ideal world. It is about people who in their own time saw danger in administration policies that could lead to war and were not afraid to express their views. Essentially, it is a book about judgment, foresight, and freedom of thought about controversial issues. Some of the people in the book were in positions of great responsibility. Others were only

Introduction

voices of the time and remain obscure. Because their backgrounds and political associations differed, they cannot be considered a homogeneous group. They were all, however, individuals with broad experience and cannot be classified as intellectual pacifists who oversimplified the forces at work. Their battle was over specifics as well as philosophy, and although the group is not all inclusive, it was representative of a wide variety of thought in the country. Many of their arguments centered around absolute neutrality, travel in war zones, preparedness, mediation, and arming merchant ships, but there were constitutional differences too. Most of them detested war while denying they were "pacifists," a loosely defined word commonly linked with woolly thinking. Also, when Wilson declared war, they supported the effort, albeit some more wholeheartedly than others.

The men and women selected came from the worlds of politics, industry, press, academia, church, and social work. None of them were German-Americans. All except the Socialist Congressman supported Woodrow Wilson in the 1916 Presidential election as the best hope for the country to remain neutral. Strangely, most of them were internationalists while they were condemned as isolationists. They strongly believed in trying to build an international organization of neutral nations to help end the war. Wilson opposed the idea and preferred to work single-handedly. Although such an organization would have produced complications, it was an odd way for a man to behave who dreamed of a league of nations to build a peaceful world.

All of these opponents of war had personal and political relations with Wilson. Generally they held him in high esteem for his obvious talents as a gifted leader. His eloquence as a speaker, gracefulness as a writer, and effectiveness as a progressive reformer in his first administration were sufficient to attract them to his side. Above all, they admired his dedication to the cause of peace. For some, the association with the President was friendly and intimate for a time. For others, the connection was more remote and chilly. Yet Wilson, often portrayed as a disillusioned President, was the eventual cause of their disillusionment. Each withstood intense pressure to uphold his or her contrary convictions in a country supposedly proud of freedom of speech. They suffered from ridicule, charges of treason, stupidity, and disdain. Each was called a traitor by the President, press, or public. None of them had magical answers for the crucial problems that faced the President, but at times they were remarkably reasonable and prescient. Right or wrong, they had a legitimate case to make and deserved to be heard with respect and consideration. If nothing else, they provided a rationale for the nation to remain at peace. Their views did not prevail, but their presence raises many questions. Did Wilson give them a fair hearing? Did they have the true national interest in mind? Were they less moral than the righteous interventionists? Were they so wrong? According to Jane Addams, Wilson said that as the head of a nation participating in the war he would have a seat at the peace table, but if he merely represented a neutral nation he could only "call through a crack in the door." Was war really a requisite at that time for influence in the world?

Today World War I is seen as a line of departure for the United States from a country that shied away from European entanglements to one heavily involved in overseas affairs. Since World War II foreign entanglements have become an accepted way of life, and as a result the first World War is looked upon more sympathetically now than in the disappointed twenties and thirties. But that is unfairly looking at the past as though it were the present. There is the possibility that a neutral United States in 1917 could have served humanity better as a model of a peaceful nation for others to follow. That was the overriding idea of the Founding Fathers. Wilson forsook that idea which he once devoutly held while it was persistently maintained by those in this book. Exhausted Europeans might have come to terms earlier without victory and saved hundreds of thousands of lives. A definite victory, as some in this book argued, only laid the groundwork for another war. They believed war led to war, not peace, and was not the basis for internationalism. Wilson is known for his famous "peace without victory" speech, but it came too late. Fascism, not democracy rose from the ashes, self-determination became an excuse for more killing, and the new world order that Wilson envisioned did not function. Nevertheless, Wilson is seen as a man of vision while his frustrated supporters are considered visionaries.

There are many similarities between the years 1914 to 1917 and today. Questions remain about war by the whim of one man, the executive versus the collective thought of the legislative branch. Also remaining are ethnic hatreds, limits on freedom of speech, special interests opposed to national interests, influence of favored nations, and the power of the media to mislead an ill-informed public. Because there appears to be a Wilsonian revival today, this may be a good time to look at some of the disenchanted who reluctantly differed with his views. Were they justified in opposing their President?

Chapter 2

The Secretary of State

William Jennings Bryan, a moralist and idealist, fares poorly in the annals of American history. He appears as the perennial Presidential candidate, a three time loser, a simple rustic ridiculed for his religious beliefs, and a man who campaigned for the wrong issues at the wrong time. He is probably best remembered today as the pitiful figure in the Scopes "monkey" trial who was savagely examined by the renowned Clarence Darrow. Woodrow Wilson, the austere eastern intellectual, was a sharp contrast to the friendly, outgoing westerner. Although Wilson, another moralist and idealist, remains an enigma to many students of history, he receives more respect as a President of profound thought who struggled desperately to keep America out of war and later led the country into a new age of internationalism.

It is one more irony of history that these two men, so different in makeup, were closely associated as the United States involvement in a European war increased. Their differences, personal and political, had been distinctly defined for years. Wilson, of the two, was the more severe judge of his fellow men and he had not hesitated to express his low opinion of Bryan. In 1896, Wilson had thought that Bryan's eloquent "cross of gold" speech at the Democratic National Convention was ridiculous and was alarmed that he might become President because of his "good voice and a few ringing sentences flying forth." Wilson, the former professor and president of Princeton believed Bryan had "no brains" and was horrified "that a man with his power of leadership should have no mental rudder." [1]

Wilson could not bring himself to vote for Bryan, the young Democratic idol in 1896, and as the years passed his criticism of the Great Commoner continued. In 1908, Wilson refused to attend a dinner with him in Philadelphia. He also withdrew from speaking at a Jefferson Day dinner at the National Democratic Club in New York City when he heard that Bryan was scheduled to speak. He said, "I have even wished at times that every fool could be also a knave instead of being, as they often are, people who possess attractive manners and excellent intentions. He is the most charming and lovable of men personally, but foolish and dangerous in his theoretical beliefs."[2] There was a "vacuity" about Bryan that disturbed Wilson.

As Wilson's Presidential ambitions waxed, however, his criticism of Bryan waned. He now saw Bryan as a man of extraordinary force, conviction, and sincerity, or at least he said so. Within a span of three years from 1908 to 1911, Wilson found Bryan "truly captivating." This new admiration seemed to have dawned on Wilson with his realization that no Democratic candidate with an eye on the White House could possibly succeed without the support of Bryan and his devoted followers. His change of heart certainly clashed with an earlier letter that he had written expressing the wish that something could be done "at once dignified and effective to knock Mr. Bryan once and for all into a cocked hat." When this letter became public knowledge in 1912, the embarrassed Wilson quickly moved to join hands with Bryan as "friends of our country and the friends of mankind." The idealistic Wilson was willing to stoop to conquer and Bryan, always less sensitive to criticism than Wilson, magnanimously accepted the apology.[3]

Bryan, no doubt with his own motives in mind, became a valuable ally who put his enormous energy to work for Wilson in both the 1912 convention and campaign. His powerful speaking contributed heavily to Wilson's eventual success against the split Republicans, Roosevelt and Taft. During a seven-week period the vigorous Nebraskan spoke about ten times a day. But even in the midst of the campaign, when Bryan's help was so important, Wilson had misgivings about his new friend. "If I am elected," he asked Albert Burleson, "what in the world am I going to do with W. J. Bryan?"[4] His lack of respect for Bryan had not really changed.

Wilson, the victor, reached the White House and captured the prize that had eluded Bryan. Yet Wilson's vote in the three-cornered race was less than Bryan had ever received in defeat. Although Bryan did not seek an appointment to office, Wilson owed him a huge debt and knew that it had to be paid. He thought about naming him ambassador to Great Britain as a way to acknowledge his help and exile him, but that was an insufficient gesture. Colonel House advised Wilson that it would be safer to keep Bryan in Washington rather than outside the administration where he might become a critic. A Cabinet post was essential, but where in the Cabinet was the question. Wilson feared that his relations with such a prima donna would eventually reach a politically disastrous breaking point. Mrs. Wilson considered a clash between the two men a foregone conclusion. Henry Watterson, a one-time Bryan supporter said, "Two dogs and one bone—the saying hath it—two cats and one mouse, two women and one house can never agree. As to Mr. Wilson and Mr. Bryan that appears to be the size of it."[5]

Although Bryan undoubtedly hoped for a role in the new administration, he graciously gave the President an opportunity to ignore him. In a front page editorial in his paper, *The Commoner*, he said that Cabinet positions should not be used to pay political debts and that the President needed to look to the future instead of the past. This was a generous gesture, but Bryan, the advocate of silver, had a sublimated desire to become Secretary of the Treasury. Understandably that was too risky for the new President. Instead, Wilson asked Bryan to become Secretary of State, the premier position in the Cabinet. It can only be explained as a pure political payoff. Wilson, holding Bryan's judgment in low regard thought this was the safer place. The world was relatively peaceful and Wilson's mind focused on his dreams for domestic reforms. This cynical decision went against widespread opinion that Bryan was unfit for the place. Nonetheless, Democrats acknowledged that this was a sensible move for the sake of party harmony. Anyway, Wilson intended to conduct foreign relations from the White House. Yet Wilson's experience with foreign policy was equally meager, and he had seen less of the world than his well-traveled Secretary of State. Bryan, an inveterate traveler, had made several trips to Europe and met many government leaders who received him with the greatest respect. He was also well acquainted with Latin America and in 1905, devoted a full year to a world tour.

Bryan, surprised and delighted by the invitation, brought up two subjects that Wilson might disapprove and affect a final decision. One was trivial and the other was at least noble in aim. Bryan, a devout prohibitionist, said that he would refuse to serve alcoholic beverages at state functions. The other was his deep interest in negotiating peace treaties based upon international mediation. Wilson had no objection to these high-minded thoughts. Later, Bryan's disapproval of alcoholic beverages at diplomatic affairs, literally a tempest in a teapot, brought frowns from Washington's smart set and provided another reason to ridicule a bucolic Bryan. A little less alcoholic consumption at diplomatic dinners was not a bad idea. But if legend is correct, Bryan was thwarted by dignitaries who took an extra nip or two before making their official appearance.

Upon assuming office Bryan surprised political seers by not making any effort to upstage the President. To the contrary, he served the President loyally and deferentially, and for a man who loved to talk so much he never leaked confidential information. Although an excess of courtesy between the two men may have hidden inner suspicions, they remained outwardly friendly, and there was never any political embarrassment. The Nebraskan also provided an extra benefit to Wilson by helping with controversial domestic legislation. Bryan was the political creator of more than one Congressman, and his influence still carried weight. None of this made a great Secretary of State. In some ways his efforts were detrimental, especially in promoting the spoils system in the State Department. In Latin America, neither Wilson nor Bryan added luster to their reputations. Perhaps Bryan's grandest effort was a number of peace treaties that placed their faith in conciliation. There was common sense in the fundamental idea that disputes should be investigated by an international commission during a one year "cooling off" period. They were no more effective than Taft's arbitration treaties, but similarly they sincerely sought ways to establish enduring peace.

Bryan's intense desire for peace brought him the most cutting criticism. Then and later, he was accused of being a "pacifist," a word that carried a derogatory connotation of fuzzy mindedness for most people. Even an excellent biographer, Louis Koenig, refers to him as a pacifist Secretary of State. *American Heritage*[6] magazine once asked leading diplomatic historians to rate the ten best and five worst Secretaries of State. Bryan was among the worst with particular reference to his "unbending pacifism." In the light of Thomas Jefferson and John Quincy Adams, Bryan remains a dim bulb.

Bryan detested war with all his might, but in reality he was not a pure pacifist. Although he may have been an Army misfit, he had, unlike Wilson, served in the Spanish-American War as commanding officer of the Third Nebraska Volunteer Regiment. As Secretary of State he reserved

The Secretary of State

the right to intervene in Nicaragua to preserve that country's independence, life, and property. In Haiti, Bryan reluctantly concluded that it might be necessary to use force to maintain effective supervision. In the tense Mexican situation, Bryan, despite personal misgivings, supported military action at Vera Cruz. When the United States entered World War I, Bryan, no longer Secretary of State, rallied around the flag. These were not the acts of a true pacifist.

From the start, Colonel Edward M. House, the President's intimate adviser, and Walter Hines Page, American Ambassador to the Court of Saint James, did their best to undercut Bryan. On July 2, 1914, House wrote in his diary that Prime Minister Asquith "cast the usual slur upon Mr. Bryan" and he heard similar comments in Germany and France. He did not believe they did justice to Bryan, but he decided that it was "absolutely useless to fight his battles." Popularity of the Secretary of State weighed heavily on the Colonel's mind. He feared that the "least gaucherie" could cause an incident. The following month, before hostilities had begun, House wrote to Wilson, "Please let me suggest that you do not let Mr. Bryan make any overtures to any of the powers involved. They look upon him as purely visionary and it would lessen the weight of your influence if you desired to use it yourself later." In the same letter, House, who had no special qualifications for engaging in foreign affairs, did not exhibit any talent for prevision when he expressed the feeling that war might not take place because "they are all very much afraid of one another."[7]

With the outbreak of war in Europe in 1914, both Wilson and Bryan desperately wanted to remain neutral. Yet it soon became clear that the two men had degrees of difference in their devotion to peace and neutrality. Wilson wanted to remain neutral as long as the Allies, especially Great Britain, were winning. Wilson made clear within his family circle that his sympathies were with the Allies. Still, both men received severe criticism for their strong desire to remain aloof from the war. When reports of German atrocities, true or false, reached the United States, the administration was silent for the sake of neutrality. The bombastic Nobel peace prize winner, Theodore Roosevelt, already prepared to go to war, said, "What can you expect when the Secretary of State lives in the clouds—no, not in the clouds, in a world of tenth-rate fiction."[8] Frustration led Roosevelt to bitterness and bitterness to perpetual rage. During these years, his many talents took a holiday as he became a man of wrath, quick to condemn anyone who did not see the world through his eyes.

Lord Bryce, British Ambassador to the United States from 1907 to 1913, once wrote, "He [Bryan] struck me, when I had dealings with him as being almost unable to think in the sense in which you and I would use that word. Vague ideas float through his mind but did not unite to form any system or crystallise into a definite practical proposition."[9] Bryce, of course, was hardly an objective observer. The records reveal that Bryan's correspondence with the President was literate and well reasoned for a man who supposedly felt rather than thought. Although eastern sophisticates might frown upon a comparison between Princeton and Illinois College, a perfectly respectable institution, critics overlooked the fact that Bryan graduated at the top of his class while Wilson, the scholar, was only forty-first in a class of a hundred and twenty-two.

Bryan's faith in peace and lack of embarrassment in proclaiming Christian principles was almost more than some Americans could stand. "Simplistic" is the popular word to describe such attitudes today. As sympathy for the Allies gathered momentum, Bryan's brand of neutrality became more unpopular, and much of the criticism against him became personal. Hardworking and determined to play a worthwhile role subordinate to the President, he was attacked as lazy and incompetent. Wilson's doubts about Bryan had probably never faded and by the end of 1914 there were indications that he wished his Secretary of State would resign. But, he never asked him to resign. Wilson considered Bryan's judgment faulty, particularly in thinking the best about everybody, a characteristic lacking in the President. Although Bryan had gone the extra mile to be nothing more than a lieutenant, he was not devoid of his own ideas, and apparently Wilson saw him as a rival in 1916. He told a friend, "If I run again for the Presidency, it will be only to keep Bryan out. I feel like a pig when I sit in my chair and look at him and think, I musn't let him be President: He would be ruinous to the country, ruinous to his own reputation."[10]

Despite the disappointments of both men in their efforts to find peace, it is frequently forgotten that they were in fundamental agreement on many critical questions during the early stages of the war. Initially, both agreed that loans by American bankers to nations at war were inconsistent with neutrality. Later, as it became less feasible economically for the United States to maintain that position, both relented. They also refused to restrict arms sales to belligerents because it would harm the spirit of neutrality by hurting Great Britain which produced fewer weapons than Germany. Wilson and Bryan supported the Declaration of London of 1909, an unratified code of maritime warfare, as a

The Secretary of State 11

basis of conduct for war. When the British refused to adopt the declaration that their foreign minister, Sir Edward Grey, had once strongly urged upon the international community, Wilson and Bryan gave way. Probably more important, neither the President nor Secretary of State protested the British mined war zone established in the North Sea.

By the end of August, after war had broken out, Bryan persistently urged that the President aggressively pursue mediation between the antagonists. Others close to the President claimed that they favored mediation too, but for them the time would come sometime in the vague future. Nevertheless, Wilson offered the services of the United States to Great Britain, France, Russia, Germany, and Austria-Hungary. Each nation replied, as Bryan informed Wilson, that it opposed the war and then blamed someone else. Undaunted, Bryan thought that these discouraging replies against war would be useful when "a way opens to present the matter again."[11] His natural optimism bolstered by deep religious faith was a never failing foundation for hope.

In the next few weeks, Bryan proposed that Wilson send a note to the belligerents reviewing the horrors of battle and emphasizing that they all denied responsibility for the war and desired peace. The Secretary of State wanted to focus attention on the thought that the continuance of war was just as undesirable as starting one. "Even if it fails," he concluded in his letter to Wilson, "and that cannot be known until the offer is made, you will have the consciousness of having made the attempt." At about the same time, however, House had forwarded a letter that he had received from Page to Wilson which said that the Germans were "fooling Bryan." The Ambassador, ever compliant to British wishes, reported that the Allies were determined to uproot German militarism, and he did not believe this was the time to begin mediation. He feared that "we shall not be wanted when a real chance for mediation" arrived. Bryan, more realistic, knew that there would never be a "right" time for mediation.[12]

Wilson also rejected a Bryan proposal to reduce U-boat attacks on Allied merchantmen. It was a suggestion for a modus vivendi whereby Allies would disarm their merchant ships and Germany, in return, would stop surprise attacks. Later in the war, Secretary of State Robert Lansing made the same proposal in an attempt to prevent the renewal of submarine warfare and Wilson then considered it "reasonable and thoroughly worth trying".[13]

By December 1914, four months of brutal combat had failed to produce success for one side or the other. Both sides had failed in their calculations and a decisive victory faded. The first battle of the Marne had caused hundreds of thousands of casualties and stunned the entire world. The Germans, crashing through Belgium, were fifteen miles from Paris before the Allies repulsed them. The German plan for a quick end to the war was finished, but they made an orderly retreat and entrenched themselves along the Aisne River in Belgium. Bryan saw the stalemate as an opportunity to approach the warring nations again and harped on the belligerents' responsibility for continuing the war. The appalling loss of life was in itself a reason for a truce. Since both sides had to admit failure, it seemed to be the moment to prevent more bloodshed. "Now when the cup of sorrow is overflowing and when new horrors are being added daily," he wrote to Wilson, "it would seem to be this nation's duty, as the leading exponent of Christianity and as the foremost advocate of world-wide peace, to approach the warring nations again and earnestly urge them to consent to a conference."[14]

Bryan also offered more mundane reasons for another peace effort. The prosperity of a war economy had not yet taken hold, and he argued that American self-interests justified mediation. Cotton growers had suffered a loss of not less than a hundred million dollars, and numerous industries were hurt by suspension of credits and market restrictions. Other neutral nations undergoing similar economic hardships looked to the United States to serve as a referee; nevertheless Bryan's proposal, considered too naive, led nowhere.

The Secretary of State may not have been as capricious as his critics claimed. He had also discussed the possibility of mediation which would include Latin American and European neutrals and was not alone in holding this view. Many prominent citizens regarded a joint effort practical. Jacob Schiff, an international financier not given to idle dreams, wrote to Bryan in the early days of the war that the United States should lead the way with other governments. But such suggestions were looked upon with suspicion. When Oscar Straus, another respected financier, showed an interest in mediation, he was called a "dupe" of the German Ambassador. One paper wrote that his interest in mediation had been prompted by German banking interests. Straus wrote Bryan, "You and I know they have nothing to do with this at all."[15]

When Bryan brought up the possibility of joint mediation, Wilson replied confidentially that he favored action by a single nation rather than several. He saw the South American countries as possible obstructionists, and European neutrals were linked to one belligerent or another. It was conceivable that the United States could be outvoted in

The Secretary of State 13

such a gathering. He may have been right, but this was the man who dreamed of a league of nations working for peace. If the problems were complex in the present, and they were, was there any reason to believe that a multinational league in the future would be more feasible? It was much easier to talk in generalities about internationalism in the future than to cope with specifics in the present.[16]

On February 11, 1915, James Gerard, American Ambassador to the German Imperial government, wrote to Bryan that he had heard from unofficial sources "that if a reasonable peace proposition were offered Germany very many men of influence would be inclined to use their efforts to induce Germany to accept the proposition." On February 19, Gerard cabled urgently, "Favorable moment passing."[17] But Wilson had no confidence in Gerard's sources. He had heard otherwise from House. Bryan knew that the longer the war went on, the greater the dangers for any policy of neutrality. The best way to stop a war was before it started; the next best time was before it reached a point of no return. While fanciful ideas of others circulated that an Allied victory would lead to eternal peace, he advised Wilson that a complete victory for either side would mean preparation for another war. On that score, Bryan's prescience has been confirmed. Much later, in February 1917, after Bryan left the administration, Wilson made a major speech calling for "peace without victory." It was too late. Too much death and destruction in the intervening years prevented enemies from thinking about an end to the war without conquest.

Wilson grew weary of Bryan's advice and according to Colonel House, the President "spoke with extreme regret of Mr. Bryan's unsuitability for the office of Secretary of State, but did not know what could be done. He intimated that it might be well to let him leave the Cabinet in the event he desired to do so because of some policy with which he might disagree."[18] Wilson did not have any intention of placing the least confidence in Bryan, but he shut out the thought of asking for his resignation. The Secretary of State had simply become a bore to the President.

At the same time, House cynically noted in his diary that Bryan was quite useful because "everything that was unpopular was laid to Bryan." Later, Wilson said privately, not publicly, that it was unfair that Bryan "should be made the target for everything, and most of the time unjustly so."[19] Nevertheless, it was handy to have a scapegoat when the brickbats were thrown. Criticism of Bryan ran from the ridiculous to the sublime and included the complaint that the Secretary lacked dignity because he worked in his shirtsleeves and on hot, air-conditionless days, placed a handkerchief under his collar. A large part of the eastern press was continually distressed by him. At the end of 1914 (December 2), however, the *New York World*, no friend of Bryan's, wrote, "there has been no instance since he became Secretary of State in which his political influence, which the East used to regard as a menace to the Republic itself, has not been used to promote the common good." In contrast, the *New Republic* (March 13, 1915), a publication read by Wilson, commented, "For the extraordinary tasks of the great war, he is a disaster, a humiliation to himself and to the whole American people . . . Mr. Bryan is an unnecessary peril injected into a situation that is already perilous enough." Bryan's struggle for absolute neutrality did not even make him popular with German-Americans. During his tenure as Secretary of State he was frequently hissed at gatherings of friends of Germany. Some who saw Bryan work at closer range, however, held higher opinions of his ability. Secretary of Interior Franklin K. Lane, often called the most capable Cabinet member, regarded him as a "very much larger man and more competent man than the papers credited him with being." William C. Redfield, Secretary of Commerce, thought the way Bryan understood the common man was uncanny.[20]

Wilson looked more and more to Robert Lansing, Counselor in the State Department, for information and advice rather than consult his Secretary. Lansing was certain in his own mind that United States entry into the war was a necessity even though he realized his attitude was in advance of public opinion. As a precise lawyer, he recognized that British violations of law were indefensible. He knew that British interference with American maritime commerce by detention and seizure incensed many citizens. Still, he hated carrying on diplomatic relations with Germany. "How much more satisfying it would have been to have denounced the whole wicked business," he wrote, "to have sent Bernstorff [German Ambassador to the United States] home, and to have declared war against the government which was the instigator and defender of the barbarous outrages." He did not shrink from hostilities.[21]

Bryan, less interested in the legalisms of Lansing and less entranced by Wilson's assumption of British morality, did not see war as a way to reach peace. He wanted to stop the shooting regardless of terms because he did not see any vital American interest at stake. To him, peace not war, would make the United States the most powerful nation on earth. War only bred more war. Bryan was not an "appeaser," a damning word

The Secretary of State 15

since Chamberlain returned from Munich in 1938. The word had no meaning for the American diplomacy of 1914–15. Germany, despite its militarism, was a far different nation from the Germany of Hitler. Although the country was not a constitutional monarchy in the modern sense, the people took pride in their enlightened and progressive government. The United States had a long history of friendship and strong commercial ties with the country. Another word "isolationist" had little critical bearing upon Bryan's activities. Some able scholars have called him a "missionary isolationist" or an "idealistic isolationist," but deprive him of the more estimable classification of "internationalist." These fine distinctions lose meaning.

Historians are too apt to categorize public figures with restrictive labels. Bryan, aware of the world around him, was a practicing politician, sometimes inconsistent and controlled by events, who did not think war was the road to international leadership. After the war it would be the more practical Bryan, not Wilson, who supported a compromise ratification of the Treaty of Versailles so that the United States could take its place in the new world for the sake of peace.

Bryan was neither anti-British nor pro-German. He was anti-war and hoped that he might soon leave on a peace mission to Europe and serve as a truly neutral mediator. Instead, he learned that Colonel House, not he, would leave on such a mission. Bryan, a veteran of three Presidential campaigns was a thick-skinned politician well versed in the pitfalls of politics. He had been introduced to intrigue, disloyalty, and other unpleasant aspects of high stakes political behavior long ago. Nevertheless, he was deeply hurt by Wilson's lack of confidence in him and realized that his influence at the White House was barely existent. He did not even hear of the colonel's trip from the President. The news came to him from House. When Wilson learned from House of Bryan's reaction, which was actually that of a gentleman, the President petulantly said that the Secretary of State would prefer not to have peace if he could not bring it about himself. Then he quickly corrected himself by saying that Bryan was obsessed with the idea of mediation.

If Bryan had visited Europe he might have horrified the British, and possibly the Germans, but there was little likelihood that he would have been enchanted by British charms or intimidated by Prussian arrogance. And he would have commanded attention, mocked or not, because after all he was a major political phenomenon unafraid to give offense in the cause of peace. His enormous energy, ego, and underrated shrewdness could have reflected a realism that was lacking in Colonel

House's tiptoeing among the great and near great. The mission may have been doomed before it began, but Wilson's selection of an emissary raises the question whether someone devoted to absolute neutrality might not have been more effective than one well known to the Germans to be committed to the Allied cause. The President, according to House, was instructed to tell Sir Edward Grey, the Foreign Minister, "his [the President's] entire mind so he would know what his intentions were about everything." He also wanted House to mention his relations with Bryan and the conduct of the State Department under him. "'Let him know,' House quoted Wilson, 'that while you are abroad I expect to act directly through you and to eliminate all intermediaries.'" House had already concluded that it was not a good idea to achieve peace until Germany was sufficiently beaten. This was in accord with the opinion of Sir Cecil Spring-Rice, the British Ambassador to the United States.[22]

The break between the President and the Secretary of State in their approach to war, if not in their mutual courtesy, was increasingly obvious. While Wilson ignored Bryan, he sent the Secretary of State a birthday note in March expressing his value as a "friend and counselor" and the "very strong affection for you growing in my heart." Nothing could have been more false.[23]

A few days later, on March 28, 1915, a German U-boat prowling in Saint George's Channel off the Welch coast sank a small British passenger ship, the *Falaba*, headed for West Africa from Liverpool. On board was Leon Thrasher, an American mining engineer returning to work in the Gold Coast, who was killed. Although the event presented grave questions about international law, experts in the State Department disagreed about the proper response. Lansing was ready to take steps that could lead to war by demanding that Germany disavow the act, punish the U-boat commander, and pay damages. Wilson, inclined to agree, took a lofty stance in the "interests of mankind" and was intent upon upholding the legal right of Americans to travel on belligerent ships.

Bryan looked upon the affair differently. As a lawyer, he believed the doctrine of contributory negligence had a bearing upon the case. It did not seem to him that the actions of one man, serving his own interests, without consulting the government, should involve the entire nation when he knew the danger. Bryan advised Wilson that the government had the duty to prevent citizens from taking unnecessary risks. If a riot occurred, officials ordered citizens to remain home to avoid an incident. Any government, he argued, was justified in keeping citizens away from danger even if they ordinarily had the right to go on the streets. Bryan felt citizens had a moral duty to keep out of harm's way at a critical time so that the government would not have to accept the responsibility for their safety. It was obvious that no one on board the U-boat knew that an American was on board the *Falaba*. There was no question of a deliberate attack against the United States. The main question for Bryan was whether the submarine, a new and horrifying form of warfare which is now callously accepted, acted lawfully in sinking the ship and took every precaution to save Thrasher's life. His aim was to reduce the strain by making it a legal matter to resolve between two nations.

Bryan saw additional difficulties if the United States condemned the Thrasher incident as inhuman. No protest had been made against the British for blocking food shipments to the continent for noncombatants. He reminded the President that the United States had proposed the British stop their food blockade if the Germans abandoned their torpedo attacks on merchant ships. Germany, sincerely or not, had appeared willing to negotiate while the British refused to consider the plan. Bryan also noted that the United States had not challenged Britain's deceptive use of American flags on its ships. "If we allow the use of our flag," he wrote Wilson, "how can we complain if in the confusion one of our boats is sunk by mistake?" The sale of arms and ammunition to Great Britain also gave Germany sound arguments that the United States favored the Allies. It was time to "cease export of arms."[24] Wilson seemed somewhat impressed by Bryan's opinion, but the *Falaba* was soon overshadowed by graver events and no note was sent. The British jurist, Lord Devlin, wrote about the *Falaba* incident in his book, *Too Proud to Fight*. It appeared to him that there was no lack of incisiveness in Bryan's argument when his reason and feelings went together.

In an attempt to avoid a crisis, Bryan repeated his threadbare appeal for mediation. Almost nine months had passed, and the war was a draw after the sacrifice of millions of men. "Surely the most sanguinary ought to be satisfied with the slaughter." The loss of one man was nothing compared with tens of thousands dying daily in a "causeless war." He did not know what the result of such an appeal would be, but he wrote the President, "if it is *right* there ought not to be lacking the faith to try. You have such an opportunity as has not come to any man before."[25] Bryan was willing to fail in the attempt to mediate. Wilson was not.

Wilson courteously replied to Bryan that his letter had made a deep impression upon him. "I wish I could see it as you do. But in view of what House writes me I cannot . . . To insist [on mediation] now would be futile and would probably be offensive." The question was whether Bryan's obsession was magnificent or foolish, workable or unworkable, attainable or unattainable. No one would ever know. Bryan, frustrated once more, could not understand Wilson's reluctance to act. He said to his wife, "Mary, what does the President mean! Why can't he see that by keeping open the way for mediation and arbitration, he has the opportunity to do the greatest work man can do! I cannot understand his attitude." Not long after, Bryan wrote to the newspaperman David Lawrence, "the Lord does not require us to win—He simply requests us to do our duty as we see it. We can never tell in advance what we can do—we can only tell by trying. If after trying we find we have failed we have nothing to regret."[26]

Oddly, House had consistently opposed Bryan's efforts for mediation. But during the summer of 1915, looking backward, he wrote to Page, "I believe if we could have started peace parleys in Nov. [1914] we could have forced . . . a peace which would eliminate militarism on land and sea."[27]

Colonel House, involved in his European mission, informed Sir Edward Grey that he had no intention of pushing the question of peace. The time was not ripe. He did not believe it could be brought about "in any event" before the middle of May or first of June. This viewpoint delighted Page who had no interest in mediation. Page's illusion, more unrealistic than Bryan's, was that the United States could enter the war and achieve peace without a large loss of American lives. Apparently not too concerned with more slaughter, he believed the Allies should try their new armies in the spring. In the latter part of March, House also indicated to the German Foreign Office that the time for peace had not yet arrived. Such talk did not have the ring of a peace emissary.[28]

On Friday, May 7, 1915, a horrendous event aroused all Americans. It was the torpedoing of the British passenger ship *Lusitania* off the Irish coast by a German U-boat with the loss, according to official British figures, of 124 Americans. Although the German Embassy had taken ads in American newspapers to warn against travel on Allied ships in a war zone, this tragedy was a turning point in American public opinion. Theodore Roosevelt wanted to go to war immediately. Wilson, initially, remained inaccessible. He needed time for reflection. The news arrived about two o'clock in the afternoon. Earlier in the day he had held a Cabinet meeting. Now he cancelled his date to play golf.

Bryan was having lunch at the Shoreham Hotel with some Cabinet members. His colleagues may have disagreed with his policies, but they

The Secretary of State

always enjoyed the pleasure of his company. A reporter came over to their table and told them the sad news. He rushed to the State Department to see if there were any official cables and waited in expectation of a call from the White House. No call came. Later in the day, Wilson took an automobile ride. In the evening the President learned the large number of lives lost and was so upset he went out for a brief walk in the rain. The next day, Saturday, no call came for Bryan. Wilson played golf and took a longer automobile ride. Bryan, talking to his wife, wondered if the *Lusitania* had carried munitions. "If she did carry them," he said, "it puts a different light on the whole matter."[29]

On Sunday, Bryan sent Wilson a clipping from the Washington *Post*, a newspaper that the President did not read. It was an editorial suggesting that ships carrying contraband should be prohibited from sailing with passengers. "This idea occurred to me last night (it was *not*, of course, communicated to the Post)," he wrote the President, "that some such rule should be adopted. Germany has a right to prevent contraband going to the Allies and a ship carrying contraband should not rely upon passengers to protect her from attack—it would be like putting women and children in front of an army." He also sent another clipping about the ship's manifest which showed 4,200 cases of cartridges and ammunition. He added, "I learned from Mr. Lansing last night that the *Lusitania* carried ammunition."[30]

On Monday, there was still no call from the President to his Secretary of State, but Bryan sent Wilson a note with three memorandums by Lansing which opposed his thought about warning Americans not to travel on belligerent ships with contraband and advised sending a strong protest to Germany. Bryan did not see Wilson until a regular Cabinet meeting on Tuesday at 11:00 A.M. During the conference, Bryan heard Wilson read a rough draft of a diplomatic note to Germany for the first time. It must have occurred to Bryan that if Wilson had followed his advice and previously issued a stern warning against American travel on belligerent ships, the lives would not have been lost. Bryan, uncharacteristically quiet, privately said, "This is no time to rock the boat." Some newspaper editorials were inflammatory, others were restrained, but the American people were morally outraged. Still, most Americans had no desire to go to war.

During these tense and delicate days, House, in London, told British friends with an air of authority that he believed the United States would soon be in the war. He cabled Wilson from abroad, "If war follows, it will not be a new war, but an endeavor to end more speedily an old one.

Our intervention will save rather than increase the loss of life." America, he went on, had to decide whether it stood for "civilized or uncivilized warfare." Later, as he prepared to sail home, he wrote in his diary that he intended to persuade Wilson to conduct a vigorous war to establish a new world order of peace and security. That appeared to be the end result of his peace mission. The lure of a civilized war had ensnared him.[31]

The preparation of a proper statement to Germany about the *Lusitania* presented a multitude of problems. Varying shades of opinion, all well intended, complicated the uncertain task. In this high pressure atmosphere, Bryan held to his vision of absolute neutrality and wanted to deal evenhandedly with all belligerents. At first it seemed as though the President was ready with a Bryan statement proposing arbitration, but the note eventually sent to Germany took a different tone. It stated the essential right of American citizens to sail on the high seas and demanded a repudiation of the act and reparations. Bryan signed the note, but told Wilson he did so with a heavy heart. He had wanted to send simultaneous notes to the British and Germans. Great Britain had used Americans, including women and children, to gain immunity for its ships carrying munitions without even a convoy, misused the American flag, and interfered with neutral trade. He wanted frankness with both sides. The President's note would be popular, but he saw "peril in this fact." He wanted the final accounting postponed until after the war. This was in keeping with his peace treaties which gave a year's time for investigation, and Germany had endorsed that principle. He thought the term "strict accountability" would be construed by some papers as a call for immediate settlement and feared the jingoes would assume the note meant war. The Allies would applaud the American demand and make Germany increasingly bitter. There was nothing strident in Bryan's tone to Wilson. He admitted that he might be mistaken and prayed that Wilson's judgment would be vindicated by events.[32]

The stern German reply to the American note underlined that the *Lusitania* was not "an ordinary unarmed merchant vessel." The note resolved nothing, but Bryan pleaded for time in the heated situation. Wilson did not agree. He said the German Foreign Office "always misses the essential point involved, that England's violation of neutral rights is different from Germany's violation of the rights of humanity." Wilson, taking the high ground, locked himself into principle and became more rigid and uncompromising. Bryan, regarded as more visionary, was ready to reach a practical solution for the sake of peace.[33]

The Secretary of State became a loner in the White House and Cabinet circles with a policy of his own that few appreciated. He was not insensitive to the politically unfriendly surroundings and the strain became almost unbearable. When the draft of a reply to the German note came up in a Cabinet meeting on June 1, Bryan suggested a strong note at the same time to Great Britain protesting its interference with United States trade. Several members opposed his proposition and he said, quite correctly, that his colleagues were pro-Ally. The President rebuked him for his remark as unfair. Later, Bryan asked "if we thought we ought to ask the British authorities what we might do" which was another impertinence not appreciated by Wilson. After the ordeal of long Cabinet meetings, Bryan returned home completely drained with bloodshot eyes. At night he lay awake in bed for hours at a time mulling over problems and occasionally jotting down a note or two.[34]

On June 4, when the draft of the second note to Germany was near completion, Bryan decided to refuse to sign it and then resign. His last futile effort to persuade the President was June 5 when he continued to seek arbitration, prevent passenger ships carrying munitions, and favor a note of protest to Great Britain. Although Wilson disagreed with Bryan he replied, "I am inclined to think that we ought to take steps, as you suggest, to prevent our citizens from travelling on ships carrying munitions of war, and I shall seek to find the legal way to do it. I fear that, whatever it may be best to do about that, it is clearly impossible to act before the new note goes to Germany." This was the nearest he ever came to restricting American travel.[35]

Bryan knew that he would be condemned in many quarters for his resignation, but he saw no alternative. He told Wilson of his intentions and the President reacted with surprise. Wilson sent his son-in-law, Secretary of the Treasury William McAdoo, to let Bryan know that he preferred to have him remain in office. If Bryan left, there were possible political losses for Wilson, and Bryan's usefulness in the next Presidential election could not be forgotten. McAdoo had some regard for Bryan's shrewdness, and told him that his resignation would lead to his political oblivion. Bryan agreed without any sense of martyrdom and answered, "Whether it does or not, I must do my duty according to my conscience."[36]

In a final effort to keep Bryan in the Cabinet, the Secretary of State and McAdoo met with Wilson in the White House. Bryan did not change his mind, and in a frank moment said to Wilson, "Colonel

House has been Secretary of State, not I, and I have never had your full confidence."[37] His assessment was correct, but it was not one the President had wanted to face. Nevertheless, the two men parted company with their usual courtesy and wished each other well. Despite their differences, Bryan departed as a man who had served the President loyally and always made certain that he was fully informed of events. That loyalty and access to information had not been reciprocated by the President who repeatedly went behind Bryan's back to House and Lansing.

When Bryan left office he received a gold watch as a gift from all members of the State Department from messenger boys to Assistant Secretary of State. Each had contributed twenty-five cents. At the presentation, William Phillips, Third Assistant Secretary of State, noticed that many in the department could not hold back the tears. The Bryan personality still affected people. No other Secretary had received such a present, and it became a treasured possession which Bryan wore the rest of his life and showed off with pride. Perhaps it meant so much to him because he had been belittled so often as Secretary of State.

Wilson's courtesy to Bryan hid bitter inner feelings which he revealed to Edith Bolling Galt, a widow with whom he was carrying on a courtship. His wife had died the previous August. Each day he devoted hours to writing to Mrs. Galt. On June 9, he wrote to "My precious Darling" with an air of wounded nobility. "It is always painful to feel that any thinking man of disinterested motive, who has been your comrade and confidant, has turned away from you and set his hand against you; and it is hard to be fair and not think that the motive is something sinister."[38] Wilson's words were either self-deception or an affected attempt to seek pity. Three days later, he wrote to her that the desertion was an experience that brought them closer together by their intimate sympathy.

When Wilson called at Bryan's home after the resignation in a calculated gesture presumed to be friendly, he hoped Mrs. Galt would not chide him. Although he felt uneasy about the visit, he explained that it was a practical mission. He made it "on the best political advice!" Wilson recognized Bryan's value and did not want to antagonize his following. "If we treat him with perfect generosity (and in the midst of it all he is praising me, you know, very generously indeed) the least bit of reaction against us on the part of his friends (whose name is legion) is prevented and absolutely all his guns are spiked . . . No stranger man has lived, and his naiveté takes my breath away."

Mrs. Galt, staunchly supporting Wilson, was incensed by Bryan's behavior. She called him "that awful Deserter" and when she learned about Wilson's courtesy call she wrote, "And I will be glad when he expires from an overdose of peace or grape juice and I never hear of him again." During the summer she wrote to "My precious One," and referred to Bryan as "that *Traitor.*" If it were left to her, she would "put him where the world would never be troubled with him or his 'peace' sheep clothing again." The President was not taken back by her harsh words. Instead, he responded, "For he is a traitor though I can say so, as yet, only to you."

Bryan had his defenders, mainly from small town newspapers and mail from citizens. One wrote that his father said, "'I've abused him [Bryan] for 20 years, but I'll vote for him if I get a chance now!'"[39] But the criticism of his resignation was far more widespread. The *New York World* of June 12, 1915 made the common charge among eastern newspapers that he had betrayed Wilson. Henry Watterson wrote in the *Louisville Courier Journal* of June 12, 1915 that "Men have been shot and beheaded, even hanged, drawn and quartered, for treason less heinous." Other comments were equally extreme. Ironically, the eastern newspapers that attacked him as a traitor for leaving his post had repeatedly urged him to resign in the past. Interpretations of his resignation covered a broad range of opinion and illustrated how little the press and public understood their political leaders. Cynics saw Bryan's resignation as his first step in another campaign for President. Others were sure that the reelection of Wilson was improbable. The most common complaint against Bryan was his disloyalty. It raises the question whether or not a Cabinet member should sacrifice his principles and remain in office as a matter of loyalty to his President.

Privately, Lansing and House were certain that Bryan's policies had endangered the peace of the country. Ambassador Page reached new heights of scorn when he wrote, "Of course he's a traitor; he always had a yellow streak, the yellow streak of a sheer fool." Senator Albert Fall, an infamous player in the Teapot Dome scandal a few years in the future, expressed relief that Bryan's departure would not harm the honor and dignity of the nation. The Senator from New Mexico would soon do more damage to honor and dignity than William Jennings Bryan. Secretary of the Navy Josephus Daniels and his young Assistant Secretary Franklin Roosevelt were among those who made the more mild comment that Bryan had lost a chance to keep America out of war by resigning. Such talk, probably politically motivated to gloss over an awkward situation, was sheer absurdity. Bryan had been blocked at every turn and realized that any influence he might have would come from altering public opinion.[40]

One distinguished historian, Ernest R. May, wrote in the post-World War II era that Bryan's policy would have led to unrestricted U-boat warfare and a series of humiliations for the United States. He claimed that by 1916 the country would have elected a chauvinist to the White House.[41] But, that is all speculation. It might be imagined just as easily that Bryan's policy would have kept the nation out of war by restraining U-boat warfare, developing an effective organization of neutral nations, and remaining a model peaceful nation sufficiently strong to negotiate terms among weary enemies. In the doing, the Allies might have averted further tragedy by saving hundreds of thousands of lives and ending the war in a healthier economic position. Germany might have prevented the rise of Hitler. Without a victor in World War I, another war might have been prevented as Bryan had predicted. Both speculations are flights of fancy. They did not happen. The magnetic attraction of war proved irresistible and the willingness to sacrifice for war was stronger than any desire to sacrifice for peace. Bryan's goals may have been unattainable, but he fought a frame of mind that precluded the possibility of attainment.

When Bryan left office he spoke out for absolute neutrality and mediation and against Wilson's preparedness program. During the 1916 Presidential campaign, however, he put aside his grievances and fought for the reelection of Wilson as the best hope for peace. But his dream that America would become the moral arbiter of the world's disputes vanished.

Chapter 3

The Chairman

William Joel Stone had a way of keeping his thoughts to himself and mystifying opponents who wondered what was going on behind those gray, inscrutable eyes. Sometimes in conference he gave an impression of sleepy indifference and then, with the gift of a true negotiator, came to life with a terse, decisive comment. Envious rivals had tagged him with the nickname, "Gumshoe Bill." In time the title became a proud distinction for his skill, discretion, and quiet way of working. Many Missourians believed that no one had made a deeper impression upon the political life of the state since the renowned Thomas Hart Benton. Nevertheless, Stone, a Democrat of Jefferson County, Missouri, is not a name known to most Americans today. Volumes have been written about President Wilson and his intimate adviser, Colonel Edward House, but Stone, despite his prominent position as chairman of the Senate Foreign Relations Committee during the World War I years, is rarely linked to the White House. At best he has become a passing reference in history books. Colonel House, a man of innumerable opinions, frequently without basis in fact, dismissed Stone as merely a machine politician. It was a questionable assessment for a man who had been generally regarded as a leading legislator and effective Governor.

Stone, born in Kentucky, graduated from the University of Missouri and began the practice of law shortly after the Civil War in the small town of Nevada, Vernon County, near the Kansas border. It was the land where bushwackers, jayhawkers, and desperadoes such as the Quantrell, James, and Younger boys had roamed only a few years before. Bitter memories and divided opinions about the war still scarred the minds of men and women, and Stone saw at first hand the tragic aftermath of a tragic war caused by powerful passions. By the early seventies, the tall, slim young man entered politics and became prosecuting attorney at the age of twenty-four. In the eighties he served three terms in the United States House of Representatives before becoming Governor.

Stone's political strength came from rural Missouri. He was active in the Farmer's Alliance, knew the magnetic appeal of populism in the nineties, and looked to the plain people for support. Win or lose, he said, he would not beg St. Louis for help. His four years as governor were a time of economic hardship and industrial unrest. Nonetheless, Stone ably managed the state funds, adeptly mediated fierce labor disputes, and became known as a moderate liberal. Upon retirement from office he practiced law in St. Louis, the city he so harshly criticized. Later, in 1903, he moved to Jefferson City and did not return to public life until his election to the United States Senate in 1908. Stone was neither a provincial midwesterner nor a blind isolationist. Personally, he and his charming, well-educated wife, Sarah Louise Winston, had insisted upon their children broadening their horizons by learning about other cultures. Their two daughters, Mabel and Mildred, attended the Ecole Normale in Paris, and later, Mabel studied music in England and Germany. Kimbrough, their son, a graduate of Harvard Law School, also traveled abroad. Economically, Stone recognized the importance of international trade and staunchly fought for low tariffs. "Isolationist," like most labels, failed to define the sensitivities and complexities in Stone's mind about America's place in the world.

During the hectic political year of 1912, Stone, an influential party leader in the nation as well as the state, first supported his fellow Missourian, Champ Clark, Speaker of the House of Representatives, for the Presidential nomination on the Democratic ticket. When that movement failed, he joined forces with Wilson. After forty-six ballots, Wilson won the nomination and Stone moved to make the vote unanimous. When Wilson arrived at the White House after his victory over the Republican Taft and Progressive Roosevelt, he soon realized that Stone was a team player who could be a useful ally. Despite their different backgrounds, the President went out of his way to cultivate a friendly personal and political relationship with the midwestern Senator. He recognized that Stone was a valuable legislator because fellow

Senators respected his calm, considerate manner, clear-headed thinking, and ability to act. During Stone's campaign for reelection to the Senate in 1914, Wilson wrote in a well publicized letter that "No member of the Senate has been a more consistent nor generous supporter of this administration than William J. Stone ... His action in all public matters since my inauguration has bound me to him by ties of admiration and friendship."[1] Once reelected, Stone's utility increased in his key role on the Foreign Relations Committee. For the past ten years he had taken a close interest in foreign affairs and was well versed in international law.

The outbreak of war in Europe strengthened the partnership between Wilson and Stone. They shared a common purpose and worked together harmoniously. Both men were determined to keep America out of war and Stone, as spokesman for the President in the Senate on foreign affairs, fought effectively for his policies. Wilson appreciated the cooperation and prided himself on having made Stone, once a party rival, into a friend. At the start of the war, the political problems were relatively simple. The American people had no interest in becoming involved in a foreign war. Soon, however, complications multiplied. Although Wilson had called for citizens to observe neutrality with strict integrity, ethnic and divisive partisan sympathies became more apparent. Stone, from a state with a substantial German heritage, reminded everyone that above all they were Americans. He appealed to them to keep their obligations in mind and bluntly spoke out against newspapers that fomented factional strife. The great hope for Wilson and Stone was that the United States would be the mediator to bring about peace.

As more complex and controversial legislation inevitably came before Congress, Stone reaffirmed his loyalty to Wilson. During an early battle over the ship purchase bill to establish maritime independence, he said, "There can be no middle ground. Either you are with the Administration or against it. The issue is clear cut."[2] Wilson's leadership was far preferable to him than that of Republican interventionists such as Theodore Roosevelt or Henry Cabot Lodge who seemed itching to go to war. In turn, the President congratulated Stone on his "sound and statesmanlike conception of how a party must act in order to govern a great country and really determine legislative policy."[3] Stone was always ready to express his opinion, but he showed no interest in infringing upon the President's conduct of foreign affairs. When news arrived in February 1915 that the captain of the *Lusitania* had raised the American flag on his ship as a ruse of war, he called at the White House to express his objection. Although he would have had no trouble passing a resolution of protest in Congress, he believed the incident should be properly handled by the executive branch.

Early in 1915, Stone wanted to explore the pros and cons of a bill proposed by Senator Hitchcock of Nebraska to prohibit the export of munitions to belligerents. He knew the President opposed the bill because it would presumably affect America's neutrality by favoring a well armed Germany and depriving the British. At best, Stone had mixed feelings about the bill, but there were many sides to consider, especially the views of other Senators. Some members of the Senate noticed that neutral nations in Europe and South America refused to sell war materials to either the Allies or Central Powers without jeopardizing their status. Stone's interest, as he made clear, was to strengthen the President's hand on this debatable question. As Stone studied the bill, he developed the opinion that it would be beneficial to go beyond the Hitchcock bill by empowering the President to control the export of munitions. If an occasion arose, it could be used to compel belligerents to respect the commercial rights of neutrals and reduce U-boat warfare. He was aware that it would be "a dangerous power to place in the hands of a rattle-head like Roosevelt or in the hands of any impulsive or indiscreet man."[4] Stone had confidence in Wilson's judgment and believed that a diplomatic warning by him would probably accomplish the desired result without resorting to drastic means. Stone expressed the hope that they could have a full discussion on the subject. Wilson, however, never found the time. Under the circumstances, Stone simply continued to reassure his colleagues that the difficult problems facing the country would be solved satisfactorily by the President. Although not sensed by fellow Senators at this time, the President called on Stone for support, not counsel.

In a moment of discouragement, Stone realized that Wilson did not favor absolute neutrality. He said to Senator Lodge, the ranking Republican member of the Foreign Relations Committee, "The President down at the bottom of his heart is for the English, just as you and Root are." Stone had many Republican friends in Congress, but Lodge was not among them. During their days in the House, Stone, a fluent speaker capable of cutting someone down to size, had once referred to Lodge as the "Oscar Wilde type" of statesman who "moves with an air of lugubrious pedantry and a solemn sense of weighty responsibility about the aisles of the Chamber." Now, as war tensions increased, Stone's disdain for Lodge deepened. He could not understand a Senator who seemed to him to be more concerned about the interests of another country than his own. Stone considered Lodge's lack of alarm over British ships flying American flags for their protection one manifestation of his attitude. Soon, Stone concluded that Lodge could not uphold the British more "if he were a member of the British House of Lords." He shuddered when he heard the conservative Lodge, never known for his compassion for the common man, talk of a war for democracy.[5]

The sinking of the *Lusitania* intensified the political atmosphere as jingoes called for immediate intervention and more moderate citizens feared the country was on the brink of war. Stone, obviously concerned when the news arrived, went to the White House to see the President, but was only turned away. Wilson was not seeing anyone that day and Stone was no more welcome than Bryan. This was a peculiar position for the President who had written a well known book, *Congressional Government*, that placed so much significance upon the leadership of the legislative branch.

Stone was always considerate of the time pressures upon the President, but he felt that he was working in the dark and frankly sought a better avenue of communication. By the end of 1915, he wrote to Wilson asking for a meeting to learn more specifics about his foreign policy. He wanted to know more about current circumstances so that he might form his own opinion. He had a more urgent reason, too. Senators, seriously concerned, sought him for information about recent developments because of his responsibility as committee chairman. The trouble was, he wrote Wilson, "I know nothing that is not generally known through the Press and am as much confused as those who come to see me." He wanted to help the President and hoped for "a good long talk with you as soon as possible"[6] to help clear the air in the troubled Senate. Two days later, Wilson saw Stone briefly, but the President was pressed for time. Wilson, occupied with his wedding plans and imminent marriage to Edith Bolling Galt, passed the Senator off to Secretary of State Robert Lansing and suggested that Stone and he get together at a later date.

Stone's conversation with Lansing did not go well. The Secretary of State wrote to Wilson about his concern for Stone's views. Lansing reported to Wilson that Stone believed the United States government was "bearing too strongly upon the Teutonic Allies" and was not "pressing" Great Britain sufficiently. When the Secretary argued that the loss of life by U-boats was more important than loss of property, Stone replied that German babies were dying because Great Britain blocked the shipment of condensed milk. Lansing thought the Senator's "considerable German constituency" influenced him, but that was not an opinion generally accepted by Stone's opponents.[7] Stone had never relied on German-American voters because they were traditionally Republicans. Although numerous in the state, they were not sufficient to sway an election and their stronghold was St. Louis where he was not held in high affection. Despite Lansing's imputation, Wilson remained confident that he could handle Stone. Both men wanted to stay out of war even though Wilson's neutrality, despite frequent and profound irritation with the British, depended upon the success of the Allied powers.

While Stone conscientiously continued to keep Congress "cool" so that it would not embarrass Wilson's diplomatic efforts, a thorny issue based upon American rights attracted increasing attention. It was the problem that had plagued Bryan: citizens sailing on armed belligerent ships susceptible to U-boat attacks. Recklessly risking American lives which could plunge the nation into war struck many members of Congress, including Stone, as foolhardy. He knew that Americans had a technical right to travel anywhere and the government was obliged to protect them. Nonetheless, he believed that Americans who sailed into war zones on belligerent ships were committing a crime against the government whose protection they sought. During February 1916, the debate grew sharper when the popular McLemore and Gore resolutions were offered concurrently in the House and Senate to warn Americans against traveling on passenger ships of nations at war.

Once again there were conflicting reports in Congress about where the administration stood. One morning, February 21, 1916, Stone visited Wilson at the White House and reiterated that he had no clear picture of his policy, particularly in relation to the McLemore and Gore resolutions. Again, he stated that he had a right to know so that he could carry out his responsibilities. Confronted by Stone, and concerned about congressional opposition, Wilson suggested that the Senator, John Kern, the Senate majority leader, and Hal D. Flood, chairman of the House Foreign Affairs Committee, meet with him the same day. In the afternoon, Stone returned to the White House with the other leaders. Someone asked what the President would do if a U-boat sank an armed belligerent ship with American passengers. Wilson answered that he would hold Germany strictly accountable. This was too much for Stone who banged his fist on the table and vehemently said, "Mr. President, would you draw a shutter over my eyes and my intellect? You have no right to ask me to follow such a course. It may mean war for my country."[8]

Despite this heated meeting, Stone tried to reassure the President that he would stand by him. "I mean to do so," he wrote Wilson two days later, "up to the last limit; and I want to talk with you and Secretary Lansing with utmost frankness—to confer with you and have your judgment and counsel—and I want to be kept advised as to the course of events, as it seems to me I am entitled to be." It was a reasonable request. Wilson, in reply, reassured Stone that he would do everything in his power to keep the United States out of war. He remained inflexible, however, about freedom of the seas including the right of American citizens to sail on armed belligerent ships. He could not consent to any abridgment of American rights. "The honour and self-respect of the nation is involved." Concessions, he feared, only led to further "unpalatable" concessions. Wilson ended his letter on a personal note, "If we should differ, we shall differ as friends, but where issues so momentous as these are involved we must, just because we are friends, speak our minds without reservation."[9]

For Stone there was more than a personal difference of opinion between two men. He was sensitive about constitutional questions that involved a declaration of war. In an effort to emphasize his anxiety, Stone sent Wilson excerpts from the works of Supreme Court Justice Story on the Constitution that related to the declaration and execution of war. Story served on the court for thirty-three years during the nineteenth century and had written that by severing diplomatic relations with a foreign nation, the President could force Congress to declare war. Justice Story added that Congress should be kept fully informed even given a voice in such decisions. That was what Stone wanted, close communications between the executive and legislative branches in a time of crisis. Stone's well-intended gesture drew a noncommittal reply from Wilson that ended, "Please take care of your health and be sure that nothing will ever mar our delightful relationship."[10] Stone told the President that the situation in Congress was "such as to excite a sense of deep concern in the minds of careful and thoughtful men."[11] Democratic members of the House Foreign Affairs Committee had unanimously approved the McLemore resolution and sought its fast passage. Speaker of the House Champ Clark estimated the favorable vote would be two to one. In the midst of such sentiment, Stone recognized the President's right to conduct foreign affairs and did not want Congress to hinder him. With a sense of loyalty to the President he again subordinated his own views and used his influence in both houses of Congress to defeat the similar McLemore and Gore measures. He was typical of many members of Congress who inherently believed they should defer to the President in a diplomatic crisis.

After tabling the resolutions, a relieved Wilson called Stone to the White House for a talk. The Senator had served the President well and in the glow of this legislative success, Wilson spoke effusively of his desire to stay out of war. The differences between the two men were now more widely known, but Stone continued to look upon the President as an advocate of peace. The veteran politician had his own ideas, but he was always ready to discuss, listen, and if possible, meet others half way. The press continued to believe that Stone would remain at the President's call. *Current Opinion* wrote, "Those who know him best say that Stone's policy is and will be whatever the Democratic administration policy may be . . . The Democratic party is his religion, first, last and all the time. As a matter of fact, positive leadership does not seem to be expected of him by the administration." The article also quoted Mark Sullivan who had written in *Collier's*, "On no foreign policy does he appear to be handicapped with commitments against the wishes or judgment of President Wilson."[12]

Although Wilson had resisted many suggestions for mediation, the subject was never far from his mind. Since the start of hostilities, he had hoped to save humanity as a peacemaker. It was his great goal, but the timing had seemed wrong so he resorted to waiting. By the end of 1915, however, the President believed the time had come to sound out the belligerents about the possibility for mediation on the basis of disarmament and a future league of nations. Wilson discussed his thoughts with House with whom he believed there was a complete meeting of the minds. As a result, House was delicately to approach the topic on his next visit to England and the continent. One hopeful sign, House told Wilson, was that Bernstorff, the German ambassador to the United States, had indicated the Foreign Office wanted to talk peace on the basis of disarmament.

House left the United States on December 28, 1915 and arrived in England on January 5, 1916. He soon broached the subject of a peace move with Grey, the Foreign Minister, and Balfour, head of the Admiralty, who seemed to him to be in a receptive mood. Later, House met with Lloyd George who spoke effusively of a peace founded on conciliation. Within the next few days, however, the conversations turned out to be idle talk that had quickly evaporated. A meeting with Prime Minister Asquith was equally unproductive.

Despite Bernstorff's optimistic report that the Foreign Office wanted to talk peace, House made no progress in Berlin. Bethmann-Hollweg, the Imperial Chancellor, expressed the usual desire for peace, but German demands were not acceptable to the Allies. Worse still, the Germans began a massive attack in February against the French fortresses at Verdun that commanded the Meuse Valley. Peace talks were inconsequential. The battle would rage for more than six months and cost about a half million lives. The resolve of the Germans to take the city was matched by the French resolve to hold on. It was at Verdun that the French cried, "They shall not pass."

The French had not shown any interest in a negotiated peace, and under the cloud of Verdun their resistance to the idea increased. While in Paris, House intentionally dropped any pretense by telling Jules Cambon, a former French Ambassador to Germany, that the United States would certainly enter the war on the Allied side before the end of the year. Cambon could not believe his ears and asked House to repeat his statement. The Ambassador wrote the remarks down and read them back. The Colonel apparently believed that he could build French confidence in the United States by making such a frank statement. Nevertheless, French officials, including Premier Briand, did not move an inch toward a negotiated peace. The military situation was too grim. House reported to Wilson that he had spoken to Cambon quite freely, but he did not present the full picture. He did write, however, that he had said the President could intervene by the end of the summer.

Colonel House continued to search for an avenue to a peace conference when he returned to London. He received no assistance from Ambassador Page who objected to the President's policies and considered attempts at mediation to be "moonshine." House looked upon his fellow American as nothing more than a hindrance. Grey appeared to be more sympathetic to mediation proposals, but in reality he did not take them seriously. British officials were skeptical about the American commitment to the Allies. House, however, did not leave London empty-handed. The result of his talks was the House-Grey Memorandum, agreed on February 22, 1916, which proposed a conference to end the war. It read:

Should the Allies accept this proposal, and should Germany refuse it, the United States would probably enter the war against Germany.

Colonel House expressed the opinion that, if such a conference met, it would secure peace on terms not unfavorable to the Allies, and if it failed to secure peace, the United States would leave the Conference as a belligerent on the side of the Allies, if Germany were unreasonable. . . . [13]

On March 7, the same day Wilson had a "frank talk" with Stone, he approved the secret House-Grey Memorandum with merely the insertion of "probably" before the words "leave the Conference as a belligerent." Wilson was pleased with the House mission. The President did not mention this subject to Senator Stone. The memorandum, which was close to a commitment to war, was in complete conflict with Wilson's assurances to keep Stone informed as well as his statements to the public that he would not go to war unless American interests were involved. What Stone, so concerned about constitutional war powers, would have done if he had known of this behavior can only be left to the imagination. In the end, nothing came of the memorandum in which Wilson had concurred except that it was more difficult for him to make any progress in gaining concessions from the Allies. Wilsonians, of course, defend the House-Grey Memorandum as a way the President hoped to stay out of the war.

On March 24, 1916, another critical event loaded with diplomatic significance arose. A German U-boat damaged an unarmed French Channel steamer, the *Sussex*. Four of twenty-five Americans on board were injured. Lansing, House, and Mrs. Wilson advised the President to break off relations with Germany or, at least, issue an ultimatum. Wilson, uncertain about taking such drastic action hesitated. Stone, as might be expected, telephoned the President and urged caution. Wilson agreed not to take any precipitous action without the approval of Congress. Stone also wrote to Lansing requesting a conference before "anything is done." He wanted to discuss the entire situation with both the Secretary and the President.

After struggling with the problem, Wilson was ready with an ultimatum to Germany denouncing submarine warfare. The statement warned the German government that if its inhumane acts did not stop, there would be no alternative except to break off diplomatic relations. Wilson, however, had avoided any conferences with congressional leaders in developing his ultimatum. Contrary to Stone's request, Wilson sent his note to Germany on the evening of April 16. The next morning, after the deed was done, the President called Stone, Flood, and some of their associates to the White House to be told of the action. This was hardly in accord with Wilson's promise to Stone and the Senator was not pleased. It was not the kind of mutual communication he had expected. At 1:00 P.M. on the same day, almost immediately after their meeting, Wilson appeared before a joint session of Congress to inform it of his decision.

Disturbed and offended by Wilson's treatment of him personally and as a Senator, Stone wrote to the President again to avoid any misunderstanding. Frankly and directly, he did not leave much doubt that he had been dealt with unfairly. "You did not ask my opinion about your message to Congress on your note to Germany before the message was written or note dispatched; but I am going to follow a different course with you with respect to my attitude." He did not want to discuss the situation as Senator and President. Instead, he wanted to talk as one sincere man to another, "just a plain, frank, heart-to-heart talk, so that each may fully understand the feeling and attitude of the other ... Out of this situation to which I refer has grown the only serious difference of opinion between us on great questions of national policy. I fear that we have not discussed this great question with that fullness and frankness that should have characterized either our personal or official relations to each other. . . . " Wilson responded politely and the two men conferred a few days later at the White House. Reassurances were given without any fundamental change in their views. The more expressions of mutual friendship were exchanged, the more they grew apart.[14]

Wilson's ultimatum, however, met with some success and there was a temporary release from tension. In May, the German government pledged it would follow rules of search and visit in and outside the war zones. Better still, the Germans appeared to keep their word and no perilous incident took place during the ensuing months. Meanwhile, British-American relations grew stormier. The British economic warfare created considerable animosity among Americans, including Wilson. Adding to the problems was the resentment in America against the British caused by their brutal behavior during the Irish rebellion.

Another Presidential election approached and Stone, the party man gave his wholehearted support to Wilson. "He Kept Us Out of War" was an ideal campaign slogan, and Stone did his best to convince dubious elements of the electorate that the President meant what he said and deserved their vote. Apparently at the behest of the Democratic campaign headquarters, Stone's electioneering extended beyond the borders of Missouri. He held several meetings with prominent German-Americans and Roman Catholic leaders and this met with no objection from Wilson. In New York, Stone met with Victor F. Ridder of New Yorker *Staats-Zeitung*, Henry Abeles of Germania Life Insurance Company, George Sylvester Viereck, editor of *Fatherland*, and Joseph Frey, president of the German-American Catholic Societies. The Senator's missionary work in Chicago included a meeting with the editor of *Amerika* to draft an appeal to German-Americans to avoid segregating themselves from other Americans. Stone kept the White House informed about his campaigning and expressed the hope that the President would speak up with a little more "punch" against British interference with mail, commerce, and freedom of the seas. Stone also wanted Joe Tumulty, the President's secretary, to "Take my voice to the President." He thought that Wilson had been mistreated by the press in the Midwest and wanted him to speak across the country. "Dignity is all right," he said, "but it will not in this instance compensate for defeat. Too much is at stake. The leader must lead."[15]

After the election, Stone still had no desire for Congress to interfere with the President's constitutional conduct of foreign affairs and continued to praise his efforts for peaceful mediation. He even gave a friendly nod to the idea of an international league for peace when another Senator charged that Wilson thought he was President of the world. Late in 1916, Stone supported Wilson's exertions for a negotiated peace and confidentially assisted him in arranging to address the Senate in January 1917. Wilson's masterful speech stressed the need for a community of power, not a balance of power. It would be based upon a "peace without victory" and the United States would participate with other nations to guarantee permanence. "Victory," he said, "would mean peace forced upon the loser, a victor's terms imposed upon the vanquished. It would be accepted in humiliation, under duress, at an intolerable sacrifice, and would leave a sting, a resentment, a bitter memory upon which terms of peace would rest not permanently, but only as quicksand. Only a peace between equals can last, only a peace the very principle of which is equality and a common participation in a common benefit."[16] They were noble words, but ironically Wilson had rejected Bryan's proposal to pursue peace without victory in 1914. Now, in 1917, too much blood had been spilled for enemies to listen to the idea of a war ending in a stalemate. Generally, however, the speech was well received in the United States. One exception was Wall Street. A *New York Times* headline read, "Stocks Fall on Peace Efforts." Although Stone supported Wilson, his approach would have been different. He wanted to join other neutral nations in an attempt to mediate a peace.

Soon a new crisis developed. In a desperate attempt to end the war, Germany designated war zones to block trade with the British Isles, France, and Italy. A warning went out that neutral ships would venture into the areas at their own risk and advised them to take other routes. A new U-boat campaign had begun. The *New York Times* banner headline on February 1, 1917 read, "Germany Begins Ruthless Sea Warfare; Draws Barred Zones Around Allies; Crisis Confronts the United States." The next day, the *Times* declared, "Wilson Silent, Washington Expects Break With Germany." When Wilson broke his silence, he called Stone back from St. Louis to fulfill a promise. He had told the Senator that he would not break diplomatic relations before advising him. It was a promise, according to Colonel House, that he regretted making. Now, he made the gesture of keeping his word. But this was a courtesy, not a conference. During the afternoon of February 2, Wilson met at the Capitol with Stone and they were later joined by a number of other Senators who happened to be in their offices at the time. The President discussed relations with Germany and most Senators favored an immediate break. They were weary of diplomatic notes, but the practice of breaking relations was usually a futile gesture that came at a time of strain when more, rather than less, communication was needed. Stone and J. Hamilton Lewis of Illinois were the only members who suggested postponement until Germany actually committed a hostile act in violation of the *Sussex* pledge. Stone also believed that this was a proper occasion to join with other neutral nations to advise belligerents that the United States would lead the way to arbitration.[17] If terms of an agreement were not accepted, all neutrals could then initiate a complete embargo. If one side accepted the terms, it would receive economic assistance. But Stone made no headway with Wilson who had no intention of trying united action and economic sanctions. The President's mind was made up.

The next day, the President informed the Congress of the break with Germany in a joint session, and the announcement met with enthusiastic acclaim. Stone was not one of the enthusiasts. He told Senator La Follette confidentially that he thought the President's decision was "a blunder worse than a crime."[18] Wilson's diplomatic action was within his constitutional rights, but he also sought a congressional resolution to endorse his decision. He wanted confirmation, not argument. Senator Gronna of North Dakota, a believer in a strong executive, was skeptical about Wilson's request. If the President was so interested in the approval of Congress, Gronna wondered why he had not called the joint session before, rather than after, he had advised the German government.

Stone introduced the resolution Wilson wanted much to the surprise and disappointment of Senator La Follette and others who believed it was unnecessary. Stone made the motion reluctantly with the discomforting support of Henry Cabot Lodge as an ally, but he felt obligated to the President as the foreign affairs floor leader. He may also have been trying to reaffirm the role of Congress in foreign policy. In doing so, however, he assured his fellow Senators with the utmost sincerity that in the future the President would submit important questions to Congress before acting upon them. Passage of the resolution was no problem because the outcome was obvious.

Debate still consumed five hours as Senators made their remarks for the record. Some Senators expressed the belief that the vote would commit the Senate in advance to a declaration of war. Stone answered that the world should know that Congress backed the President when he acted within his constitutional power. After many speeches, a few with justification, only five Senators voted against the resolution. One of the negative votes came from Senator Works of California, a Civil War veteran. This distressed Senator Lodge, a man unfamiliar with gunfire. He considered Works an "upright man" who was "perfectly unreasonable about peace."

As war came closer and tempers grew shorter, Stone stood between interventionists like Lodge and noninterventionists like La Follette who he often thought talked too much. He tried to maintain a semblance of steadiness. "There are two things we should do now," he said, "keep our heads level and our mouths closed."[19] No politician could have been more self-effacing, but even he became incensed with false reports that continually appeared in major newspapers. He suspected without proof that a "cabal" of big newspapers in the country sought to influence unduly or coerce the government into a hostile attitude. Stone served the President well, but the thread that held them together stretched to the limit and finally snapped. The eventual break between them came with Wilson's request to arm merchant ships just as Congress was about to adjourn. Wilson called Stone to the White House on February 26, 1917 and told him that he intended to address Congress that afternoon to recommend passage of such a statute. Stone, taken aback, replied that the move was a serious blunder that

The Chairman 39

would inevitably lead to war. He opposed plunging the country into war without greater provocation and also thought such a law would be in direct conflict with the Constitution. Stone left the meeting with "ominous apprehension."

When Wilson made his armed ship speech to Congress he said that it was his "duty to keep in close touch with the houses of Congress so that neither counsel nor action shall run at cross purposes."[20] Despite declaring these sentiments, the President had shown little inclination to receive counsel from Congress.

Within two hours after the President spoke to Congress, Stone gathered his committee to consider the bill to arm merchant ships which included suggestions from the White House. The following day, in committee, Stone offered an amendment to the Senate bill that would have made it acceptable to him. It was a provision to prohibit armed merchant ships from transporting munitions to the armed forces of a belligerent government at peace with the United States. Although it was reasonable, the majority opposed the amendment and decided to introduce the bill without alteration. Stone could not support the bill, but he did nothing to block the presentation. After introducing the bill to the Senate, he punctilliously turned over the floor management to the next ranking member of the committee, Senator Gilbert Hitchcock of Nebraska. Early in the war, Hitchcock had sponsored the bill to place an embargo on the export of arms and munitions and his opinions had seemed further from Wilson's than Stone's. Now, Wilson looked to him.

During these eventful days, news of the Zimmerman telegram arrived in the State Department on February 24, but Wilson did not tell Stone or Flood, the Senate majority leader, about it when they met at the White House on February 26. The German telegram, a bungling effort of the German Foreign Secretary, had proposed an alliance with Mexico in the event the United States entered the war. In turn for entering the war against the United States, Mexico would receive "the lost territory in Texas, New Mexico, and Arizona." In calmer times it would have been seen as a ridiculous ploy. On February 28, Wilson released the telegram for publication the next day which appeared to be carefully timed to sway the public and press in favor of armed neutrality. That same day, February 28, Wilson told a delegation at the White House that included Jane Addams and Joseph Cannon, a Socialist candidate for the Senate in 1916, about the telegram in confidence. But he did not inform the chairman of the Senate Foreign Relations Committee. Stone learned of the incident when he read the newspaper. Wilson had instructed Lansing to show the message to Hitchcock, not Stone. Utterly dismayed, Stone had no doubt that it was part of the White House strategy.

As the debate on the armed ship bill began, everyone in the chamber felt the tension. Many members feared violence. At times the Senate was in an uproar. Senator Ollie James allegedly carried a gun under his coattails. Senator Harry Lane, a physician, had a sharp file in his pocket in anticipation of trouble. He knew the file could be slipped inside a man's collar bone on the left side and reach his heart with one thrust. In this high pressure atmosphere, Stone presented his case. He had much to say and spoke four hours which, with some reason, attracted criticism that he was filibustering. But he never wandered from his subject and did not regard his speech as part of the planned filibuster of Senator Norris and others. At the outset, he diplomatically expressed his trust in the President to keep the country out of war. "I would rather trust him than all that horde of official weaklings who daily fly their kites to see which way the wind blows." Stretching a point, he added that he had worked by the President's side and enjoyed both his friendship and confidence. They had not always agreed, he explained, but as a rule he followed the President's lead. This was the first disagreement with Wilson that he had not been able to reconcile. On any lesser matter, he would again support him, but this subject was vital and he profoundly regretted the parting.[21]

To Stone the bill was an "unpardonable and perilous mistake" that violated the Constitution. It destroyed the war making power of Congress and set a dangerous precedent by giving too much authority to the executive. The country could find itself in a war begun by the President, and it would be too late for the Congress to disapprove. Stone recognized that formal declarations of war were in danger of falling into disuse and he again turned to Justice Story who had written that the history of republics "proved that they are too ambitious of military fame and conquest and too easily devoted to the view of demagogues." It should therefore be difficult in a republic to declare war, but not to make peace. The Senator also supposed that some people considered Washington's advice obsolete, but he referred to the first President's warning against changing the Constitution by usurpation. Washington had said, "for though this in one instance may be the instrument of good, it is the customary weapon by which free governments are destroyed." It seemed to Stone that these were fundamental concerns for the nation that rose above faith in any one man.

Stone's fervor increased when he spoke of the current clamor for war. He had heard little in favor of peace in the Senate. Lies he charged were continually repeated. Senator Lodge, for example, had told about the detention of Ambassador Gerard in Berlin for a week without the right to communicate with the State Department. It was absolutely false. Yet the story was exploited to inflame public opinion. "Unadulterated mendacity," he said, "oozing like filth from vindictive invention, supplemented by the most reckless and ferocious appeals to passion, have filled the country with loud alarms of war."

Stone had little doubt about the instigators of war. They were the munitions manufacturers with annual dividends above 250 percent. There was the shipping trust headed by International Mercantile Marine organized by J. P. Morgan & Company with associates in England. Then there was J. P Morgan himself who was the American fiscal and business agent for the British government. It was through him that the British made almost all contracts with Americans for war supplies. At the start of the war, Wilson had advised citizens against investing in war securities of belligerent nations. It still seemed obvious to Stone that Americans who were financially interested in a country at war were no longer impartial. Finally, there were instigators of war who were neither greedy nor sinister. They were citizens who were susceptible to the "beating of the war drums" because they had succumbed to their strong sympathy for a particular European nation.

The United States had faced serious provocations for war in the past and Stone cited such incidents in administrations from George Washington to Benjamin Harrison. In their time, they were as critical as anything the country coped with in 1917. He reminded Senators that Canadian militia had boarded the USS *Caroline* in American waters, killed a crew member, set the ship on fire, and sent it adrift over Niagara Falls. He continued with other incitements and set up a refrain, "But we didn't go to war. [The President] settled our troubles by negotiating, just as the President of the United States is trying to do today." Fighting over every injury would mean perpetual war. Such a policy, he said, would make the United States "the policemen of the world." The words "national honor" were bandied about and he wondered where, when, and from whom these persons received the commission to be keepers of the nation's honor. The Constitution gave Congress the power to declare war instead of the President because national honor should not be a whim of an individual.

In his plea to retain the traditional policy of neutrality, Stone admitted that the country had suffered from the actions of both belligerents. Britain and Germany had declared war zones that undoubtedly violated maritime law. The Germans had a submarine blockade, the British, over a larger area, had a mine blockade. A few days before he had read in a Washington newspaper that six American ships had been sunk by German U-boats and five ships by Allied mines. He did not see much difference between being killed by a mine or a torpedo. Although he knew that some isolated incidents were inexcusable, both sides sought to remain friends. Neither one side nor the other deliberately chose to injure or insult the United States. That was not the case with the historic incidents he had just reviewed. Then the injuries were intentional, not incidental.

As Stone approached the end of his long speech he delved into the much discussed doctrine of freedom of seas. He approved the principle, but there was also a matter of common sense. He did not think much of citizens who wrapped themselves in an American flag and sailed into submarine infested waters. Such behavior clearly endangered the country. There was also much irony associated with the practice of freedom of the seas. While the United States permitted its citizens to incur hazards, Canada, New Zealand, and South Africa prohibited their noncombatant people from sailing on ships bound for war zones. Stone had noticed an obscure report within the past few days that a ship en route from Boston to Liverpool had stopped at Halifax. When the examining officers found a number of British subjects aboard, they had to disembark. In contrast, the Americans on board were allowed to continue their dangerous voyage. This dumfounded the Senator.

Stone's controversial speech was intelligent and reasonable and upheld Wilson's belief of a month earlier in a peace without victory. As an American and United States Senator, he had every right to make his argument, right or wrong, popular or unpopular. Although a losing cause, he felt the case had to be made. Oddly, the opposing Senators did not disagree with his essential point that the bill would lead to war. Stone had said nothing treasonable and assured everyone that if war came he would give it his full support. Nevertheless, he did not want to join a bloody struggle that was neither the responsibility of the United States nor in its interest. His greatest crime was to express an opinion in conflict with a determined President. The speech took a lot out of Stone. By the close he was near collapse as he held onto his desk for support.

When finished, he sat down a moment and then with bowed head started to leave the chamber. Moses Clapp, a nearby Republican, noticed his weakened condition and kindly put his arm around Stone and walked out with him.

Although Stone was widely denounced for his public opposition to the President, a friendly Kentuckian sent a sympathetic letter to the editor of the *Lexington* (Kentucky) *Herald*. It included a quotation from Tom Corwin of Ohio who once disagreed with his President during the Mexican War.

> If it be my duty to grant whatever the President demands, for what am I here? Have I no will upon the subject? Is it not placed at my discretion, understanding, judgment? Have an American Senate and House of Representatives nothing to do but obey the bidding of the President? With these doctrines for our guide, tell me, tell the American people, what is the difference between your American democracy and the most odious, most hateful despotism that a merciful God has ever allowed a nation to be afflicted with?[22]

Senator Stone had done his best to avoid a personal feud with the President. The President looked upon the episode differently. It was a personal affront. When eleven Senators finally prevented a vote and the sixty-fourth Congress ended without passing the armed neutrality bill, he was infuriated. He resented the audacity of Senators who had disagreed with him and taken an independent stand. The fury of the President during this time of high tension may have been understandable, but intellectually he was in an odd position. During the Senate debate, Norris of Nebraska read from a book which declared, "It was something more than natural that the Constitutional Convention in 1787 should desire to create a Congress that would not be subservient and an Executive that could not be despotic." The book was *Congressional Government: A Study in American Politics*, by Thomas Woodrow Wilson.[23] Yet it was also true that Wilson tended to regard the President as a Prime Minister and saw himself as the legislative leader.

Wilson showed his true feelings when he issued his famous and acrid public statement devoid of any generosity. "A little group of willful men, representing no opinion but their own, have rendered the great Government of the United States helpless and contemptible."[24] Stone's loyal services to the President were forgotten and his effort to keep the debate on a professional level was unappreciated. Their "delightful relationship" was over and they could no longer "differ as friends." Admiral Cary Grayson, the President's physician, once said that if someone urged Wilson to do something contrary to his own conviction, he stopped liking the person. Now, the incensed Wilson told David Houston, Secretary of Agriculture, that Stone was "slippery" and he said to Joe Tumulty that he would never shake hands with Stone again. Senator Gronna, one of the "willful men" said, "In the words of the Master, forgive them, for they know not what they're doing."[25]

Stone believed that he spoke for a vast number of Americans, but he was also aware that his speech would be costly. War hysteria was now rampant and newspapers in his own state carried vicious attacks that showed no sympathy for their Senator. Little attention was given to his specific arguments in Missouri or elsewhere, but he suddenly appeared as a traitor. An editorial in the *Joplin News-Herald* of March 2, 1917 called his speech a "final act of treachery." The paper carried a cartoon of "Von Stone on a pedestal with the Kaiser who referred to the "willful men" as his "jewels." The *St. Louis Post-Dispatch* pronounced Stone's conduct as "the climax of a wabbling, contemptible course . . . He has always been dickering with and coddling with the pro-German traitors." The *Kansas City Star* indignantly wrote, "Missouri is no mollycoddle state . . . In times of international crisis Missouri follows the flag which is in the President's hands. If Senator Stone cannot follow it, he ought to withdraw from the Senate." Other newspapers across the state were equally severe. Stone had become the "shame of the people."[26]

Denunciations of Stone beyond Missouri were just as extreme. Democratic editorials referred to him as a "scandal" and an "offense to the country." The *Atlanta Journal* wrote, "The Kaiser has no cause to regret the dismissal of von Bernstorff [the German Ambassador] from Washington as long as William J. Stone is there." The *Duluth News-Tribune* considered Stone "a poltroon as well as a dastard." The *Chicago Evening Post* wrote, "Stone must go." The *Philadelphia North American* did not hesitate to call his act "treason," and the *New York World* saw him as a "partizan of Germany . . . as intolerable as an avowed secessionist at the head of the Union armies would have been in the Civil War." To the *New York Times* Stone's defection was an "astounding circumstance" for a man who had been the President's "trusted mouthpiece." The *Times* also condemned Stone in an editorial for divulging a navel secret about anti-submarine patrol boats after the paper had previously reported in its own pages that the information was public knowledge.[27]

A number of state legislatures added to the furor with resolutions attacking the "willful men." The Kentucky Senate stingingly referred to "certain un-American, disloyal, unpatriotic, traitorous, and cowardly Senators." Stone was also hung in effigy as a traitor for the first, but not the last time. Worse for him were the friends he had once helped who now turned against him. There was nothing too mean to say. A more steadfast friend wrote, "I know how brave you are, but matters of this sort cannot but worry you and you are not physically able to stand it."[28]

The realization that a dividing line in American history had arrived weighed heavily on Stone's mind. When the country joined forces with the Allies militarily, political involvement was bound to follow. He was aware that the President looked forward to playing a leading role at the peace conference and that he was in the way of Wilson's evolving dream for a new world order. The President, beginning his second term, considered armed neutrality so vital he cast aside his concern for Congress, ignored the Senate's obstruction, and on his executive authority armed merchant ships. Once accomplished, only a few weeks passed before Wilson called his armed neutrality program "worse than ineffectual."

In mid-March, Germany sank three American merchant ships in its designated war zone. The *City of Memphis*, after a warning and evacuation of crew, went down without casualties. The *Illinois* received no warning and was sunk by gunfire which wounded one crew member. The *Vigilancia* was torpedoed and suffered the greatest loss when fifteen of the crew drowned while trying to lower lifeboats. The banner headlines stirred the rage of Americans once again. Press accounts underplayed the fact that the United States recognized the British war zone and steered clear of its thousands of mines while the German war zone was ignored.

During these difficult days, Senator James Reed spoke bluntly to Stone, "It is the decree of fate, war will be declared. A vote against it will mean your political ruin. You are old and have no property." Stone, according to Reed, replied, "I know what it means to me. I know this war is coming. I know the people are aflame with . . . battle . . . But would you have me consider my personal welfare in a case that involves the loss of millions of men? I cannot vote to send our boys into this conflict."[29] Many Americans thought the U-boat sinkings were sufficient reason to go to war, but it was not so cut and dried in the world of international law and politics. The President still resisted the final step while he considered the ramifications of this new crisis. Short of war, however, he did not know what else he could do. On March 19, he conferred with Lansing for about an hour. Wilson did not believe the sinkings were enough reason to declare war. He searched for a higher purpose. Lansing was certain that war was now inevitable and the time had come to publicly admit that fact. Still, the President remained noncommittal. Lansing wrote to Colonel House immediately after his White House visit. The Secretary mentioned that Wilson resisted calling Congress. "He indicated to me," he wrote, "the fear he had of the queries and investigations of a Congress which could not be depended upon because of the out-and-out pacifists and the other group of men like Senator Stone." Lansing urged House to "put your shoulder to the wheel" if he agreed that this was the time to act.[30]

The next day, the President met with the Cabinet which favored a declaration of war. In its discussion, Lansing agreed with Wilson that the sinkings were insufficient cause for war because they would create debate. The sounder reason, which he knew appealed to Wilson, was the duty of a democratic nation to suppress autocracy. The time was ripe since the Russian Revolution appeared to clarify the battle between democracy and absolutism. The hope for permanent peace depended upon the establishment of democratic institutions throughout the world. This kind of thinking struck a chord with Wilson and a discordant note with Stone and others who were touched with wonder when they contemplated their future Allies. The United States would now keep company with such democrats as the King of England and Emperor of India, King of Italy, King of Rumania, King of Belgium, King of Serbia, King of Montenegro, and the Emperor of Japan as well as a chaotic Russia. Admittedly the kings of England and the Belgians were constitutional monarchs, but it weighed heavily on Stone's mind that the United States, once in the war with such Allies, would be involved in European politics. According to the *New York Times* of April 1, 1917, he sarcastically asked, "Are we to be as successful in the internal affairs of European nations as we have been in Mexico?"

On April 2, the President appeared before Congress to ask for a war resolution. Stone offered his hand at that time in a gesture of friendship and support. Wilson coldly took his hand, but he did not speak. When the war resolution came before the Senate, La Follette, who had been denied the right to speak during the armed ship debate, made a long, impassioned speech. Norris, the most bitter, said, "We are going into war upon the command of gold." Stone's remarks were brief, but no one expressed greater depth of despair than Stone who concluded, "I shall vote against this mistake, to prevent which, God helping me, I would gladly lay down my life."[31]

Stone cast his negative vote with Gronna of North Dakota, La Follette of Wisconsin, Lane of Oregon, Norris of Nebraska, and Vardaman of Mississippi, and fifty Congressmen from more than twenty states. Senator Reed said that Stone had told him he would refuse to vote for war "not because this war will cost billions, which these fools think will cost only millions; it's not even because of the loss of American lives although I would not sacrifice one American boy for all the European belligerents. I won't vote for this war because if we go into it, we will never again have the same old Republic."[32] Unlike Wilson who envisioned a war that would create a democratic new world, Stone foresaw a Pandora's box of problems beyond anyone's ability to predict.

The Senators received the most scathing criticism for their vote against war. They were better targets for the press and public because they were so few. There were too many Congressmen for a sharp attack. Despite wild accusations heaped upon the Senator from Missouri and talk in the Senate cloakroom of ousting him from the chairmanship of the Foreign Relations Committee, he retained the respect of most of his colleagues and remained in his post. This came as a surprise. The *Literary Digest* of March 24, 1917 had noted, "Grant had his Sumner and Wilson had his Stone." When Charles Sumner, chairman of the Foreign Relations Committee clashed with the President, fellow Senators removed him from the chairmanship. Democracy in action seemed to work better among those who knew Stone best rather than among those who knew him least.

Stone supported the war effort conscientiously as he had promised. On the way to work at the Capitol one day in 1918, he died of a heart attack. Vice President Marshall said of Stone, "Beneath that brain, which was a wonderful one, there beat a heart full of affection for his fellow man . . . Right or wrong I loved William J. Stone; had an intense admiration for his ability."[33] The President sent flowers.

For courageously expressing his honest convictions Stone received the President's scorn and the public's censure in a country that prided itself on freedom of speech. Both Wilson and Stone had a vision for a peaceful world. The President saw the way to peace through war and a place at the conference to follow. He was to be the leader of a new world. The Senator, a dying man, had no personal ambition. He pictured a strong America that remained aloof from the fray and became a model for a devastated Europe that might learn war was futile. The practical politician was as idealistic as the professor in the White House. After the sinking of the *Lusitania*, Wilson said, "The example of America must be a special example. The example of America must be the example, not merely of peace because it will not fight, but of peace because peace is the healing and elevating influence of the world and strife is not." When Charles Eliot, former president of Harvard, had once suggested intervention, Wilson replied that it would be an added burden to mankind, "if the only neutral nation should withdraw from the position of influence afforded her by her neutrality." Stone understood those Wilsonian words.[34]

In the rush of events that followed the declaration of war, the destruction of the working relationship between Wilson and Stone was a minor affair in the cruel business of politics. But the constitutional jurisdictions of the executive and legislative branches in matters of peace and war remain ambiguous and troublesome. Late in the twentieth century they remain questions to ponder.

Chapter 4

The Publisher

William Randolph Hearst was neither a moralist nor an idealist, and he was certainly not a pacifist. He liked to think of himself as a realist, but in reality he was the spoiled son of very rich parents who went through life simply wanting his own way. Frequently, and sometimes unfortunately, he succeeded. His motivations, hidden in a complex personality, defied comprehension and confounded analysis. He was living proof that shyness, for which he was famous, did not exclude an aggressive, crusading spirit. His overly generous father, George Hearst, was a rough, self-taught geologist who made a fortune in mining and later turned to politics and became United States Senator from California. His family heritage was mainly Scotch and English. The former Phoebe Apperson, young Hearst's devoted mother, was a sparkling woman who became a philanthropist and regent of the University of California. Her family background was English.

William Hearst was well acquainted with Europe from boyhood where he had lived as well as visited for long periods of time. As he grew into manhood, he was tall, slim, with pale blue-grey eyes, and hair distinctively parted in the middle. When he spoke, his voice was surprisingly high. At Harvard, he became one of its more outrageous students, and in turn, one of its more outrageous alumni. When interested, he was capable of being a good student, but he was frequently uninterested. His greatest collegiate achievement was his tenure as business manager of the humor magazine, Harvard *Lampoon*. Near the end of his junior year he played one practical joke too many for the college administration and was invited to leave. His crime was said to be that he had presented hand painted chamber pots to some prominent faculty members with their pictures painted inside the bottom for Christmas. Apparently, the departure did not devastate him. He was probably bored by then and knew what he wanted to do with his life. After a year as a reporter for Joseph Pulitzer's *New York World*, he convinced his father to turn his newspaper, the *San Francisco Examiner*, over to his son. It was a losing proposition anyway and the father obliged. Soon the turbulent young man made the *Examiner* the lively talk of the town.

Anyone casually acquainted with Hearst's career knows that he is looked upon as the man who started the Spanish-American War. Although the claim may be exaggerated, there is no doubt that he stirred the emotions of the American people against the Spanish in Cuba with stories of fake atrocities and other imaginary incidents. By the time the battleship *Maine* blew up in Santiago harbor, his sensational headlines had helped to create an atmosphere receptive to war. If Hearst's sole purpose was to boost the circulation of his newspapers in a battle with his rival Joseph Pulitzer, he accomplished the feat. When he bought the *New York Journal* in 1895, the circulation was a mere 77,000. Within a brief three years, sales increased to more than a million. Gullible, and not so gullible readers, could not resist the exciting news, true or false, that blared across the country. Such headlines as "The Warship Maine was Split in Two By an Enemy's Secret Infernal Machine" had no basis in fact.

Nevertheless, it proved that Hearst, a skilled promoter and propagandist, had a gift for fanning the flames of war. Lurking in the recesses of his peculiar mind may have been other reasons for his behavior such as dreams of greater power, political glory, and even, quite possibly, sympathy for the Cubans. Whatever his whims, he got his war and profits and by 1908 he had a network of newspapers in New York, Boston, Chicago, Los Angeles, and San Francisco.

To think of the war monger of the nineties as a man of peace less than twenty years later is a contradiction in terms, but Hearst was a mass of contradictions. The only consistent elements in his makeup were inconsistency and ability to shock. He delighted in going against the tide and took pleasure in perversity. By 1917, Hearst, a frustrated politician who had failed to reach the White House, the Governor's mansion in New York, or even the Mayor's mansion of New York City, did not think kindly of Woodrow Wilson. He considered him a "sham progressive" as Governor of New Jersey, and his distaste increased in 1912 when Wilson won the Democratic nomination for President over his candidate, Champ Clark. Although Hearst supported the Democratic ticket in 1912, his low opinion of Wilson still lingered when war broke out in Europe in 1914.

The war clearly delineated the differences in temperament and judgment between the rough, tough publisher and the scholarly President. Hearst, the westerner, feared the "yellow peril" in the Pacific. Wilson, the easterner, feared German militarism in Europe. Hearst's British heritage meant nothing to him. He did not care for arrogant British manners and he worried about foreign entanglements. Wilson cherished his British heritage which was an inherent influence upon his life. Hearst's personal prejudices became his principles. Perhaps the same could be said for Wilson.

When the President delivered his first message to Congress in 1913, Hearst was quick to criticize this British practice. No President had addressed Congress in person since Thomas Jefferson had renounced the ritual as too reminiscent of the King addressing Parliament. Jefferson, not a particularly good public speaker, was probably relieved to escape the chore, but his precedent had remained in effect in the intervening years until Wilson decided to assert his authority. The former professor of political science favored the British parliamentary system and that did not conform in Hearst's mind with the Jeffersonian idea of political simplicity. Wilson's recent admission that he received much of his information about world events from the London *Times* was another irritant for Hearst. "There is no publication on the face of the earth," he wrote, "so completely and absolutely saturated with English prejudice toward all other countries, and toward America in particular, as the London *Times*. . . ."[1] To make matters worse, Wilson was an English free trader in the tradition of Cobden and Mill. Hearst's anti-British sentiments were baffling because he had favored the British not too many years before during the Boer War.

Soon after the outbreak of war in 1914, Hearst tried to organize a peace campaign among newspapers. He believed the power of the world press was sufficient to stop the war. It was an appealing dream. The press played an important role in inciting wars and unifying public opinion for battles to come. As an agent for peace the press could exert untold pressure in molding the public. Theoretically, he may have been right. Practically, it remained a dream. Hearst, the imperialist jingo was now on the side of the angels who were more than a little suspicious about their new found friend. Andrew Lawrence, one of Hearst's editors, sought support from Chester Wright, managing editor of the Socialist *Call*. He replied, "The *New York Call* and the great Socialist movement for which it stands have fought too long for peace not to be able to continue the fight without the aid of unclean hands. . . . "[2] The thought of a pacifist Hearst was incredible to Wright. Hearst papers had "left no type unset" to drive the country into war with Mexico and Japan. Now, suddenly and supposedly sincerely, they were proponents of peace. Wright had no doubt that this was another escapade to build Hearst circulation. Incredibly and illogically, however, Hearst appeared to be sincere. Nevertheless, other idealists were equally dubious about the new voice for peace. Even William Jennings Bryan shied away from Hearst's friendly overtures after he resigned as Secretary of State. Their doubts were understandable. While Hearst pushed for peace in Europe, the imperialist in him was willing to invade and annex Mexico. Besides annexation would protect Hearst's Mexican holdings.

Hearst never had the reputation of a man to be trusted. The publisher once offered to help his fellow Californian, Franklin K. Lane, who replied, "If you ever get a telegram from me asking you to do anything, you can put that telegram down as a forgery." Lane thought Hearst had a "great capacity for disorganization of any movement that is not his own, and an equal capacity for organization of any movement that is his personal property. He feels with the people, but he has no conscience." At times he could act like a "queen dove," but in reality he was arbitrary and overbearing.[3]

Hearst may have entered the battle for absolute neutrality to boost circulation, but the decline became clearly evident as he opposed Allied loans and contraband shipments. It would have been much more profitable to have enlisted in a less contentious crusade. Profits aside, it must have been a severe sacrifice for the sensationalist to pass up so many heaven sent opportunities for sensationalism. The pages of Hearst papers were never dull, but it would have been much easier to sound a clarion call for intervention, especially after the loss of the *Lusitania*. The cry for war could have filled the need for a simple solution accompanied by much flag waving. Instead, Hearst, the old jingo, functioned as the sober publisher who called for restraint when more dignified rivals spread a war fever. Hearst papers were quick to condemn the sinking of the *Lusitania*, but soon added qualifications. Hearst wrote, "whether the *Lusitania* was armed or not, it was properly a spoil of war, subject to attack and destruction under the accepted rules of civilized warfare . . . The *Lusitania* incident is, of course, no cause for a declaration of war."[4]

The Publisher

Unlike most proponents of absolute neutrality, Hearst supported Wilson's preparedness program. He believed the best policy was to avoid entangling alliances that would lead to war. Armed neutrality, however, made sense to him as long as Europe's "revolution" was underway. He even went so far as to approve conscription. When a new democratic continent arose out of the chaos, the United States could then negotiate the peace of the world. He did not mind spending huge amounts of money for defense, but he did not want to contribute to the "universal wreck." Another reason for interest in preparedness was his continuing fear of the Japanese. When three U-boats reportedly sank nine merchant ships near the East Coast, his *New York Evening Journal* commented on October 10, 1916 that Japanese submarines might do the same in the Pacific. "The Japanese are good imitators. . . . "

The *New York American* was accused of being "for war with Great Britain at any cost and for peace at any price with Germany," but Hearst's anti-British attitude made his papers seem more pro-German than they were in reality. He considered his campaign to stay out of war as pro-American. In his opinion, he spoke for a large silent segment of American society. Despite the impression he created, he bought the news services of the London *Times*, London *Daily Telegraph* and paid substantial fees for pieces by such leading British writers as Rudyard Kipling, H. G. Wells, Bernard Shaw, G. K. Chesterton, and Lord Northcliffe. One analyst claimed that Hearst papers published about 4,000 columns of pro-German articles and 10,000 columns of pro-Ally articles during a two-year period. *The American Press Resumé*, issued by the British Foreign Office Office for Cabinet members included an appraisal that stated it was not fair to charge Hearst as pro-German. "He is ever ready to receive into his papers and to give prominent display to special articles of any and all partisanships whenever the interest, or repute of the author make a fair claim upon him." The *Resumé* also wrote, "To say that he [Hearst] is pro-German is at once to over-credit his integrity and to undervalue his importance . . . No more do I believe that Hearst can be 'bought' in that sense; certainly I am sure that he would not be a safe or dependable bargain for any purchaser."[5]

Hearst's reputation was not improved when it was learned that his foreign correspondent, William Bayard Hale, unknown to the publisher, was a paid propagandist of the German government. Ensconced in regal surroundings, Hearst ignored much criticism, but as time went on even he felt the harsh blows that came his way. His greatest comfort came from a young chorus girl and future Hollywood star, Marion

Davies, whom he, a married man, met in 1915. She remained with him for the rest of his life. Fellow publishers bashed his views, friends fell by the wayside, political ambitions were shattered, and he became a lonely figure in disgrace accused of treason and near-treason. Yet he stubbornly pursued his neutrality policy with such mottoes as "America First" with red, white, and blue titles, little American flags, and verses of "The Star Spangled Banner" decorating his pages. Orders went to his editors to present pro-American editorials. Perhaps the German propaganda director, Dr. Albert Fuehr, analyzed the Hearst papers more clearly than American critics. He wrote to the Imperial German Government that they were not blind champions of the German cause. "They stood upon sound American policy, but their sharply anti-English tendencies are much more effective in support of our cause than newspapers with pronounced German orientation could be."[6]

Hearst, the skilled propagandist, was particularly galled by the subtle British propaganda in the United States which no one seemed to challenge. Since he knew how to rouse emotions, he recognized their clever ability to prey on gullible minds. He was shocked that there was no organized effort to expose false atrocity stories and well-placed insinuations that were so effective. When the dreadnaught, HMS *Audacious* was sunk by a German mine off the northern coast of Ireland, the Admiralty under Winston Churchill, attempted to keep the loss a secret. The incident had been observed by a passenger liner and Hearst published a photograph of the sinking much to the embarrassment of the British. He also took pleasure in reminding readers of British paradoxes. A few years before, the British had regarded the Belgians as bloodthirsty savages for mutilating and killing natives in the Congo. The sudden British admiration for the Czar's highmindedness seemed absurd, too, when they hated Russia's threat to India.[7]

The volume of British news arriving in the United States also created a favorable propaganda edge for the Allies. One analysis indicated that during the first year of the war, seventy percent of front page war news originated in Allied countries while comparable German stories were not more than four percent. Since the British blocked German use of transatlantic cables, their only immediate access to the United States was by wireless. Unfortunately for the Germans, atmospheric conditions sometimes knocked out wireless transmissions at critical moments. That happened to them during the *Lusitania* crisis and placed them at a great disadvantage.

Hearst could not understand why England complained about American neutrality. It was far from absolute. The United States had loaned hundreds of millions of dollars to the British, turned the country into a munitions factory for their benefit, and allowed them to seize ships, hold up the mail, and take goods from American ships. What more could the United States do? When Hearst attacked British censorship, interference with American commerce, and cruelty in the Irish rebellion, he was promptly counterattacked. His anti-British stance resulted in the British government banning Hearst's International News Service from its cables and mail in October 1916. The thought that a foreign nation would edit his papers sent him into a rage. "I would shut down every publication I have first, and I don't intend to shut them down." The incensed Hearst wrote to J. J. Harris of INS, "I am convinced that the exclusion of the International News Service is not due to delinquency on its part or on the part of the Hearst papers, but is due to the independent and wholly truthful attitude of the Hearst papers in their news and editorial columns." His *New York Journal*, with a touch of bravado, said on October 12, 1916 that it would print the news exactly as it happens "not as England would like to have it twisted, painted, distorted and arranged to suit British vanity or British incompetency." In the following month, Canada was sufficiently exercised to ban Hearst newspapers and any Canadian reading their papers could be fined $5,000 or sentenced to up to five years in prison.[8]

By 1916, Hearst had lost almost all faith in the President and it is safe to say that Wilson's faith in Hearst was nonexistent. Despite the serious divergence of their views, Hearst supported Wilson because he was among the many who saw no alternative. His support, however, did not mean the absence of criticism for the Democratic candidate. When Jeremiah O'Leary, president of the American Truth Society, a vehemently anti-British organization, sent Wilson a telegram attacking his pro-British policies, war loans, ammunition traffic, and dictatorship over Congress, Wilson came out the victor in a well-publicized exchange of messages. The President replied to O'Leary, "I would feel deeply mortified to have you or anybody like you vote for me. Since you have access to many disloyal Americans and I have not, I will ask you to convey this message to them."[9] The scathing response, so uncharacteristic of politicians, met with widespread approval from the public, press, and later, historians who considered O'Leary's telegram offensive. Colonel House thought Wilson's forthright reply was the turning point of the campaign. It came as a relief to many voters that a candidate could cast aside pussyfooting and make an unequivocal statement; however, Hearst reacted differently. An editorial in the *New York American* read, "Political Opposition to President Must Never Be Construed as Treason in America." With an appreciation for free speech, the editorial declared, "We are sure that no American President ever before advanced such a definition of treason or such a doctrine of lese majeste. If an American citizen who strenuously objects to the welfare of England being put above the rights and the dignity of the sovereignty of the United States is disloyal to his country, then the majority of us Americans are disloyal." In the light of the First Amendment, the *American* was more statesmanlike than Wilson.[10]

Hearst's low opinion of Wilson, as he later wrote, was based upon his belief that the President was a theorist without deep conviction, "certainly none that interfered with his personal advancement." He admitted that Wilson was a brilliant speaker, but he thought he was "an unstable thinker, and an unreliable performer ... an opportunist in his support of any principle at any time."[11] It was bad enough that Wilson's theories were "theories of books, but worse, they were theories of British books that were outdated and not even in tune with progressive Englishmen. "Professor" Wilson became a standard character in the stinging portrayals by Winsor McCay, one of Hearst's keenest political cartoonists.

The line between courage and unmitigated gall is sometimes very thin. Whichever quality Hearst possessed, he remained resolute in opposition to Wilson's policies as United States entry into the war became almost a certainty. Hounded by government agents and pilloried by hordes of Americans, Hearst retained his cool demeanor and held on to his views as the personal, political, and financial costs mounted. Among his stray opinions there was some common sense and he had a large audience for what he had to say, but his passions ran too rampant for the intellectual elements of society.

After the United States broke diplomatic relations with Germany, Hearst insisted that the country was "gold bricked." In his opinion, "Notes are better than bullets; ink is better than blood." He was convinced that if there had been more writing in Europe there would have been less fighting. Sending food, munitions, and money abroad only prolonged the agony for the belligerents. Why, he wondered, were we wasting our wealth? If it were for some noble purpose the country could afford to go poor for a generation and find comfort and consolation in a worthy deed. But this was a "carnival of murder," a "dance of death."[12] He wanted to build and conserve the resources of the nation. Loans to the British, forced upon Americans by munitions makers, were unsafe. He was sure the British would be exhausted and bankrupt at the end of the war and unable to pay. The British were near defeat, and this was no time for the United States to be used by them as a mere reinforcement in their war. Anyway, he did not see how the United States could join hands with the British ally, Japan. He believed then and later that the war would end democracy and war would be perpetuated. As war approached, he joined the quixotic call for a popular referendum. He wanted people to look behind the war talk and underneath the alleged patriotism. Democracy was slipping away from Americans. His special target became the highly respected corporation lawyers such as Joseph Choate, a former ambassador to Great Britain, and Elihu Root, a former Secretary of State, who had become so militaristic. He asked where they were during the "big war," the Civil War. As young men, he charged, they and others like them stayed home and lacked the courage to fight. Now, "in their well paid old age cheerfully plan the war wanted by corporations that hire them." The complaint may have been low brow, but there was some truth in what he said. During the Civil War, young Joseph Choate, for one, expressed some qualms about his comfortable life while others sacrificed their lives. Nevertheless, his uneasiness did not prompt him to join the Union army. Choate was now one of the vigorous members of the National Security League along with a blue ribbon list of capitalists such as Henry Clay Frick and Cornelius Vanderbilt who had shown their militaristic and unneutral sympathies since the earliest days of the European war.[13]

Hearst was also a rare exception among opponents of war who was not impressed by Wilson's "peace without victory" appeal. The *New York American* reflected his skepticism in writing, "we do not have any faith that another alliance for the enforcement of permanent peace, organized at this time, would result any better than the effort at The Hague or the effort of the Holy Alliance." But Wilson's belated effort soon washed away with America's declaration of war.[14]

When war came Hearst papers entered into the spirit of the time by favoring fund-raisers for the Red Cross and Liberty bond drives. Yet Hearst's obstinate nature had not changed. Wilson's war was not the kind Hearst had in mind and he continued a barrage against the administration. As a starter, he wanted to keep the armed forces on this side of the Atlantic. If Germans were a threat, let them come over here.

Almost as soon as the war began, he was ready for peace. By early 1918, the *New York Tribune*, admittedly a biased observer, claimed that Hearst papers had made seventy-four attacks against the Allies, seventeen defenses or praise for Germany, and one deletion of a Presidential proclamation. Hearst immediately denied the charges as falsehoods while he marched to his own drummer.[15]

Hearst's stubborn convictions brought wrath upon him from a variety of places. He was an easy target for angry Theodore Roosevelt who said he was "one of the efficient allies of Germany on this side of the water" and he was included in his select group of "Huns within" who were more dangerous than "Huns without." Samuel Seabury, the lawyer and big time investigator, always ready to pass moral judgments on others, considered Hearst "false not only to his own country but to every ideal of decency." The Justice Department scanned Hearst papers for signs of sedition, tailed his movements, and planted a federal agent in his home as a butler. Private clubs in Los Angeles burned his papers and the Boston Club denied him admission. Many cities, forgetting the First Amendment, blocked distribution of his papers, used them for huge bonfires, and held anti-Hearst demonstrations. A delegation of women demanded that he be interned. All this went on while Hearst thought of himself a representative of a respectable viewpoint. As his profits and political ambitions plummeted, he took the punishment and did his best to appear unfazed. Years later, he wrote, "The great war was not a war to end war and perpetuate democracy. It was rather a war to end democracy and to perpetuate war. Permanent peace will come not through war but through civilization. Civilization is slow. We have not yet emerged from savagery."[16]

Hearst was a peculiar, perverse person and much of his behavior was inexcusable. Yet, oddly, when he sacrificed the most for his beliefs, he drew the greatest condemnation. For all of his many faults, he had a lively brain and rousing perspectives that should have received a more broad-minded reception, if not acceptance, by his critics. Hearst may not have been a moralist, but those secure in their self-righteousness who intolerantly refused to listen to him may have denied themselves a refreshing idea or two. Perhaps his views were best summarized in a letter he wrote in 1934 to the president of the Association of College Editors when he said, "I personally believe in nationalism *and* internationalism—each in its proper place. I believe in benefiting all the people of the earth whenever and wherever we can do so without sacrificing the interests of our own people."[17]

Chapter 5

The War Hero

Isaac Sherwood always attracted attention. Bright, handsome, and opinionated, he was the sort of man that people tended to call a natural leader. In 1917, Congressman Sherwood represented the Ninth District in Toledo, Ohio, and he was more commonly known as General Sherwood. The title was neither honorary nor empty. To the contrary, he had risen from private to brigadier general in the Union army, fought in more than forty battles in the Civil War, spent 123 days under fire, and endured some of the fiercest fighting in the Atlanta campaign. War was not an abstraction to him. He had seen blood flow, heard cries of the wounded, and smelled rotting bodies of the dead. Somehow he survived the horror and received ten citations for gallant conduct in special and general orders and on the battlefield by commanding generals.

Sherwood took pride in his heritage which began with the arrival of Dr. Thomas Sherwood who had left Ipswich, England, in 1634. Both of his grandfathers and one greatgrandfather served in the American Revolution, and his father, Aaron Sherwood, enrolled in the army during the War of 1812 but did not see service. His mother, Maria Yeomans Sherwood, a native of New York City, came from a family that had originated in Scotland.

Sherwood was born in Stanton, Dutchess County, New York, on August 13, 1835. Although his father died when he was only nine years old, the family had sufficient means to see that he received a good education. He attended Antioch College when the famed educator, Horace Mann, was president and obtained a law degree from Ohio Law College in 1859. But the law did not hold sufficient attraction for him. While still a law student, he bought a small paper, the *Williams County Gazette*, in Bryan, Ohio, and it soon reflected his decided views. When John Brown carried out his insane invasion of Virginia at Harper's Ferry, Sherwood portrayed him as a hero to the consternation of more moderate anti-slavery Republicans.

Publishing, politics, and personality went together and despite his critics, Sherwood, twenty-six years old, won election as a Republican to the office of probate judge of Williams County in 1860. The young judge had married Katharine Margaret Brownlee, a striking young woman, not quite eighteen, the year before. She was a descendant of a long line of Scottish lairds and shared her husband's literary interests and strong-mindedness. The future was filled with promise. Soon a family was on the way, but the attack on Fort Sumter shattered their immediate dreams as it did for tens of thousands of others.

On April 16, 1861, the day after President Lincoln issued a call for volunteers, Judge Sherwood, as might be expected of a man with his impetuous qualities, was the first to enlist in Bryan. He became a private in the Fourteenth Ohio Infantry and took part in the earliest battles of the war at Philippi, Laurel Mountain, and Carrick's Ford. At the end of his three months enlistment, the new soldier, still full of energy, returned home to help recruit the 111th Ohio Infantry. During the intervening months his first child, a son, was born, and he also had his wife and widowed mother to consider. Nevertheless, he promptly resigned as probate judge, closed down his newspaper, and moved his wife and child back to her parents.

Isaac Sherwood believed in the noble cause of preserving the Union, and he was incapable of remaining a bystander. In September 1862, he accepted a commission as first lieutenant in the 111th and took off again without the faintest notion of what was in store for him. In the years to come, one out of every five officers and men of his regiment would become casualties of war.

Promotions came rapidly for Sherwood, partly because of the high casualty rate and illness. By 1863, Major Sherwood commanded the regiment in Kentucky and East Tennessee and remained the commanding officer until mustered out in 1865. During the winter of 1863 and 1864, he and his men suffered the additional hardships of heavy sleet and snow as well as short rations, clothing, and tents, but still volunteered for reenlistment. At Knoxville, the regiment covered General Burnside's retreat from the Holston River to Strawberry Plains without rest for three days and nights as Longstreet's cavalry pursued them. At

Campbell's Station, Sherwood, not quite unscathed, lost the hearing in his right ear from the concussion of a shell. It was at Campbell's Station that Burnside personally complimented Sherwood before the troops.[1]

For "gallant and meritorious services" at the bloody battles of Resaca, Franklin, and Nashville, Sherwood became a brevetted Brigadier General. It was at Franklin that Hood ordered the Confederates to take the offensive. Although the rebels broke the Union line, savage hand-to-hand fighting drove them back in what was probably the most intensely fought battle of the war. Hood, as James McPherson noted in *Battle Cry of Freedom*, had more of his men killed at Franklin than Grant at Cold Harbor or McClellan in all Seven Days. Among the Confederate casualties were twelve generals and fifty-four regimental commanders.[2] Sherwood's promotion came as a result of a paper written by the officers and men of the regiment which was addressed to President Lincoln. "It has been the good fortune of the regiment," the paper said, "to be led by him in every engagement in which we have participated since we entered the field, and the cool, determined bravery displayed by him on every occasion, particularly that on the bloody field of Resaca and the terrible struggle at Franklin, is an example worthy of emulation of all true soldiers."[3] The testimonial was signed by every officer of the regiment and the line officers of the brigade. Clearly, Sherwood was no run of the mill man. In all, he commanded the regiment in thirty-one of their forty or so engagements which included eleven bayonet attacks.

Sherwood, only thirty years old, returned home a hero, but the war left its mark. Years later he said the experience had saddened all of his life. "I had my soul rent with indescribable agony, as I stood in the presence of comrades who were maimed, mangled, and dying on forty-two battlefields of this Republic." He knew what war meant. The romance and glory had disappeared.[4]

In the years that followed the war, Sherwood combined his interest in newspaper work with politics. At times he was a newspaper owner, at other times an employee. He was an editor of the *Toledo Commercial* and an editorial writer on the *Cleveland Leader*, and later an owner of the *Toledo Journal*. Still later, in the eighties and nineties he was editor of the *Canton News-Democrat*. During those years he also carved out a political career. In 1868 he was elected Secretary of State of Ohio and reelected two years later. From there he won election as a Republican from the Sixth District to the Forty-third Congress. But his independence on currency questions differed from John Sherman's, the Ohio Republican leader, and cost him renomination in 1875. Once again he served as probate judge, this time in Lucas County as a candidate of the Greenback party. In 1881, he was elected as a Democrat and Independent.

As the years passed, Sherwood became a leader of progressive Democrats in Ohio and in 1906, at the age of seventy-one, ran for Congress in the heavily Republican Ninth District. In the Presidential campaign two years before, Theodore Roosevelt carried the district with a majority of almost 20,000. Sherwood won the election by a slim forty-one votes, but retained the seat with increasing margins for seven terms. In 1920, he lost election, but he was not a man to give up and returned to Congress at the age of eighty-seven for one term in 1923 to become one of the oldest Congressmen on record. During his political career he ran for office fourteen times and proudly claimed that he never accepted a dollar from an individual or corporation for his campaign fund. Champ Clark, Speaker of the House, described a Sherwood in his eighties who was straight as an arrow, read without glasses, and looked fifty.[5]

Many of Sherwood's constituents were Civil War veterans including some who served with him in the 111th. It was probably a foregone conclusion that he would become chairman of the House committee on Invalid Pensions. He was an astute politician keenly aware of the value of veterans' votes and sponsored a dollar-a-day pension for Civil War veterans who had served a year or more. The legislation, called by cost conscious President Taft one of the worst measures ever proposed, may have been one of Sherwood's greatest claims to fame. A compromise bill eventually passed, but in the meantime the nickname "Dollar-a-Day Sherwood" served him well. He firmly believed in the personal touch and his activities for veterans were not lost on him. Every veteran who received a pension increase could count on receiving a letter as a gentle reminder of who was responsible.

Unlike many politicians who used veterans' affairs then and later to advance their careers, Sherwood was never a militarist. By 1917, he would be accused of following the wishes of his strong German-American constituency. His antiwar sentiments, however, were of long standing and touched him much more deeply. Long before war broke out in Europe in 1914, he opposed increases in Army appropriations as a member of the House Military Affairs Committee. From 1907 to 1909, he actively advocated universal peace and fought any trend toward militarism. In 1908, he was the only member in the House to vote against a large expenditure for a drydock at Pearl Harbor. In 1913, he supported a one-year naval construction holiday which he believed was in keeping with Democratic ideas on economy and humane Christian concepts. He said, "I was for war myself when I was a semibarbarian and did not know it . . . but after I had been in some 30 or 40 battles I was convinced that war is hell, and I have been a Quaker ever since. And what we need now, and need more than anything else to advance our much-boasted Christian civilization, is more Quakers and fewer battleships." Sherwood, a Presbyterian, was never a member of the Society of Friends, but in spirit he vigorously shared their distaste for war.[6]

Sherwood was certain that the war in Europe was the definite result of the armaments race that had been going on there for years. When calls for preparedness in the United States became more strident, he became equally vocal. He had once admired Theodore Roosevelt. Now, as the former President was among those who frantically preached preparedness and intervention Sherwood, not shy about tossing back epithets, called them alarmists and "mental inebriates." He did not believe it was necessary to create "military idols" to vitalize the national life. The United States was not in danger of attack from any European nation. To his populist nature, munitions makers were "blood-money gangsters." When Sherwood voted against a half billion dollar expenditure for national defense in November 1915, a critical editorial in the *New York Times* correctly stated that his opposition to preparedness was not unexpected. Sherwood's outspoken opinions attracted sufficient attention throughout the country for him to be mentioned as a vice presidential candidate with Henry Ford on a peace ticket. Nothing came of the talk, and anyway, he said the idea did not appeal to him."[7]

Early in 1916, Sherwood regaled the House for almost an hour in eloquent opposition to the President's preparedness program. At the start he expressed the obligatory regret that he could not support the administration's plan and quickly paid homage to Wilson for his "superb poise and masterful grasp of the many diplomatic problems" he had faced in the interest of peace. Sherwood believed, however, that the President had mistaken the popular judgment. The Congressman had asked his constituents for instructions on how to vote on the issue, and he claimed that not a single letter or telegram arrived to approve the huge expenditure. Specifically, the farmers in his district were against "preparedness" and the State Grange of Ohio formally expressed its opposition at a recent session. Labor unions shared this same sentiment. The Central Labor Union of Toledo, representing 10,000 organized workers and ninety-one locals, passed a resolution against the proposed legislation without one dissenting vote.[8]

The request for vast sums of money for defense perplexed Sherwood. Although he had a long record as a peace man, he had never been for peace at any price. His trouble now was that he could not find any enemy. The American people did not perceive an immediate German military threat, and in truth, neither did Wilson. The President's concern was a long-term German attack on the economic interests of the United States and the loss of a British-American balance of power despite his idealistic talk about a community of power.

If an enemy existed, Sherwood had been assured that the nation could ably defend itself. Only a year ago, the President and the Secretaries of War and Navy had announced that the country was fully prepared for any emergency. Then European armies were more powerful, numerous, and less exhausted, and were a greater potential threat. The present contradictions were incomprehensible to him. He also charged that for ten years before the war in Europe broke out, the United States had expended 300 million dollars more than Germany in strengthening the Navy. The nation had also spent large sums over the past thirty years on coastal fortifications, and the disastrous Allied campaign in the Dardanelles proved that naval guns were no match for strongly armed forts and mines. He claimed that prior to the passage of any preparedness legislation, the United States was producing more war materials than any two armies now fighting each other. Gun and ammunition factories, he said, produced at least five million cartridges each day and would soon be capable of manufacturing 50,000 artillery shells daily. Hence the alarm about unpreparedness seemed to him to be criminal foolishness.

Sherwood agreed that the submarine was a horror for those sailing on belligerent ships, but 153 Americans had been brutally killed in Mexico recently without reason. Yet there was no war. Not one of the "whole array of pretending patriots" had pointed to an enemy hostile to the United States. He had no criticism for the Army or Navy. It was the war-scare newspapers and "armor plate" magazines that misled the people. It was war hysteria and the nation had suffered from that disease in the War of 1812 and the Spanish-American War. In the War of 1812, the United States had 2,000 soldiers killed, built an enormous war debt, and then made peace with Great Britain with a major cause of the conflict, impressment of American seamen, unsettled. In the Spanish-American War he was certain, and most historians agree, Cuba could have been freed without the loss of an American life or the residual expenses. One ramification, the Philippine Insurrection, had cost 16,000 lives, a billion dollars to date, and a long pension list. In 1916, thirteen thousand experienced soldiers could be brought home from the Philippines to bolster the Army at home. It would also "lift the white man's burden in the tropical Orient and shorten our battle line some 10,000 miles should Japan seek to dominate the Pacific Ocean." That would save about forty million dollars a year.[9]

Sherwood would have preferred to reduce the standing Army and strengthen the National Guard. The money saved could establish the foundation for a social security plan such as Bismarck had instituted in Germany. Such a humane program, he argued, could save money, maintain preparedness, and relieve the tax burden at the same time. He reiterated that no European nation with a worn out army, paralyzed industry, huge debt, ruined foreign trade, and millions of maimed soldiers and widows would cross the Atlantic to attack a hundred million people when there was no quarrel. He wanted America to become the beacon for social and moral betterment and prayed that the war hysteria would soon pass. His long speech drew considerable applause that did not reflect a hostile audience, but it was the beginning of a Presidential election and peace was popular.[10]

During the 1916 Presidential campaign, Sherwood remained a loyal Democrat and supported Wilson despite their differences. Although he rationalized that support for the President was necessary, he also said with a touch of ambivalence, "I cannot seek reelection on a platform that pledges the party to militarism. My convictions are such that I cannot and will not seek reelection on the preparedness platform." When Wilson arrived at Union Station in Toledo to briefly address a political rally, Sherwood confirmed his loyalty to the President by emphasizing that they agreed on many things. Wilson politely rebuked Sherwood by expressing regret that he disagreed with him on preparedness. The President claimed that advocating preparedness was not advocating hostility. "I represent and am the servant of a nation that loves peace." It was necessary that part of the world keep cool, while all the rest of the world was hot. He stole the center stage as the peace candidate while Sherwood, a mere Congressman, was an insignificant factor.[11]

In an effort to avoid American involvement in a European war, Sherwood flailed around for possible solutions in the coming months. For awhile he hoped that arbitration could solve the tensions between the United States and Germany. And early in 1917, he introduced a resolution with many adherents that called for a popular referendum before a declaration of war. It went nowhere. In the late nineteenth and early twentieth centuries, referendum along with recall, initiative, and direct primaries were the great hopes of progressives for achieving direct democracy. The fulfillment of such hopes for these political techniques were never realized, even in matters much less critical than war, but a referendum did not seem so impractical in 1917.

When the bill to arm American merchant ships came before the House in 1917, Sherwood opposed the bill because it gave too much power to the President and was a first step toward war. The "willful men" in the Senate who blocked passage of the bill attracted more of the public and Presidential wrath. Nevertheless, Sherwood was one of only fourteen members of the House and the only Ohioan to vote against the bill. Back home he received his share of angry complaints. The local chapter of the Sons of Revolution lost faith in him and veterans of the Forsyth Post of the Grand Army of the Republic censured Sherwood, their honorary member. Two hundred local businessmen and professional leaders, indignant and exasperated, called upon him to resign. Through all of the heated words he remained unmoved.

Righteous abstractions were favorite arguments on both sides. Interventionists were repelled by those who righteously agitated for peace because they would not combat concrete evil. Noninterventionists were repelled by those who righteously called for combat because they saw a threat to American rights.

Only a few weeks passed before the President asked Congress for a declaration of war. Once again, as in 1861, Sherwood showed the courage of his convictions. In his speech before the House in opposition to the resolution he argued that freedom of the seas was always subject to the law of blockade. In contradiction to this traditional practice, Americans were now told that they had the right to ship munitions to Great Britain and permit American citizens to sail into the war zone. "War-crazed enthusiasts" who talk about national honor, he said, would make Americans believe that the submarine was aimed at the United States. He also pointed a finger at international financiers and munitions makers such as DuPont which paid a hundred percent dividend on its common stock in 1916. Then there was an argument forgotten by the average citizen that war would be in violation of the Monroe Doctrine. It was usually overlooked that the historic hands-off warning to Europe in the Western Hemisphere also announced a noninterventionist-policy for the United States in Europe. President Monroe said:

Our policy in regard to Europe, which was adopted at an early stage of the wars which have so long agitated that quarter of the globe, nevertheless remain the same, which is not to interfere in the internal concerns of any of its powers; to consider the government de facto as the legitimate government for us; to cultivate friendly relations with it, and to preserve those relations by a frank, firm, and manly policy, meeting in all instances the just claims of every power, submitting to injuries from none. But in regard to those continents, circumstances are eminently and conspicuously different.

Sherwood, the descendant of British ancestors, reminded his listeners that England had tried to destroy the republic during the Civil War. The old soldier's recollections were still vivid, and he had not forgotten the English antagonism against the Union. He recalled, too, that Missouri and Maryland would have been lost to the Union if it had not been for German-Americans in those states. "And now," he said, "we are going to war as an ally of the one nation in Europe that has always been our enemy and against the nation that has always been our friend." He wondered, as a constituent had written to him, "Why attempt to overthrow 'Prussian militarism' abroad and intrench it within our doors?" The arguments and accusations that Sherwood made were not particularly original or profound. Others had made similar statements. The difference in his speech was his character and the weight of his military record.[12]

German-Americans in Sherwood's district may have appreciated his stand, but condemnation rained down upon him that reflected strong Allied sentiment. Nevertheless, he was not an easy target for his emotional critics who would have been delighted to tar him with un-Americanism, disloyalty, and dishonor. Charges of cowardice, yellow streaks, and burned effigies against other antiwar members of Congress were not so easy to fling at the war hero.

The fifty dissenters in the House who voted against the war resolution were an unusual lot. Forty-eight of the fifty would seek reelection and twenty-one were defeated. Two-thirds of them lost in primaries which showed dissatisfaction in their own parties. Congressman Edward King of Illinois, in contrast, was reelected with a greater majority than he ever had before. Nevertheless, he found in common with other antiwar Congressmen that his political enemies who held grievances against him for other reasons could now oppose him on the grounds of "patriotism." Jeannette Rankin of Montana had been elected to Congress prior to the passage of the Nineteenth Amendment to the Constitution that granted women's suffrage. She was probably the only pure pacifist among them and would live to cast her vote against war after the Japanese attack on Pearl Harbor. Fred Britten of Illinois was more prescient than even he realized when he spoke against entering the war. He had been impressed by the President referring to a "partnership of democratic nations—a league of honor." That league included Japan. Britten said, "And, just at a time when Japan was hoping that she might take over the Philippine Islands, Guam, and the Hawaiian Islands . . . Their plans also include the taking of the island of Java which will come under Japanese rule at the very first opportunity.[13]

Sherwood had no influence upon Wilson in his effort to keep the United States out of war. For the President, he was at most a minor gadfly. Primarily, Sherwood was a local politician without a voice in foreign policy, but he was a rare man who did not glorify war to advance his own career as a spokesman for militarism. It would have been so easy for him. It is also an established cliche that old men send young men to war. Sherwood was not one of those old men. After more than half a century his memory had not become colored or grown dim. The tendency of veterans to forget the pain and magnify their heroics were not among his transgressions. He still remembered that the romance of war was fiction. His vote against war was not a vote based upon intimate knowledge of international politics, economics, or dreams of a new world order. It represented the judgment of a man who knew war. The list was so long of men ready and even anxious for war who knew nothing of combat. Wilson could speak eloquently about the evils of battle, but it was nothing more than rhetoric.

Sherwood's long career came to an end in 1925 when he was ninety. Until the final months, he remained spry, energetic, and optimistic. When he died, the commander of the Forsyth Post of the Grand Army of the Republic forgot the harsh words against him and recalled, "He was a most wonderful man." A past president of the local chapter of the Sons of the Revolution, recently so bitter about his fight for peace, eulogized him as "one of the greatest patriots in American history" and "an inspiration to all lovers of their country." The mayor said, "All Toledo will mourn his loss."[14] Tributes flowed in from around the nation and newspaper obituaries devoted columns to his magnificent war record. There was scarcely a mention of his hatred for war or his courageous vote in 1917.

Chapter 6

The Women at The Hague

There was nothing in Jane Addams's appearance that suggested a dynamic leader. She was about five feet three inches tall, had dark eyes and complexion, and by middle age was slightly stooped. When she spoke, her voice was soft, calm, and unemotional. Her temperament and habit, she admitted, "had always kept me rather in the middle of the road in politics and social reform." Yet there was an indefinable quality in her presence that was appealing, and her ability as an administrator and shrewdness as a negotiator could never be underrated. Perhaps too, the mission at Hull House uplifted her. She knew how to get along with all kinds of people, young and old, rich and poor, educated and uneducated. She had, as the journalist Walter Lippmann once said, "compassion without condescension." When someone was needed to lead the way at hearings and conferences, she seemed to be the natural choice. Sometimes she received vicious letters from those who disapproved of her efforts at betterment, but many more saw her as a sensible woman of good will.[1]

By the beginning of the twentieth century, almost everyone in the country had heard about Hull House in Chicago where Jane Addams worked to build a better world for the poor and downtrodden. Her sense of mission introduced her to a squalid world, and she had the skill to dramatize her role in battles over child labor, unhealthy housing, long hours for working women, and discrimination. Every day she coped with confused immigrants, people from broken homes, prostitutes, thieves, and crooked politicians. The dignified, reserved young lady had shown no compunction about working as both a street and garbage inspector to learn how "the other half" lived.

As Addams's reputation grew, admirers called her a saint more often than any other woman in America. She was not a saint, but she was a good woman of many talents who deserved the recognition she ambitiously sought. Much of the attention that she received came from self-promotion in speaking and writing about her experiences in books and leading magazines such as *Ladies Home Journal, Atlantic,* and *American.* Her sense of drama and her way with words always made good copy and she pronounced her achievements while retaining an aura of modesty. Nevertheless, the achievements were real, the causes were noble, and her motives were pure. She had courage and a level head that was always practical in seeking tolerance for all.

Jane Addams was born in Cedarville, Illinois, in 1860, the eighth child, one of four to survive. Her father, John Addams, as Abraham Lincoln once wrote to him, was the one with the "two d's." He was a prosperous miller and grain merchant who served as a state senator during the Civil War and raised a military company even though he was a Hicksite Quaker. Her mother, Sarah Weber Addams, died when Jane was little more than two years old. The young girl, often plagued by poor health, had a pleasant childhood despite her ailments and graduated from Rockford Seminary in Illinois in 1881. In the years that followed she traveled abroad and searched for a mission in life. Among the places she visited was Toynbee Hall in London, the world's first settlement house, which made an indelible impression upon her. Eight years after graduation from Rockford, she and her classmate, Ellen Starr, under the influence of the Social Gospel, founded the settlement house at Polk and Halsted Streets in the nineteenth ward of Chicago. It was known as Hull House, the name of a previous owner, and it became the basis for the fame of Jane Addams, the more outspoken of the two founders.

At Hull House, Addams and Starr, initially at their own expense, provided health services, child day care for working mothers, English classes for immigrants, boys clubs, and a variety of other programs to help improve the quality of life for the impoverished. The neighborhood consisted mainly of newly arrived Irish, Italians, Russians, and Poles. Helping the poor meant combating local politicians to clean filthy streets or improve the sewer system, street lighting, and housing conditions. Addams's running feuds with Johnny Powers, the corrupt boss of the nineteenth ward, became legendary, and she occasionally won a battle. These political scraps led to her appearances before the city council, state legislature, and Congress.[2]

The work and publicity that surrounded Hull House attracted a wide array of volunteers who came and went. Some were young, idealistic college women, others were older, more experienced social workers. Dr. Alice Hamilton, who became the first woman on the faculty of Harvard Medical School, was a specialist in industrial diseases; Julia Lathrop, later the first chief of the United States Children's Bureau; and Florence Kelley, a well-known student of industrial conditions, were among those who lent their support. Even Governor John P. Altgeld had an interest in Hull House. There was a depth to Jane Addams that attracted men as well as women of achievement to her side.

Addams had held a passing interest in the subject of peace for a long time. In 1896, she met Leo Tolstoy during her travels in Russia and was impressed by his pacifist views even though she did not accept his more extreme ideas of nonresistance and passivity. She preferred action and once wrote, "Aristotle is reported to have said that politics is a school wherein questions are studied, not for the sake of knowledge, but for the sake of action."[3] She agreed. She was not one to sit idly.

The Spanish-American war may have raised her consciousness about the immorality of war, but at the time she was primarily busy with her own war against poverty and corrupt politicians. Still, her activity in mutual understanding, growth of democracy that would include women's suffrage, and belief in progress eventually led to increased involvement in the many ramifications of war and peace. Peace societies flourished after the war and their goals were quite acceptable for respectable people to ponder. Woodrow Wilson, for one, was a member of the American Peace Society. In 1899, Addams optimistically wrote, "Peace is not merely something to hold congresses about as an abstract dogma. It has come to be a rising tide of moral feeling, which is slowly engulfing all pride of conquest and making war impossible."[4]

Her opinion was not uncommon that as society improved, war was bound to disappear. In the following year, she joined William Jennings Bryan's campaign against imperialism and this added, rather than detracted, from her knowledge of the world. But she was wise enough to recognize the irony that "We bless peace and preach peace when all is peaceful; we justify and even uphold the necessity and beauty of war when war rages about us. It simply means that our religion and philosophy have no virility."[5]

Addams knew that war, with all of its horrors, brought out some of the noblest qualities of men. In 1903, she gave a speech called "A Moral Substitute for War." Since war had a dramatic appeal because it was "so much more magnificent to do battle for the right than patiently to correct the wrong,"[6] young men needed another road to adventure. The labor movement, social reform, and internationalism, she thought, might serve as that substitute. Four years later, her book *Ideals of Peace*, expressed faith in "constructive labor" which could replace destructive war. The book prompted Theodore Roosevelt to refer to "foolish Jane Addams." He had no sympathy for those who did not see the morality in war.

Although Addams never believed that women were superior to men, she was sure they held the key to a more peaceful world. Maternal instinct meant that women had an inherent interest in abolishing war. They were the life givers, the nurturers, who by nature opposed the barbarity of war. In the latter part of the twentieth century the argument has a quaint ring as women in their quest for equality now fight for the right to engage in combat. In the early part of the twentieth century, she spoke for most American women. As a consequence, in 1908, she was selected to represent women at the first National Peace Congress held in the United States and found herself in the company of such luminaries as William Howard Taft, Nicholas Murray Butler, Elihu Root, and William Jennings Bryan. Her stature rose to such eminence that she became the first woman to receive an honorary degree from Yale University, and other accolades followed.

Despite Roosevelt's snide remarks about Addams's peace efforts, she turned to him in the 1912 Presidential election. She was aware of his military spirit, but as President he had used the World Court of Conciliation and Arbitration at The Hague to settle a dispute with Mexico. That was the kind of pragmatic approach to peace that made sense to her. In the three-cornered race with the Republican Taft and Democrat Wilson, the Progressive Party appealed to her as the best alternative. Roosevelt also stood for women's suffrage, labor legislation, and social reform. At the national convention of the Progressive Party there were many distinguished professional women in attendance to lend their support. According to William Allen White, the Kansas newspaperman and ardent Progressive, "Our prize exhibit was Jane Addams."[7] As the best known woman in America, she received the assignment to second Roosevelt's nomination. She may have served as a token female, but she had also become an influential political figure before the Nineteenth Amendment gave women the constitutional right to vote. Always well organized and well informed, she campaigned vigorously. Someone claimed her help was worth a million votes which she immediately denied. There was no question, however, that she was a political force as she approached the peak of her career.

The new President, Woodrow Wilson, impressed Addams in the early days of his administration for his progressive interest in social reform, and when war broke out in Europe she approved his determination to remain neutral. By the end of 1914, Carrie Chapman Catt, the energetic leader of the suffragist movement suggested that Jane Addams join her in a conference that would organize women across the country to help find a way to peace. Catt said that when war came, the women waited for the peacetime pacifists to move, but they heard nothing from them. Even though it was the "eleventh hour" she thought it was time for women to act. Addams had her doubts about a separate women's movement, but she succumbed to the idea despite her misgivings. Her practical mind wondered if it could accomplish anything and she undertook the task "with a certain sinking of the heart."[8]

When the group met at the New Willard Hotel in Washington D.C., on January 10, 1915, Addams presided over 3,000 women. Among those present were Mrs. Robert La Follette and two militant pacifists from overseas, Madame Rosika Schwimmer of Hungary and Mrs. Emmeline Pethick-Lawrence of England. Schwimmer, in her late thirties, was an engaging speaker who knew how to rouse an audience and had traveled around the United States enlisting women to work for peace through mediation. Pethick-Lawrence saw the opportunity for a "woman's war against war." Another delegate, Fanny Garrison Villard, daughter of the abolitionist, William Lloyd Garrison, agreed. She said, "The fear of being called 'peace at any price men' made cowards of them all."[9] Addams showed her aptitude as a parliamentarian and desire for moderation in directing the gatherings along a middle path. Aside from her natural temperament, she had learned from experience that extremists usually hurt their own cause.

The outcome of the meeting was the formation of the Woman's Peace Party with Addams named as chairperson. There were eleven planks to a platform that included the need for convening neutral nations to engage in peace efforts. It also supported "continuous mediation," arms limitation, women's suffrage which was linked to peace, and a world organization that would substitute law for guns. Other planks favored democratic control of foreign policy, economic pressure instead of military force, removal of economic causes of war, and the appointment by the government of a commission of men and women to promote international peace. The aims of the huge meeting in the nation's capital were noteworthy, but not earthshaking and appeared to be one more ineffectual attempt to find peace that attracted little publicity. Later, Carrie Chapman Catt said working for peace was like "throwing a violet at a stone wall."[10]

The most practical suggestion of the conference was the call for "continuous mediation." It was the result of a plan developed by Julia Grace Wales, a Canadian who taught English at the University of Wisconsin. The idea differed from other mediation schemes in that experts would explore issues involved in the war and serve as a clearing house for both sides. It would invite suggestions from belligerents and submit proposals on such complex subjects as territorial boundaries, indemnities, and postwar problems. The hope was that these technical discussions would eventually lead to peace negotiations. Because commercial and scientific experts worked on an international level to solve their problems in the modern world, it seemed reasonable to her that the same practice could achieve a more peaceful world. The plan had been endorsed by the Wisconsin legislature and sent to President Wilson who showed no interest.

In the ensuing months, membership in the Woman's Peace Party grew rapidly and Addams's leadership foisted her into the forefront of one more movement. Shortly after the formation of the party, Rosika Schwimmer sent Addams a quote from George Bernard Shaw that appeared in the Woman's Suffrage number of the British magazine *Puck*. He asked, "When are the women going to tell us what surely they must have to say about war and how soon do they intend to stop it, or have they all become childish, or unreasonable or villainous or cowardly or romantic and impossible like the other sex?"[11] It was a flip challenge, but Addams accepted it.

In March, Addams attended an emergency peace conference in Chicago which adopted an arbitration plan to proceed without an armistice. A committee that included Addams requested an appointment with President Wilson to present the plan. Their thought, as they advised Wilson, was to help, not interfere or criticize. But the President had no desire to meet with pacifists. He believed such meetings only raised false hopes that peace could be attained soon. Wilson, always friendly and courteous to Addams, replied that he dare not meet with her. He received similar requests every week "and I should have to draw some distinction which would become invidious before I got through with them, unless I granted interviews to all who applied for them in this matter. I should welcome a memorandum from you with all my heart."[12] The President's predicament was understandable, but the arbitration plan, however presented, did not move forward.

Dr. Aletta Jacobs of the Netherlands, a physician and pacifist, invited the Woman's Peace Party to send a delegation to an International Congress of Women at The Hague from April 28 to May 1, 1915 with Jane Addams to preside. The meeting's vague objectives were limited to a protest against war and a discussion of how to make war impossible in the future. Women's suffrage was considered one of the ways. The distinction may have been insignificant, but it was never officially called a "peace congress."

Once again, Addams had doubts about the effectiveness of such a meeting at The Hague. It struck her as "hopelessly melodramatic and absurd." Nevertheless, she wrote to her friend Lillian Wald of the Henry Street Settlement in New York City, "that women who are willing to fail may be able to break through that curious hypnotic spell which makes it impossible for any of the nations to consider Peace."[13] She had touched on a profound consideration. Statesmen were afraid to act because they were afraid to fail. Practicing politicians, including Wilson, survived on success or the appearance of success. Failure was their death knell. The women were not afraid to face the danger of futility. Addams also knew, as many men did, that every day's delay meant the heightening of hatreds that would make any solution impossible. She decided there might be "just one chance in 10,000" to do some good.

Addams and the Executive Council of the Woman's Peace Party knew that the caliber of women who would go to The Hague was of paramount importance, and they strived to round up the best and brightest. Addams wished Ida Tarbell would attend because of her knowledge of economics, but the famous "muckraker" of the Standard Oil Company showed no interest. In urging Emily Balch, a professor of economics at Wellesley College, to attend, Addams wrote, "I am especially anxious that we should have delegates conversant with the racial and nationality situation, and I know of no one who would meet these requirements better than you would." In trying to lure the professor, she did not exaggerate the chances for success. They might "easily fail— even do harm. Our chance of success depends largely upon the personnel of the women who would go."[14] She believed there was a certain obligation for women who had the proper training and background to help out.

Emily Balch was exactly the kind of woman who appealed to Addams. She had a brilliant mind, broad experience, a quick wit, and modesty without fear of speaking out. As her biographer, Mercedes Randall, wrote, "She was popular in school even though 'smart.'"[15] At Bryn Mawr, where she graduated first in her class, she just missed the opportunity to study history under Professor Wilson who left before her senior year. At college she studied the classics and literature and later concentrated on economics and sociology at Radcliffe, the University of Chicago, and the University of Berlin. The use of economics to improve relations among people was one of her major interests. She was well traveled in Europe and well acquainted with Slavic people. Her great natural gift was linguistic ability. Aside from Latin and Greek, she knew French, German, and some Dutch, Swedish, Polish, Russian, and the common Slavic roots. For a time she had done field work with Jacob Riis, the well-known reporter for the *New York Sun*, who wrote about New York slums and was the author of *How the Other Half Lives*, and she worked at a Boston settlement house. This gave her an additional bond with Jane Addams.

Balch came from an old, upper class New England family and was one of five sisters and a brother. Her father was a lawyer who once served as secretary to Charles Sumner, the early antislavery Senator from Massachusetts. Perhaps she inherited his instinct for humane causes. Her mother was Ellen Maria Noyes of Newburyport. Emily was tall, slim, and usually quiet, but when she spoke her voice rang as clear as a bell. She was the sort of young girl who suffered at dances and later described herself as "only the plainest of New England spinsters and ex-teachers." Nothing could have been less true. The appearance may have been plain, the reality was a rare woman of the world.

Balch was active in the Wellesley branch of the Woman's Peace Party, but did not suffer from false illusions. She was aware of the dilemma that "too much demonstration of unwillingness to fight under any circumstances may weaken the hands of the Washington authorities in trying to get foreign nations to behave themselves decently."[16] It was not her aim to be an obstructionist. She knew that peace was a delicate, complex problem with many subtleties and ambiguities. Nonetheless, she cast aside her doubts and accepted the invitation to attend the meeting at The Hague.

Alice Hamilton also accepted an invitation to The Hague. She made her mind up quite suddenly and feared that her grounds were not exactly noble. She looked forward to the excitement. She had worked at Hull House and was well acquainted with Jane Addams. She was also well acquainted with Europe. After taking her medical degree at the University of Michigan, she had studied pathology at Leipzig and Munich as well as at the Pasteur Institute in Paris. While at Hull House her interest in occupational safety had led her to make a specialty of safety laws for industry and factory inspection systems. In 1908, Governor Charles Deneen of Illinois appointed her Commissioner of Occupational Diseases. After World War I, she wrote a classic text, *Industrial Poisons in the United States*. In a long life that ended in her hundred and first year in 1971, she always showed her independence and love of pioneering. As a young woman she became a doctor because "I could go anywhere I pleased . . . and be quite sure that I could be of use anywhere." And in the pursuit of industrial toxicology, she went everywhere. She was not afraid to explore deplorable conditions in mines, visit unhealthy saloons, or climb dangerous catwalks. Early in her career while living at Hull House and working as a professor of pathology at the Woman's Medical School, she also found time to start a baby clinic and investigate cocaine addiction. A handsome woman with a gracious manner and strong mind, her Harvard friend Felix Frankfurter, called her "the finest combination of exquisiteness and expertness."[17]

Among other American delegates were Dr. Sophonisba Breckinridge, an assistant dean of women at the University of Chicago, who taught social economy and was author of a weighty book, *Legal Tender—A Study in American Monetary History*; Alice Carpenter, director of the women's department of a New York investment house; Madeleine Doty of the Woman's Lawyer Association; Mrs. Lucy Biddle Lewis, a trustee of Swarthmore College; and Julia Grace Wales of Wisconsin University who Addams had urged to attend because she saw an opportunity to push the plan for continuous mediation. Others in the group of forty-seven Americans, who paid their own expenses, had equally distinguished careers. There were also a few who were well-meaning dilettantes. The misconception that most of the women were naive and inexperienced was false. Many of them had more intimate knowledge of Europe, the economy, and human nature than some leading male politicians.

The unrestrained Theodore Roosevelt was quick to condemn the undertaking. He wrote a public letter to Mrs. George Rublee, one of the delegates, "Pacifists are cowards, and your scheme is both silly and base." All the critics were not men. Mrs. William Lowell Putnam, sister of the president of Harvard University, spoke for many women when she said the Woman's Peace Party was dangerous and condemned the movement. One sympathetic man, less vitriolic, had reservations about the overseas trip. He wrote to Jane Addams that it sounded like "'Hollow Mockery' when our government permits, and sanctions, the manufacture and exploitation of all kinds of munitions of war—by private individuals and corporations." He thought it would be better for the Woman's Peace Party "to labor with our *own* 'ruler'—if you please—Mr. Wilson."[18]

Addams acknowledged to David Starr Jordan, president of Stanford University, that The Hague conference might be a "fool's errand" and wrote to Ray Stannard Baker that success was "uncertain and has about it, of course, a certain aspect of moral adventure." Aware of the possible consequences, she was ready for the adventure. On the eve of sailing, she spoke at a farewell dinner in New York City and said that the delegates had neither quixotic hopes nor expectations of stopping the war. Their hope was that some suggestions could be brought to the attention of those who might approach the belligerents and ask what they are fighting for and their terms for peace. Despite this modest goal, the chairman of the Committee on Military Affairs in the New York Assembly considered it "amusing to think that the female sex should have the effrontery to presume for a moment that it could bring sufficient pressure to bear on the belligerents to cause a cessation of hostilities at this or any other time."[19]

That same day, Woodrow Wilson spoke at an Associated Press luncheon for editors and publishers at the Waldorf-Astoria in New York. His speech, he said, could be summed up in the motto, "America First," a phrase not usually associated with the great internationalist. "Let us think of America before we think of Europe, in order that America may be fit to be Europe's friend when the day of tested friendship comes . . . getting to help both sides when the struggle is over. The basis of neutrality, gentlemen, is not indifference; it is not self-interest. The basis of neutrality is sympathy for mankind."[20] The women on their way to The Hague did not disagree with his repeated expressions of sympathy for mankind except that they did not want to wait for the war to end to help both sides.

Forty-two of the delegates sailed the next day on the Dutch liner *Noordam*. "We are going to be 'all sorts,'" Addams wrote to Lillian Wald, "and in that, perhaps lies our greatest value." Alice Hamilton, who had looked upon the voyage as a lark, found that she was never bored and time passed quickly. She noticed that Addams enjoyed herself and made everyone feel that she was their intimate friend. Some of the delegates may not have been the most promising material, but all in all, she was pleased with the selection. At first they were a chaotic group with some half-informed, muddled enthusiasts and sentimentalists, but as time moved on they evolved into a "coherent body." Each day there were long meetings with discussion and reading about the underlying causes of the war. Hamilton's touch of cynicism and sharp perception noted that they passed through the stage of poems, impassioned appeals and "messages for womankind" with willingness to die for the cause. The exchanges absorbed her and then all of a sudden the whole thing looked absolutely futile. "I suppose," she wrote, "I shall always be a doubting Thomas and pessimist." But she was evolving too and began to take the adventure more seriously. Eventually, her commitment to peace enabled her "to leave the muddled thinking behind."[21]

Emily Balch also realized that the group became more united during the crossing. She did not believe they deceived themselves about their power or importance. "We know we are ridiculous," she wrote in her diary, "but even being ridiculous is useful sometimes and so too are enfents [sic] terribles that say out what needs to be said but is not discreet or 'the thing' to say which important people will not say in consequence."[22] She knew that lack of power did not absolve them of responsibility.

The International Congress of Women convened on April 28, 1915 in a large audience in the Zoological Gardens at The Hague with 1,136 delegates from twelve nations. Most of them came from the Netherlands. There were also almost a thousand observers. The countries represented were Austria, Belgium, Canada, Denmark, Germany, Great Britain, Hungary, Italy, the Netherlands, Norway, Sweden, and the United States. Neither France nor Russia sent delegates. Dr. Aletta Jacobs welcomed the gathering and expressed the hope that the Congress would be the beginning of a better world. The interests of humanity, she said, went beyond the interests of any nation and it was too late in the day for war. In the prevention of future wars, she believed that women's suffrage would play an important role.

The Dutch police anticipated trouble and were present in the galleries for the first two days, but no trouble arose. Jane Addams, fifty-five years old, took up the gavel and did not have any difficulty maintaining order. During the day, the delegates worked on developing a platform and in the evening there were public speeches. Alice Hamilton found the meetings interesting and sometimes moving, especially when the Belgians or Poles spoke, but there was never an excess of emotional display. Instead, she felt a restrained undercurrent of emotion.

Contrary to expectations, the Congress received considerable press coverage. It was not all favorable. The Paris *Temps* said the Congress injected a note of comedy in war-darkened days. The Dutch papers sometimes showed contempt and the English papers, according to Hamilton, were quite nasty. Five German newspapers reported each day's proceedings respectfully. Favorable or not, the European press generally treated the meetings more seriously than Americans who found the ladies amusing. Not surprisingly, the British claimed that the conference was dominated by Germans while the Germans claimed the reverse. Since there were twenty-eight delegates from Germany and only three from Great Britain, the difference in numbers could have created a false impression. Alice Hamilton found the Germans to be an "unusually fine lot of women," able, fair, and generous.

As in most such meetings, many speeches were repetitious concerning woman's revulsion to the barbarity of war and the determination to find a substitute for carnage. The remarks against the savagery of war were platitudinous, but during the Congress a horrible example of their platitudes took place. The battle at Ypres began on April 22 and the German attack introduced poison gas in violation of any human code. The British gave ground and thousands met excruciating deaths, but the Germans did not gain a permanent victory with their new weapon. Their greatest achievement was to expose Allied weakness and the myth of General Kitchener's invincible troops. To make matters worse, the Allies soon adopted the frightful use of gas and thousands of Germans then suffered the same agony and death. During this holocaust, the International Congress continued. The *New York Times*, April 29, 1915, reported, "They emphasize women's responsibility for initiating a better world order." Mrs. Emmeline Pethick-Lawrence, the militant British pacifist, added that women were unique since they could protest against war without being called cowards.

In committee meetings, Emily Balch was invaluable in struggling with thorny problems of developing a platform. She showed a quiet sense of humor, scholarly knowledge of European politics and economics, and was quick in debate while she spoke French, German, or

The Women at the Hague

English. At times the ideas expressed seemed unreal to her, "so powerless before the vast physical force of the military masses today." She had to remind herself that it was only ideas that created that force. "Let force once be disbelieved and that force melts into nothing."[23]

In contrast to Emily Balch who never sought the limelight, there was the Hungarian, Rosika Schwimmer, another gifted linguist, who delighted in the center stage. Thirty-eight years old, impatient, quick to domineer, she was always suspicious of others. She called Jane Addams, "slippery Jane." But Schwimmer, whatever her many faults, was devoted to the cause of peace and knew how to inspire an audience to new emotional heights.

Julia Grace Wales persisted in trying to take a practical step toward peace by working for continuous mediation. The differences between her plan and older methods of mediation may have seemed negligible to some, but to her the differences were preeminent. The belligerents would not accept any such offer from a neutral nation. On the other hand, if a continuous conference of neutral nations stood ready to act when the opportunity arose, it could be of enormous value. The idea was not "stopping the war," desirable as that might be. The idea, as she had explained in Washington, was to offer a steady flow of expert information and serve as a clearing house for peace proposals from both sides without an armistice. The apolitical experts could supply specific data on causes of the war or possible terms for peace. Propositions could be continually revised until a solution might be reached. Wales did not claim originality for the plan. She was a developer. It replaced the traditional plan for a truce first which was always so difficult to achieve. She said the first Balkan War had been settled by continuous mediation which had been initiated by none other than the British Foreign Minister, Sir Edward Grey. At the final session of the Congress, Rosika Schwimmer proposed the plan and Wales was the seconder. It received a unanimous and enthusiastic endorsement as a tangible resolution that could conceivably produce a positive result in the near future.

As the Congress approached the end, a message was read from President Wilson. In a carefully worded statement, he expressed sympathy for the intent of the conference while mentioning that the United States had not been consulted about the meeting. He understood that the Congress of women preferred to work unofficially.

The final resolutions passed by the Congress bore a strong resemblance to the platform produced by the Woman's Peace Party at the

New Willard Hotel and the future Fourteen Points of Woodrow Wilson. The essential provisions for an enduring peace included the following:

- Territory should not be transferred without the consent of the people in the area. The right of conquest should not be recognized.
- Governments of all nations should agree to refer future international disputes to arbitration or conciliation and to bring social, moral, and economic pressure to bear upon any country which resorts to arms.
- Foreign policies should be subject to democratic control.
- Women should receive equal political rights.
- A call for an organization of nations which would include a permanent international court.
- Other objectives were disarmament, government manufacture of arms, freedom of seas, and no secret treaties.
- The formation of the International Committee of Women for Permanent Peace. (Later, it would become The Women's International League for Peace and Freedom.)[24]

The ever impatient Rosika Schwimmer wanted more than a "paper expression of pious wishes." She wanted action and focused attention on the resolution for continuous mediation. In stirring words, she introduced an additional resolution for the Congress to select delegates to take the resolution to responsible parties in neutral and belligerent countries to sound them out. Still, the more cautious Jane Addams had doubts about the idea, and others were strongly opposed. But Schwimmer's passionate oratory won and her resolution passed. The purpose of the mission was to make clear that whatever caused the war, the time had arrived for negotiations. If there were deep-rooted injustices and some nations suffered from the loss of commercial, political, or maritime opportunities, it was implied that a solution could be discovered better by men who considered the merits of the case rather than by military victories and losses.

The emissaries to carry the message to the warring nations were Jane Addams, Dr. Aletta Jacobs, and Rosa Genomi of Italy who left the group when Italy declared war. Dr. Alice Hamilton and Mevrouw van Wulffton of The Hague accompanied them unofficially. Hamilton, still skeptical, thought it would be a "singularly fool performance." The emissaries to the neutral Scandinavian countries and belligerent Russia were Emily Balch, Chrystal Macmillan of Great Britain, Rosika Schwimmer of Hungary, and Madame Ramondt-Hirschmann of the Netherlands. Julia Grace Wales joined this group as secretary, a modest title for the major proponent of continuous mediation.[25]

The two groups of travelers had little difficulty meeting heads of governments and foreign ministers and had the additional opportunity to meet and listen to ordinary people. After a visit with Prime Minister Cort van der Linden and Foreign Minister Loudon at The Hague, the Addams group left for London. They could not have arrived at a worse time. The *Lusitania* had just been sunk and British bitterness intensified. And the unneutral American ambassador Walter Hines Page, gave grudging assistance at best. He called the Women's Congress, "The Palace of Doves." Still, the women met with Prime Minister Asquith and Foreign Minister Grey, now a Viscount. They were advised in advance that the meetings had to be entirely personal and private. Eric Drummond, writing for Grey, said, "If you wish to present to him the Resolutions of the National Congress of Women and any observations which you desire to offer on them, he must ask that this shall be done officially and in writing."[26] The meetings were courteous and inclusive, but the British claimed that a belligerent could not make a move for peace because it would be an admission of weakness. Any action would have to come from neutral nations.

While Addams was in England, Louis Lochner, a young pacifist, went to Germany as an advance man to arrange for her visit. Ambassador Gerard told him that the women did not have "a ghost of a show to be received by the German government. The Germans do not care for peace." He was also told that no one was allowed to discuss peace, but Lochner spoke at a public meeting without any interference from the police. He spoke flawless German and rode in third class railroad cars to learn what ordinary people were thinking. He found that contrary to the impression he had received in America, the German people were not as united in the war effort as they once were and that the German press did not reflect the true opinion. Many people expressed the wish for an early peace, but were convinced that Germany was fighting in self-defense and that Russians broke into Germany before Germans invaded Belgium. Much of their bitterness came from the knowledge that the United States supplied arms and ammunition to the Allies.[27]

When Addams arrived in Berlin, she found the city appeared to be functioning normally. She did not see any unusual signs of poverty or suffering. The one exception to normality was the absence of young men on the streets. She watched a parade of about five hundred young soldiers, none more than nineteen, she thought, marching down an avenue with bouquets tied to their bayonets and ribbons on their caps. "It thrilled me, shocked me, horrified me to see them march gayly toward the slaughter."[28]

Despite Gerard's discouraging attitude, the Addams group received a friendly welcome from both the people and government officials. He may have forgotten that Addams was a respected international as well as national figure. Foreign Secretary von Jagow gave the same refrain as the British. The belligerents could not initiate action for a peace conference. The gesture had to be made by neutral nations, but there was a hint in his reply that he doubted American neutrality. Still, he agreed that neutrals should organize a conference along the lines proposed by the women. The depth of such agreement was always the question.

Addams met Chancellor Bethmann-Hollweg at his official residence alone. Although she was not deceived by simple courtesy from him or other officials, he impressed her as a good man who represented civil opinion against the military which was probably too strong for him to manage. The Chancellor had lost a son in the war, and there was no reason to doubt his sincerity in wanting to end the war. He said that Englishmen always expressed the desire to crush Germany while Germans never said they wanted to crush England. Addams replied that the English wanted to crush German militarism, but he did not see any difference. Bethmann-Hollweg did not believe the English understood any government except their own. One of the strange aspects of the war was that despite their differences, Germany had more in common with England than with Catholic Austria or Mohammedan Turkey. Perhaps it was merely another gesture, but the Chancellor said the neutrals had done little to bring about peace and that they should begin to make proposals and continue to make them.

Vienna presented a different picture from Berlin. There were food shortages, the bread allowance was small, and the horses were so thin their ribs could be counted. Wounded soldiers were noticeable everywhere. Prime Minister Stürgkh listened to the women's presentation and remained so silent he unsettled Jane Addams. Never as confident as she appeared, she wondered if she had said the right thing. To fill the silence, she added, "It perhaps seems to you very foolish that women should go about in this way; but after all, the world itself is so strange in this war situation that our mission may be no more strange nor foolish than the rest." Von Stürgkh responded by banging his fist on the table and said, "Foolish? Not at all. These are the first sensible words that have been uttered in this room in ten months." People came to him for more money and ammunition. "At last the door opens and two people walk in and say, 'Mr. Minister, why not substitute negotiating for fighting.' They are the sensible ones." The unexpected reaction was the most encouraging moment of the mission.[29]

Count Burián, Minister of Foreign Affairs for Austria-Hungary, favored a conference of neutral nations, but he did not think the United States should lead the way. He wanted its participation, but he did not want it to lead because it lacked an understanding of European interests. He also thought that President Wilson's early offer to mediate was ineffective because the belligerents were forced to turn down the offer. He wanted to see neutrals offer specific proposals to both sides and if they were not accepted, further proposals could be made. This was, of course, what the women wanted to hear. During the trip there were moments of such elation when everything seemed worthwhile and then, Addams wrote to Ellen Starr, "it fades into nothing." The doubting Alice Hamilton, however, began to take their expedition seriously.

In Budapest, Hungary's Prime Minister, Count Tisza, indicated that he would welcome negotiations. Hungary would be reasonable about terms because his countrymen were not gaining anything from the war. He said they fought the Russians, but did not dislike them because Slavs understood them while Germans and Austrians did not.

A brief meeting in Switzerland with President Motta and Foreign Minister Hoffman had little meaning. The women were told that the Swiss would join other neutral nations if they acted, but they always faced the necessity of remaining friendly with their neighbors. In Rome, there was a completely different atmosphere. Italy had recently entered the war on the side of the Allies and there was a fresh enthusiasm for patriotism and militarism. The women went through the motions of a meeting with Prime Minister Salandra and Foreign Minister Sonino, but they knew it meant nothing. The meeting at the Vatican with Papal Secretary of State Cardinal Gasparre and Pope Benedict XV was more positive. The Pope believed President Wilson should lead the way in mediation and the Vatican would lend support.

The most depressing visit was in Paris where bitterness and hatred permeated the air. France was the major battlefield of the war, and the dead and wounded had affected almost every French family. Foreign

Minister Delcassé, a longtime militant, was not receptive to any peace resolutions from the women at The Hague. His aim was to destroy Germany permanently. Premier Viviani was more affable, but unmoved by anything the women had to say. They noticed, too, that for the first time in their travels the police followed them with suspicion. While in France, the visitors also met with the Belgian Minister of Foreign Affairs d'Avignon who was located in temporary government headquarters at Le Havre. Although sympathetic to mediation, he was helpless to do anything because Belgian affairs were controlled by the Allies. This was the last visit for the group.

Addams returned to England for a week and met a number of notables including George Bernard Shaw and Bertrand Russell who were hardly representative of British thought. Russell was of the opinion that his views coincided with Addams. He was ready to admit everything that was said against the Germans, but as war went on he was sure the British were becoming more like the Germans. "The faults one hates in them," he wrote, "are not confined to them . . . The belief in punishment, which all nations have, seems to me quite mistaken, an outcome of hatred, in which there is no wisdom."[30] As he looked at the world, the working classes and fighting men at the front were saner than the rulers who remained at home. From England, Addams sailed for home, anxious to meet with President Wilson.

Meanwhile, Emily Balch and her group left the Netherlands for Copenhagen. Because Chrystal Macmillan and Julia Grace Wales were citizens of belligerent countries, they could not travel by train through Germany. Instead, they took a small, uncomfortable boat and faced the danger of striking a mine or being torpedoed. Undeterred, they arrived safely. Balch, Schwimmer, and Ramondt-Hirschmann had a more pleasant train trip through Germany. In Copenhagen, their meeting with Prime Minister Zahle and Minister of Foreign Affairs de Scovenies was formal but friendly. One of the chief objectives of the women was to ask the Scandinavian governments if they, with the Swiss and Dutch, would join in an invitation for a neutral conference with the assurance that the United States would respond positively. Now, it seemed important that the President had to make clear that it would not be considered a discourtesy if other neutral nations acted.

Emily Balch talked to the United States Minister to Denmark and was disillusioned by his attitude. She thought that everything seemed incredulous to him "that does not answer to preconceived notions." He regarded anything that diverged from the past as inconceivable.[31]

In Norway, King Haakon VII talked informally for an hour and three quarters to the delegation, an unusually long time, but Balch did not believe the conversation led anywhere. He seemed to be genuinely interested in continuous mediation, but the interest did not produce action. In addition to talks with Prime Minister Knudsen and the Foreign Minister, the Norwegians extended themselves by honoring the women with receptions at Parliament House and the Nobel Institute.

The Swedish welcome was equally friendly without producing any tangible results. Foreign Minister Wallenberg gave the impression that he was the most enthusiastic official they had met who favored mediation by neutrals and expressed some willingness to initiate a conference. The lack of specific results in their talks did not necessarily mean that the women had failed. They were, after all, acting unofficially and positive follow through would have to move through established channels.

Next on the itinerary was a visit to one belligerent, Russia, which took three days to reach Petrograd by train. Since Schwimmer was an enemy, her place was taken by Baroness Ellen Palmstierna of Sweden. They spent one week in the city waiting to meet Minister of Foreign Affairs Sasanov. Privately, the Minister said continuous mediation was "not unacceptable" to him, but he did not think it would accomplish anything at that time.

Second meetings were held with officials in Stockholm and Cristiana, and then some members of the two traveling groups met in Amsterdam to compare notes. They decided that neutral nations feared calling a mediation conference because it would be looked upon as an unfriendly act by the belligerents. To clear up this possible objection, Schwimmer and Ramondt-Hirschmann met with von Jagow in Berlin and Balch and Macmillan called on Vicount Grey in London. They received written statements from both nations that gave assurance that neutral action would not be considered unfriendly.

Jane Addams arrived in the United States on July 5 and waited in the East for an appointment with the President who did not see her until the twenty-first. Because she had just met eight prime ministers or presidents, nine foreign ministers, and the Pope, she wryly observed that she had not waited more than five days for an appointment. She wrote, "such is life." She hoped to see Wilson while he was vacationing at Cornish, New Hampshire, but he could not be interrupted. A reverent fan of the President said that he was "walking with God." Florence Kelley sarcastically thought it was more likely that he was "walking with Galt."[32]

In the meantime, Addams gave a speech at Carnegie Hall about her observations during the trip. When college students in one of the balconies of the packed house sent up three cheers she was delighted. "It's a good thing," she said, "to see that peace can be as rousing as war." She returned full of hope for continuous mediation and was certain that the United States had to act if there was going to be any movement at all. She presented the complexities of the situation in a straightforward manner and stressed the similarities of opinion of both belligerents. Both sides claimed they were fighting for self-defense; both sides could not show willingness to negotiate because it would be seen as a sign of weakness; both sides expressed an interest for neutral nations to lead the way in a negotiated peace; both sides were convinced they were fighting a righteous war; both sides were bitter about atrocities. For the Allies it was the Germans in Belgium, for the Germans it was the Cossacks in East Prussia. Both sides lacked an understanding of the other. And everywhere she heard that it was an old man's war. "The old notion that you can drive a belief into a man at the point of a bayonet is in force once more." To Jane Addams, it was foolish to think that militarism could be crushed by countermilitarism. America had to lead the search for peace. But none of the significant remarks of her speech attracted the press as much as her repetition of reports that soldiers took alcohol or other substances to dull their fear before going into combat. This gave an excuse for sensationalists to charge that she had slurred the honor of troops and challenged the glory of war.[33]

The exaggerated newspaper treatment of this practice among soldiers believed to be common, reinforced Addams's concern about the press in Europe and the United States. She thought untrustworthy press reports and the war fever they generated made it almost impossible for good citizens to honestly differ. It seemed to her that the press served its own motives and did not honestly interpret public opinion. Politicians in Europe were afraid to talk about negotiations while newspapers demanded unconditional surrender. Nationalism and "patriotism" were uppermost in the press and expressions of internationalism were denounced. The modification of government policies required the mobilization of public opinion, but the press restricted the basis for intelligent opinion. Addams said the ability of the press to be selective gave it a power which the church once exercised when it disseminated only the facts it believed were fit for the people. There were times when she thought the next revolution would be against tyranny created by the unprincipled power of the press.

No one had greater respect for young soldiers than Jane Addams. During her travels she found that they did not understand why they were fighting and were more pragmatic in their outlook. Older men were inclined to place their faith in nationalistic or theological abstractions. "Tragedy after all is not a conflict between good and evil," she observed. "Tragedy from the time of Aeschylus has been the conflict between one good and another, between two kinds of good, so that the mind of the victim is torn as to which he ought to follow, which should possess his allegiance. That sort of tragedy, I am sure, is in the minds of certain young men who are fighting upon every side of this great conflict." But such thoughts were too much for the press to convey in its headlines.[34]

While Addams waited for Wilson, she visited Colonel House in Manchester, Massachusetts, in the hope that he would be helpful. Her illusion about any assistance from him was badly mistaken. After their talk, the colonel wrote to Wilson, "She has accumulated a wonderful lot of misinformation in Europe. She saw von Jagow, Grey, and many others, and for one reason or other, they were not quite candid with her, so she has a totally wrong impression. . . ."[35] The obvious reaction is to wonder if the same men were candid with House. The colonel believed that he was capable of manipulating others, but seemed unaware others might manipulate him.

After repeated postponements, Addams met the President who treated her with his usual courtesy. Their conversation, however, did not lead to any effective commitment. Wilson did not believe it was the right time to propose mediation. Addams, under the impression during their talk that he would act when that time arrived, agreed. She was wrong. All she accomplished was to present the resolutions of the International Congress of Women.

Julia Grace Wales read a newspaper account of the Addams interview with the President and his discouraging opinion that it was not wise to act at present. She realized that Wilson was a busy man and wondered if he understood the fine points of continuous mediation. She knew that it was difficult to recognize the shades of difference with other plans and reiterated some of the key points in a letter to Addams. It was not a diplomatic function, she said, and a league of neutrals was not bound to neutral obligations. It was "merely a free scientific conference, of which the members would not have to agree among themselves on any one proposition." And it did not suggest an effort for immediate peace, "but the beginning of indefinitely lengthy mediation without armistice." She was particularly disturbed by the argument that the time was not ripe. It was to her a theory without proof. The question was not whether the time was right "but whether there is an advantage in beginning to put forward proposals for consideration *before the time for peace is ripe* in the hope that they will tend to ripen them." She believed that "truth does tend to work on the mind" and that it should begin early. If there were no standing proposals, how could anyone know when the time for peace was ripe? She wanted to see a sitting commission throughout the war to put simultaneous conditional proposals before all. Neither one side nor the other could think effectively without exact data. Addams understood Wales's arguments and frustrations, but whether or not the President was aware of the fine distinctions was unknown. The presumption is that he was fully aware of the distinctions, but feared the outcome the process might produce. The real complaint was that he did not act. The man who dreamed of a community of nations hesitated to take the first step. At that time the Central Powers held a stronger military position and the Allies would not be pleased by an American peace initiative.[36]

In mid-July, Colonel House received a message from Grey that he presumably conveyed to the President about America's peace-making role. The British Minister thought it would take "very great provocation" for the United States to go to war, but if it did, "I believe it is certain that the influence of the United States on the larger aspects of the final conditions will prevail, and I am very doubtful whether anything short of being actually involved in the war will stir your people sufficiently to make them exercise, or enable the President to exercise, on the terms of peace all the influence that is possible. Personally, I feel that the influence of the President would be used to secure objects to future peace that we all desire." Grey's tantalizing letter cleverly tempted an idealistic President to enter the war for the sake of peace. There is little doubt that was one of Wilson's goals in 1917 and it may have affected him in 1915.[37]

Emily Balch met with Wilson in August. The President did not look forward to the meeting. "I know these good people are not going to let the matter rest until they bring it to a head one way or another. I must, I suppose, be prepared to say either yay or nay," he wrote to Lansing. But he did not say "yay or nay" in his hour-long meeting with Balch. Wilson's only remark that stood out in her mind was that he would not wait to be asked to mediate. Instead of taking the initiative, however, he waited for something to happen and then reacted. Many years later, looking backward, Balch wrote, "In spite of real interest in the plan in some responsible quarters, it was wrecked by President Wilson's refusing to take it up. He doubtless felt that he could act better alone when the time came, but when it came he was no longer a neutral but completely involved in the power politics of the Allies."[38]

In the months that followed, Addams, Balch, and others continued to lobby for continuous mediation without success. Meetings with House and Lansing in the hope that the two men would persuade the President to see their point of view were a waste of time. Both men used their influence in the opposite direction. The firm opposition to mediation by House was especially difficult to understand. In August, he received a letter from Grey that said, "no one could resent any efforts of neutrals which were impartial and independent to promote peace, but I did not think a conference of neutrals would be of much use unless the United States was in it. If the end of this war is arrived at through mediation, I believe it must be through that of the United States."[39]

Lansing was certain that the belligerents were against peace moves by neutral nations because he was sure that the civil leaders in the belligerent countries were opposed to the idea. He discouraged the President from any neutral movement because "it would fail and because, if it did fail we would lose our influence for the future." Wilson agreed. Once again the fear of failure hindered them from making any overtures for negotiation. When Balch met Lansing after she returned home, her reaction was disheartening. He impressed her as amoral and cynical, "however shrewd and capable he may be as an international lawyer." He ridiculed continuous mediation and said it would be meddling for the United States to propose peace terms. Balch reminded Lansing that the disinterested action of the United States under President Roosevelt brought peace between Russia and Japan. He replied that the agreement was harmful.[40]

In November, Addams, Wald, and Schwimmer called on House, and he noted in his diary that it was "the same old story of trying to get the President to appoint a peace commission jointly with other nations."[41]

Addams and Balch held other meetings with the President that were equally unsatisfying. One correspondent wrote to Addams, "If we wait until Wilson acts we will wait a long time." The writer thought he may have done nothing because he believes the side "he evidently favors" will win.[42] The women had become accustomed to agreements on broad objectives from politicians which were followed by rejection of specifics. They continued to hear that the present was the wrong time and that

Wilson needed freedom of action for the future. When Addams met Wilson early in 1916, he repeated his concern about dealing with neutrals and indicated he might take steps to mediate on his own. The difficulty was that the tides of war were always shifting and he continued to wait. During that meeting, Wilson took out the resolutions of the Women's Congress which she had given to him months before. They looked well fingered. He said to her, "I consider them the best formulation which up to the moment has been put out by anybody."[43] Since some of the resolutions would find their way into his famous Fourteen Points at the end of the war, he was unquestionably sincere. He was ready to accept their advice for the postwar world but not before American entry into the war. At the time, Addams despaired about her lack of progress with the President to make a bold attempt to end hostilities. Ironically, Addams and those progressive internationalists who shared her views receive credit from Wilsonian scholar, Thomas J. Knock, as the advance guard of the New Diplomacy. "From them," he wrote, "emanated most of the components of Wilson's formula for a new world order as well as a program for social and economic justice at home."[44]

Addams and her associates were continually accused of wanting to isolate the United States when they were trying to do exactly the opposite. They urged the United States to "lead the nations of the world into a wider life of coordinated political activity . . . that modern wars are not so much the result of quarrels between nations as of the rebellion against international situations inevitably developed through the changing years, which admit of adequate treatment only through an international agency not yet created."[45] When Addams first became interested in the peace movement, she hoped that the internationalism engendered in the immigrant sections of American cities might serve as effective instruments for peace. Her experience at Hull House convinced her that the diverse population should make it easier for Americans to form an international organization. But 1915 and most of 1916 slipped by while the President waited and the point of no return for negotiations had probably passed.

At the start of 1916, congressional hearings on Wilson's preparedness program were underway and Addams appeared before the House Committee on Military Affairs as president of the Woman's Peace Party. Previously, she had reminded Wilson of his statements to reduce the "vast burden of armaments which has crushed to poverty the peoples of the world." Now, before the committee, she said, "I am speaking for those women all over the country who can not understand what has so suddenly turned public opinion in the direction of an increase for the Army and Navy, when even hypothetical enemies are across the ocean, and nobody knows really that we have any enemies. These women can not understand why the Government should want to 'prepare' before there is a need to contemplate war."[46] Her hope was for the United States to wait until after the European war to adopt a new military policy. Then there would be a possibility to work for proportional disarmament. Congressman Tilson said that history illustrated that wars were inevitable. She replied that the lesson of this war was that preparedness did not prevent war.

Addams, like Bryan, Stone, and many others who had been disappointed by the President, gave him her support in the 1916 campaign. It was an act that he fully appreciated, and he recognized the value of her assistance. After Wilson won reelection, he sent a note to the belligerents in December 1916 asking for their terms to end the war. It seemed as though he was starting to take the initiative. He did not call for continuous mediation or ask neutrals to act, but it was a move toward mediation even if late in the day. Addams thanked him for his action and he replied, "I knew that you would sympathize and am happy to think of your sympathy."[47] She was further pleased with his "peace without victory" speech in January 1917 which aimed at a community of power and an organized peace. Her mild elation did not last, however, when the belligerents showed no interest.

Later, when Addams met Wilson at the White House with members of the Emergency Peace Federation, he showed no interest in arbitration or conciliation and she left in "deep dejection." War was at hand. She recalled him saying, "as head of a nation participating in the war, the President of the United States would have a seat at the Peace Table, but that if he remained the representative of a neutral country he could at best only 'call through a crack in the door.'"[48] She had recently heard that same remark from Colonel House which, unknown to her, echoed the sentiments of Lord Grey's letter to him in July 1915.

Addams believed that Wilson had overrated his own leadership and wondered if it was too much for one man to formulate ideals and then live by them. She was weary of the grand speeches of statesmen that had become threadbare. When she read about opponents of Napoleon talking about war aims in the early nineteenth century, they had a familiar ring. Then there was oratory about "the reconstruction of the moral order" and "the establishment of an enduring peace founded upon a just redistribution of political forces." When Napoleon met defeat, none of those noble aims was fulfilled by the Allies. It was the same old story, the same old words empty of meaning. When would anyone learn? In her book, *Peace and Bread,* she asked whether any man had the right to rate his moral leadership so high that he could consider the sacrifice of the lives of thousands of his young countrymen a necessity. War, she believed, destroyed more democratic institutions than anyone could rebuild.[49]

As war approached, Jane Addams, the so-called saint and leading woman of America, found herself transformed into a prominent villain. It was a role she did not enjoy playing. She had been a respected leader for so long, it was a rude awakening to find that she was in disrepute. When war was declared, she led a lonely life against her natural inclinations. She had always enjoyed being among people. Now she admitted that she traveled "from the mire of self-pity straight to the barren hills of self-righteousness" and despised both. She was not a woman who fooled herself. Her doubts disturbed her deeply and she asked herself if any individual had "the right to stand against millions of his fellow countrymen. Is there not a great value in mass judgment and instinctive mass enthusiasm?" She would have loved to be a part of that enthusiasm. In her fight for peace, she had become more radical, but she hated the idea of being a "crank" or a "centro-egotist." She lost many friends, and others begged her to give up her opposition to war. They said she was "committing intellectual suicide and would never again be trusted." She was not insensitive to their arguments which increased her torment and tested her courage. The luxury of smug, blind conviction was not a part of her character. With all of her inner doubts, she held fast to her beliefs and took comfort in the thought that most great changes in life came from a "variation from the mass."[50]

The American women at The Hague reaffirmed their loyalty to the country, but they were a suspect lot. A minister said, "If Jesus were living today he would be fighting in the trenches of France."[51] Addams thought it was more likely that Jesus would be under surveillance by the Justice Department. Her agony was made worse by the tragic news that her nephew was killed fighting in the Argonne. Eventually, Herbert Hoover, the food administrator, rescued her from depressing confinement and put her to work traveling around the country campaigning for food conservation.

Other women at The Hague suffered from the consequences of their convictions too. Emily Balch, for one, found that she was not reappointed to her professorship at Wellesley in 1918. After twenty years of service to the college, she left gracefully and devoted the rest of her life to the cause of peace. Both she and Addams were named in a list compiled by the Military Intelligence Bureau in 1919 which was submitted to the Senate Judiciary Committee for connections with "pro-German pacifist movements prior to entry of the United States into the war."[52] In time, both women survived the opprobrium.

By 1931, a popular magazine formed a committee of distinguished men and women to select the "twelve greatest living women of America." Jane Addams headed the list. She accepted the honor, but noticed that one member of the committee had once regarded her as a traitor, and she was sure that at least two others had never heard of her before the "contest." That same year she received a more prestigious award, the Nobel Peace Prize. It was shared with Nicholas Murray Butler, President of Columbia University to the amazement of many who remembered that he had succumbed to war hysteria when he condemned Senator La Follette and some faculty members who opposed the war. Nevertheless, it was a well-earned recognition for Addams. Professor Halvan Koht, who made the speech in her honor, said, "She clung to her idealism in the difficult period when other demands and interests overshadowed peace ... She was the right spokesman for all the peace-loving women of the world."[53]

In 1946, Emily Balch, the girl who always felt so awkward, received the Nobel Peace Prize with international YMCA leader Dr. John Mott. A patronizing editorial in the *New York Times* referred to her pacifism as the "kindly and simple sort" and expressed disappointment that a nominee was not found among the statesmen who had "done the hard and tedious work of trying to put the United Nations on its feet." They hoped that eventually "a shining name or two will be found worthy in this field." Gunnar Jahn, chairman of the Nobel Committee, held a different view. He referred to her practical work at The Hague and said of Emily Balch, "She has shown us that the reality we seek must be won through hard work in the world in which we live, but she has shown us more than this; that one does not become exhausted and that defeat gives new courage for the struggle to those who have within them the holy fire."[54]

Chapter 7

The Tycoon

Henry Ford was a mechanic, a very good mechanic, as everyone knew, but the opinion prevailed that mechanics were not the best makers of public policy. Essentially, they worked with their hands and minds on nuts and bolts which seemed to preclude them from the ethereal world of politics. Colonel House, the self-appointed political expert, spent an evening with Ford and found him crude and ignorant. How such a man amassed so many millions was beyond him. The only safe subjects for conversation were machinery and farming. But even House conceded that Ford was an idealist as well as a mechanical genius.

House did not recognize that Ford's genius was a gift for simplicity that enabled him to break down the complexities of life into fundamentals. He was a pioneer who consistently cast aside conventional wisdom, used his imagination, and scaled impossible barriers. If he had conformed to accepted thinking, there would have been no Ford Motor Company, no assembly line, no Model T. And he would not have paid his workers five dollars a day when the average wage was less than half that amount. As an idealist he thought and philosophized about the greatest good for the greatest number. It was true, however, that when he applied his particular kind of analytical mind to aspects of society outside the factory the results often shocked people who regarded them as bizarre. As House observed, Ford's knowledge of the intricacies of international politics was minimal at best. He was an intuitive thinker, prone to make judgments without deep study.

By 1914, Ford was accustomed to patronizing people who underrated his ability and overrated his money. It did not matter much. He was in the prime of life, energetic, strong willed, and always impatient to get on with the next project. At fifty-one he was trim in appearance, medium height, with keen blue eyes, and gray hair. Although not a sparkling conversationalist, he was friendly and without pretense. Never short of opinions and frequently cynical, he expected his ideas to be translated into action without delay. Everyone was in awe of his money, but he knew that achievement, not money, meant much more. Although he had contributed as much as anyone to an industrial revolution, he did not waste his time on self-congratulation.

Ford, the friend of rural America, was born July 30, 1863, shortly after the Battle of Gettysburg, on a farm in Greenfield Township, Wayne County, Michigan. He was the second of eight children of William and Mary Ford, a family descended from English freeholders who settled on Irish land confiscated by Queen Elizabeth. Ford's father made a decent living, and he hoped that Henry would follow him as a farmer, but the son's inherent interest in mechanical engineering led him in a different direction. In 1888, he married Clara Bryant who supported him every step of the way in his hectic career. He appreciated her unquestioning loyalty, especially in the early days, and called her "The Believer." They had one son, Edsel. It was 1908 when Ford introduced the Model T and 1913-14 when the moving assembly line got underway.

Mary Ford, according to some stories, instilled in her son a hatred for war. Although possibly apochyphal, it is not unlikely that living through the dark days of the Civil War had sharpened her pacific feelings. Whether or not Ford's mother influenced him, there was no question that he detested war. When hostilities broke out in 1914, Ford considered it unnecessary, immediately sensed the tragedy, and feared American involvement. In the ensuing years he issued many public statements expressing his antiwar opinions. He had no trouble reducing war to its simplest terms. War was murder. "To my mind," he said, "the word murder should be embroidered in red letters across the heart of every soldier."[1]

There was no doubt about the depth of Ford's beliefs, but too often his public pronouncements had the ring of truisms, extremism, or wistfulness. Before the war was over he would have the distinction of being the only multimillionaire to be called an anarchist. To many, the practical man offered nothing more than impractical solutions. His platitudes, however, sometimes camouflaged sensible and creative ideas. At any rate, he courageously spoke out when others who agreed with him remained silent in the face of sneers and ridicule. Most prominent people trembled at the thought of being laughed at by the crowd.

For all his pacifism, Ford did not consider himself a pacifist. It was probably a distinction without a difference. War was desolation and destruction to him, but he did not believe that his hatred was based upon nonresistant principles. He was a producer who hated waste and war was the greatest waste of all. It was an "orgy of money" and an "orgy of blood," and as far as he could see, war never settled anything. It made the world a disjointed mass. He believed the people knew that basic fact even if the politicians did not. He wanted to see a world of self-supporting nations that would serve each other because a few nations trying to grab the world's trade only promoted war. In his opinion, that was a lesson international bankers, his bête noir, had not learned. "We boast of independence," he said in April 1915. "There is only interdependence."[2]

All kinds of people opposed America's entry into the European war. No one, however, was ready to sacrifice more financially than Ford. In crude terms, he was ready to put his money where his mouth was. He knew that his factories could make huge profits from war orders, but he did not see how making money by sacrificing other men's lives was patriotism. Quite naively and erroneously he was certain that the continuation of wars would make it harder for "the upright businessman to regard war as a legitimate means of high and speedy profits."[2] At the same time he considered international bankers and munitions makers as the underlying cause of war and did not hesitate to criticize J. P. Morgan's firm for making a half billion dollar loan to the Allies. With bankers in mind, he once said, "New York wants war, but the United States doesn't."[3]

When Woodrow Wilson initiated his preparedness program in earnest, Ford responded that a nation fully prepared was a nation seeking war. He denounced the military initiative in a carefully worded statement. Many of Ford's antiwar pronouncements were written by Theodore Delavigne, a former Detroit newspaperman, whom he hired as a "peace secretary," but the sentiments belonged to the industrialist. "I have prospered much," Ford said, "but I am ready to give much to end this constant, wasteful 'preparation.' Not by building palaces of peace, not by inspiring fearful peace by powerful armaments, but by teaching men, women, and children of America that war does not threaten us, that the fulness of peace is their inheritance, not the burden of militarism, with its heavy hand that curbs liberty, and its foul sustenance upon the blood, the labor, and the toil-earned happiness and goods of the workers."[4] He admitted that he did not know the best way to undertake the task, but he was ready to do battle against the "breeders of war." The man constantly characterized as uneducated and narrowminded, believed education was one way to fight for peace. He wanted a small fraction of the energy devoted to preparedness transferred to the elimination of national and international differences that had built up over the centuries. If that were possible, there was a chance that war might cease.

The sneers came quickly. An editorial in the *New York Times* suggested that Ford was not qualified to speak with authority on anything except making and selling cheap cars. When he strayed from his business, he was not "a marvel of light and learning."[5] The desirability of Ford using his money to keep the United States out of war was also questioned. Apparently editorial writers, not always marvels of light and learning themselves, could express their opinions, but Ford should restrain himself. Ford also faced criticism within his company that proved costly. James Couzens, his invaluable and equally strong-minded associate who handled the financial side of the business, sharply disagreed with Ford's notions about peace, preparedness, war loans, and the Allies. Their differences were the specific cause for Couzens's resignation. He said, "The friendly relations that have existed between us for years have been changed of late, our disagreements daily becoming more violent."[6] His departure was a great loss.

When Ford, the impulsive man of action, assigned a job in his plant he expected immediate follow through. He placed severe time pressures on his men, and they were usually met. When he looked at the interminable war, he could not understand why a definite plan did not move forward instead of endless, meaningless talk about peace and humanity that led nowhere. He shared a widely held opinion that Wilson had lost opportunities in 1915 to end the war through planned mediation. In the fall of that year Ford met the dynamic Hungarian, Rosika Schwimmer, who was one of the leaders of the International Congress of Women which had met at The Hague in the spring. She and Louis Lochner, the young American pacifist, convinced Ford that continuous mediation could be effective. After some hesitation Ford said in his typical manner, "Well, let's start. What do you want me to do?" Later, at a meeting at the McAlpin Hotel in New York with Jane Addams, Oswald Garrison

Villard, and others, the conversation led to the idea of Ford chartering an ocean liner to promote the mission abroad. The thought of a special ship probably emanated from Lochner. It appalled Addams who believed the idea was unnecessary and too spectacular. In the end, Ford did not charter a ship, the *Oscar II*, but the effect was the same. He paid for his guests at a cost of about $400,000 and "The Peace Ship" probably made him the butt of more mean jokes than anyone else in America. He was the new Don Quixote.

Ford envisioned an expedition to Europe that would include some of the most distinguished men and women in the country to spur mediation for peace. Their distinction would presumably add weight in achieving their serious purpose. Ford knew that some of his well-known friends and acquaintances yearned for peace, and he misled himself into believing that they would enlist in his venture. Among them were Thomas Edison, John Wanamaker, the merchant prince, and John Burroughs, the naturalist.

John Wanamaker said, "Mr. Ford has three things—a mission, a generous heart, and a fat pocketbook; but he has no plan to stop the war."[8] There was no question that Ford had jumped into the project without sufficient planning, but he had a plan. Ford's intention was to form a mediating commission backed by the prestige of the United States government that would consist of responsible representatives of neutral nations. They would conduct continuous mediation, serve as a clearing house for peace proposals, and present objective studies concerning disputed issues among the belligerents. This was, of course, the plan developed by Julia Grace Wales. Because the technique had been used in labor conflicts, it did not appear to be a far-fetched idea. Ford said in his uncomplicated manner, "Men sitting around a table, not men dying in a trench, will finally settle the differences." One of his first steps was to meet with President Wilson at the White House to urge the establishment of such a commission. When the automaker sought an appointment, the reluctant Wilson reportedly said, "Mr. Ford has proved himself so unwise recently that I think this interview should be avoided if possible." But Joe Tumulty, his secretary, did not think that Ford could be ignored and an appointment was scheduled.[9]

When the two men met, Ford, according to accounts, talked to Wilson as a "plain American." Their meeting was cordial, but unproductive. Ford, breaking the ice, told the most recent joke about the man who wanted to be buried with his Model T because it had pulled him out of every other hole. Wilson responded in the same manner by reciting an amusing limerick. When they got down to business Wilson claimed that he approved the idea of continuous mediation, but he did not want to be connected with a single project in his search for peace. He felt he must be free to act. If he really considered the plan worthwhile, it is not clear why his approval would have closed other avenues to peace.

Even a friendly unofficial nod from Wilson could have reduced the ridicule and altered the atmosphere. Ford futilely offered to finance the plan. Finally, he said to Wilson, "If you feel you can't act, I will."[10] Nevertheless, the lack of government sponsorship was the death knell for the project.

Ford left the White House convinced that Wilson had missed another opportunity. "He's a small man,"[10] he said. The lack of a favorable gesture from Wilson made him more vulnerable to a multitude of jibes. Those who had kind words for his plan came from quarters not normally considered a part of his sphere. Most notable among them were the Socialists, the Jewish press, and the rabbis who expressed their admiration for his ideals and courage.

Newspapers had a field day printing quotations making fun of Ford from almost any celebrity seeking publicity. They indicted Ford for creating a farce, and he became fair game for an odd assortment of critics from the Christian evangelist Billy Sunday to Alton B. Parker, the Democratic Presidential candidate in 1904 who pictured the industrialist as "a clown strutting on the stage for a little time." Parker's adversary in 1904, Theodore Roosevelt, was delighted to agree with his former rival that Ford was not only "mischievous," but "ridiculous." In London, George Harvey, Wilson's early promoter for President, announced that he was "disgusted" with Ford which pleased the British and further diminished the mission in their eyes. "It is silly," Harvey said, "Mr. Ford has for a long time been regarded as a public nuisance in America along with Mr. Bryan. . . . No serious minded man in America or elsewhere can think of this Ford expedition as anything but ludicrous."[12]

Despite the critics, Ford sent out his invitation to prospective delegates by telegrams and letters. The telegram read: "The time has come for a few men and women with courage and energy . . . to free the goodwill of Europe that it may assert itself for peace and justice, with the strong probability that international disarmament can be accomplished."[13] Ford invited college students to join the voyage as part of an educational experience. John Hibben, president of Princeton, feared that his students might be contaminated by joining the peace ship and

The Tycoon 103

prohibited their participation. Ford seemed to be a supreme embarrassment and humiliation to the nation.

The rejections to Ford's invitation that flowed in were enough to dishearten the most ardent supporters of the project. The Governors had a ready excuse. They were too busy, but sent their best wishes. Rolland Spalding, Governor of New Hampshire, was one of the more forthright. He added that he could not accept, "even if I believed which I do not that undertaking is wise and practicable." The names of respondents who refused could have made up a directory of very important people. Colonel House, as might be expected, turned down Ford's invitation. He regarded it as a crude effort. Louis Brandeis had "imperative engagements." Helen Keller wanted more information about the practicability of the project and eventually decided not to make the trip. Clarence Darrow, the famed attorney, wrote that he did not believe he could be of service "or that it is quite right for the people of this country who so far have done nothing but make money out of the war to offer any advice in its settlement." H. J. Heinz courteously and thoughtfully replied that representations coming from private citizens of neutral nations "who speak without the authority of their governments, will be ineffective." The scientist, Charles Steinmetz, sent a sympathetic letter. He was in poor health and did not think his German name would help the cause. "You realize, however," he wrote to Ford, "that those financial, industrial and military influences, which benefit from war and destruction, will be strongly opposed to your endeavour, and only the pressure of an international people's conscience can persuade them to accept peace." He thought the people had submitted to "false nationalism and false patriotism." When David Starr Jordan, the peace-loving president of Stanford University, turned down his invitation, Lochner desperately tried to persuade him to change his mind. In his anxiety, he grossly distorted the truth. "The New York press now dead in earnest with us," he wired to Jordan. Even more outlandish, he added, "Governors of various states practically unanimous behind the proposal." The Governors were practically unanimous in their rejection. Jordan did not budge. He thought the movement had an air of opera bouffe, and that there was no evidence that the mediation commission would consist of carefully chosen experts in international law.[14]

Jane Addams found the sensational publicity distasteful and regarded some of the people surrounding Ford eccentric, but she decided to join the expedition. "I had learned from life—to use Dante's phrase, that moral results are often obtained through the most unexpected agencies."[15] Soon, however, she found that she had to undergo serious surgery and canceled her acceptance. Although her ailment was genuine, it was initially interpreted as a lame excuse. Emily Balch served as her substitute, but she did not sail on the *Oscar II*.

Ford had sought publicity for his cause, but it backfired and was abetted by his own careless statements. The remark most widely used against him was his exaggerated claim, "We're going to try to get the boys out of the trenches before Christmas."[16] Even the ever hopeful David Starr Jordan thought he was going too far. Privately, Ford held lower expectations, and he would have been much wiser to restrain his offhand comments. The chief effect he had wanted was psychological plus the possibility of driving the preparedness program off the front pages. Preparedness in his simplified terms was like a man carrying a gun. He thought men and nations with guns were bound to get into trouble. When someone told Ford that only a miracle could make the mission a success, he replied, "Miracles are only the aspiration of the many carried out by the few."[17] His experience convinced him that there was no man alive who could not do more than he thought he could do. That was his attitude as he prepared to depart on the peace ship. Mrs. Ford, "The Believer," sympathized with her husband's purpose, but not his means. She pleaded with him to stay home, but he believed it was worth a gamble. This time, however, "The Believer" stayed home.

Samuel Marquis, a former clergyman and employee of Ford's, spent most of the night before the expedition left with Ford and his old friend William Livingstone. The two men tried at that late hour to persuade Ford to give up a futile task, but they had no success. "It is right, is it not, to try to stop the war?" When Marquis answered "Yes," Ford replied, "You have told me that what is right cannot fail."[18] When they argued that right things attempted in the wrong way could not ensure success, Ford was not impressed. He had made his last will and testament that day and his mind was made up.

Marquis thought Ford had a complex mind "of strength and weakness, of wisdom and foolishness, in which the shallows are the more pronounced because of the profound depths which lie between." He wished Ford had been properly assembled.

Others commented on Ford's dual nature. Louis Lochner later wrote that the left half of Ford's face was that of an idealist, humanitarian, and dreamer while the right half of his face was "shrewd, sharp, cynical, full of cunning." By then, however, Lochner was an embittered pacifist.[19]

The Tycoon

The *Oscar II* sailed from Hoboken on December 4, 1915. It was a cold, depressing day with freezing light rain, but two bands played to try to make it a festive occasion. One of the favorite tunes was, "I Didn't Raise My Boy to Be a Soldier." There was as much confusion at the pier as there had been at the temporary headquarters at the Biltmore in New York. No one seemed to be in charge. Bryan was there. He had been invited to sail with them, but had decided to remain home to fight against Wilson's preparedness program. Edison politely smiled when Ford offered him a million dollars to make the trip with him. John Burroughs, the naturalist, Ford's presumably peace-loving friend, had developed an intense hatred for the Germans and thought the expedition was like trying to stop a surgical operation before it was finished. When he bid Ford goodbye, his words were a dismal send-off. He told Ford that he might as well try to hasten the spring as to hasten the peace.

When the visiting men of distinction left the ship, there were fifty-five delegates on board, about equally divided between men and women. There were also twenty-five college students from across the country. Even Princeton was represented despite President Hibben's ban. The press was heavily in attendance with forty-five correspondents from most major newspapers, three wire services, and a number of magazines. Aside from Ford, there was not a businessman of national consequence in the group. George Fort Milton, editor and large stockholder in the *Chattanoga News,* one of the abler men, made one of the few kindly comments. He wrote that "it was no more visionary of Henry Ford to say that wars should be settled by moral suasion than it was for Thomas Jefferson to declare that all men are created free and equal." In contrast, Judge Ben Lindsey, an authority on juvenile delinquency, one of the better known names, exclaimed to reporters, "Oh God, why am I here!" The eccentricities and squabbles of the passengers made good copy in the absence of any substantial happenings. Even Hearst's *New York American* joined in the lampoon. It became a "ship of fools" and a "comedy of errors." The stories and distortions were damaging, but Ford never attempted to stop them as they went out over the wireless. When the ship's captain showed him some of the outrageous reports and asked if they should be withheld, Ford said, "Let them send anything they please. They are my guests. I wouldn't for the world censor them." At the outset of the voyage, he had wired Wilson, "Hope you will not be annoyed by misleading dispatches from newspaper correspondents about proceedings on steamer. I shall take pleasure in informing you personally of developments."[20]

During the voyage, delegates attended daily discussions which usually ended in divided opinions. How to cope with Wilson's preparedness program caused most of the disagreement. Ford, perhaps wisely, avoided the meetings. He preferred to remain in his cabin, talk to young students, or converse with the captain, Johan Wilhelm Hempel, whose company he genuinely enjoyed. And according to Lochner, he preferred the simple meals prepared for third-class passengers while his guests feasted on the fine first-class fare. Some of Ford's aloofness may have come from an awareness that his project was doomed. The original plan had so quickly eroded. The President's refusal to give government support, the cruel publicity, and the rejected invitations were handwriting on the wall. There was also a deeper disillusion: He had sought to rally the people of Europe, as well as those at home, and he had come to realize that the common people in the belligerent countries supported continuation of the war.

Rosika Schwimmer's aggressive behavior was another negative factor. The true pacifist was not a pacifying influence among the passengers. Her dynamism was matched by autocratic ways, self-promotion, exaggerations, and falsehoods that jarred her fellow travelers. Ford was foolish to give her such a free hand. Much later, Mrs. Ford, probably more perceptive than her husband, wrote bluntly to Schwimmer, "The way Mr. Ford's name and money was used was shameful and you were the leader. . . . You and your followers cared not if he died, just so long as he went along to lend his name and provide money to be squandered."[20]

Near the end of the voyage, Joseph Jefferson O'Neill of the *New York World* who was president of the press club organized on board wrote an unusual confession in the ship's newspaper on behalf of his colleagues. "Some of us," he declared, "doubtless entered upon this expedition tainted with the spirit of jest, looking upon it as a foolish if not foolhardy exploit of an ultra-rich idealist. With the passing of each hour of time, each league of the sea, that feeling has diminished. We realize that this is a serious undertaking, from which good must inevitably come, even if the highest hopes of its projectors may not be fulfilled."[22] It was a handsome and unexpected apology, but their damage could not be undone and their coverage did not improve when the mission arrived in Europe.

In February and March 1916, after an ailing Ford had abruptly returned home, the Neutral Conference for Continuous Mediation began its work in Stockholm. Emily Balch joined the group and served on the mediation committee and a committee for constructive peace. Without official participation of neutral nations, the weakness of the meeting was immediately apparent. Nevertheless, the earnest effort of the participants resulted in introduction of bills in parliaments of Sweden, Norway, Switzerland, and the Netherlands urging mediation, though no action was taken on them. The conference also offered a set of principles for a postwar world reflecting the recommendations of the Women's Congress at The Hague which would reemerge in Wilson's Fourteen Points.

Perhaps the conference sowed some seeds for a more peaceful world, but that was little consolation. No substantial progress in peacemaking had been accomplished by Ford's expedition. He had offered an alternative that failed. He had failed many times before and took the loss philosophically. Failure was no proof to him that it was not worth trying. When he returned home, he told Samuel Marquis that he was in a peculiar position. There was nothing that he could not buy, but he did not want what money could buy. He wanted to live a life that would make the world a little better. The trouble was the people did not think. He wanted to do and say things that would make them think. Under the barrage of criticism he kept up the best front possible and claimed that he did not regret a single thing. In a serious vein, he said, "I wanted to see peace. I at least tried to bring it about. Most men did not even try."[23]

It is not inconceivable that an official conference of neutral nations engaged in continuous mediation might have picked up the meager possibility for a settlement and brought the parties together. Wilson said that the building of a league would be "a stage of development . . . built by slow habit."[24] It was not something that could be done quickly. Even failure of such a conference might have served as a beginning. That was Ford's major goal.

During 1916, Ford continued to attack the war "profiteers." He believed that much of the blame belonged to the munitions makers and international bankers and took full page ads denouncing preparedness. The fear of German militarism was not a legitimate reason to Ford for creating American militarism. He explained that Europe had been fully armed for a hundred years while America remained safe. The questions he raised in his ads appealed to the plain people, especially in the South and West, and irritated the sophisticated Anglophiles in the East. "Is it unpatriotic to wish for world peace," he asked, "instead of a universal war over commercial rights of a few men or to uphold an unpopular government? Would any man, preparing to fight a fire in his shops, store those same shops with tons of inflammables? Why not build a machinery of reason to do work machinery of force has not accomplished?" Patriotism, according to his ads, was not merely dying for one's country. It consisted "more in living for the benefit of the whole world, of giving others a chance to live for themselves, their country and the world." Write to the President, he suggested.[25]

The next day a half-page ad paid for by the American Defense Society replied to Ford. Its advisory board included such esteemed names as Perry Belmont, vice-president of the Navy League, Henry Joy of Packard, John Hibben of Princeton, and Theodore Roosevelt. This elite group announced that preparedness was vital to protect the honor of the nation. That same day, February 24, 1916, a *New York Times* editorial entitled, "Mr. Ford's Nightmare" depicted Ford as a simple mechanic. "Pacifism is right. Preparedness is wrong. That is as simple as a poppet valve and has the beautiful finality of a mechanical law. Why will the world not accept it . . . At this point . . . Mr. Ford's resources of reason fail."[26] The *Times,* however, did not represent all Americans. It was an election year and in the spring Ford's name appeared in the Nebraska Republican Presidential primary even though he was not a candidate. It was taken as a joke until he made a stronger showing than Charles Evan Hughes. Some voters considered the result a rebuke to extreme advocates of preparedness. Others regarded it as a sympathy vote for a man who had tried to achieve a desirable, but unattainable goal with his peace mission and was abused for his pains. In the Michigan primary, Ford received 5,186 votes more than United States Senator Alden Smith for the preferential nomination for President.

Wilson had feared Bryan as a Presidential rival in 1916 and it is conceivable that he saw Ford as another threat. Despite Ford's deficiencies as a politician, he had personal attributes that appealed to the public. He expressed himself in straightforward, simple language, projected a friendly manner, was a family man untouched by scandal, and had a following. As an independent candidate, Ford could have destroyed Wilson's reelection just as Roosevelt had broken Taft in 1912.

Fortunately for Wilson, Ford did not have his eyes on the White House. As the Presidential campaign got underway, Ford announced in full page ads that he had been nominally a Republican all of his life, but now he supported the President. "Special interests are demanding war," an ad read, "and the President is being criticized with many words, but stripped of all unnecessary words, their real complaint is that he has not plunged the country into war for their profit."²⁷ Ford's support undoubtedly relieved Wilson.

Despite Ford's misgivings about Wilson, he gave his full support, unlike a vast number of businessmen, to the reelection of the President. He praised Wilson's neutrality policy and showed his internationalist colors by attacking protectionism. A tariff was "a hothouse remedy. If we cannot compete on even terms with any country on earth then we ought to quit."²⁸ Democratic editorials were suddenly silent about Ford's simplistic language.

The war came and Ford, who had always said that he would throw all of his efforts into the defense effort if such an event occurred, kept his word. He rallied his organization to produce a variety of wartime products that ranged from Liberty aircraft engines, tanks, and antisubmarine boats to steel helmets and ambulances. And he did more. He entered the Democratic and Republican Senatorial races in Michigan in 1918, won the Democratic nomination, ran as "the President's candidate" and strongly supported a League of Nations. He lost in a very close race by little more than 4,000 votes in a recount. Once more, the bizarre, mercurial, Ford showed that he attracted a sizeable number of Americans. In 1925, a Ford memoir, *My Life and Work* appeared. It ended with a quotation, "'Faith is the substance of things hoped for, the evidence of things not seen.'" That was Ford's belief from 1914 to 1917.²⁹

Chapter 8

The Majority Leader

Shortly after midnight, April 6, 1917, Claude Kitchin, an impressive figure in the prime of life at forty-eight years of age, rose to a round of applause to make a prepared statement in the House. It was one of the rare times that the fluent Congressman used a manuscript. This was an occasion to be careful with words. He spoke slowly with a slight tremor in his voice. "Mr. Chairman," he said, "in view of the many assumptions of loyalty and patriotism on the part of some of those who favor the resolution, and insinuations by them of cowardice and disloyalty on the part of those who oppose it, offshoots doubtless of a passionate moment, let me at once remind the House that it takes neither moral nor physical courage to declare a war for others to fight." Again, he was greeted with applause. Only God, he told his audience, knew the depth of his sorrow and intensity of distress. He recognized the gravity of the situation and appreciated the penalties a "war-mad moment" imposed, but he had made up his mind "to walk it, if I go barefooted and alone." Kitchin did not exaggerate the pain he had undergone in deciding to vote against the United States entering the European war. He was an ambitious politician, a party man, and respected legislative leader. He was certain that his bright future, once so assured, evaporated as he spoke. Never a rebel, he now found himself in the company of outcasts during one of the great decisions of the twentieth century.[1]

North Carolinians, unlike their neighbors to the south, never pretended to possess an elegant aristocracy. If such tendencies had existed, Claude Kitchin could have staked a reputable claim to membership in an elite society. He came from an old planter family of British ancestry that settled in the Roanoke River Valley at Scotland Neck, Halifax County, North Carolina, not far from Virginia. His father was a captain in the Confederate army and served in the forty-sixth Congress. His brother, William, was a Congressman and Governor of North Carolina. Claude, born in 1869, was a product of the Reconstruction period, but he did not suffer from the deprivations of the war to the same degree as most southerners. Nevertheless, the results of a devastating war were everywhere for him to see and made a deep impression upon him as he grew up. He attended Wake Forest College and shortly after graduation, at the age of nineteen, married Kate Mills, the daughter of one of the professors. Two years later, he was admitted to the bar and began a successful legal career in his home town of Scotland Neck where Kitchins were plentiful. Claude and his wife contributed to their number with nine children.

By 1900, Kitchin, following his father's footsteps, became a member of Congress. He was a gifted speaker with a pleasant voice, congenial nature, and quick wit in debate that soon attracted attention among his colleagues in the House. As a six footer with brown eyes and dark hair, he made an attractive appearance that matched his reputation for hard work and integrity. Champ Clark, Speaker of the House, considered him a magnificent specimen of a man "mentally, morally, physically." Clark admired Kitchin's commanding presence and clarion voice that sounded to him like a silver bugle. He was also a skillful "cloakroom debater" where he could be amusing, serious, or sarcastic as the situation demanded. As a member of the powerful Ways and Means Committee,[2] Kitchin soon established himself as an authority on finance.

In the Presidential election year of 1912, Kitchin, previously a Bryan man, campaigned ardently for Woodrow Wilson and after the election he fought valiantly for the policies of the New Freedom in the House. Wilson once said of Kitchin, "I never knew a man who could state his position more lucidly or state yours more fairly."[3] Recognition of such qualities gained respect among fellow members in Congress and in February 1915 they elected him chairman of the Ways and Means Committee and Democratic majority leader. The honor was particularly significant since many observers at the time regarded the majority leader as second to the President in power and influence. That observation would come into question in the months and years ahead as the President, with his prime ministerial inclinations, increased his domination over Congress.

Kitchin, the loyal leader and strong partisan, was certain that the President would avoid involvement in the European war. Wilson's

The Majority Leader

eloquent message to Congress in December 1914 made clear that the United States was at peace with the world and that there was no reason to feel threatened by any foreign nation. "We never have had," he said, "and while we retain our present principles and ideals we never shall have, a large standing army. If asked, Are you ready to defend yourself? we reply, Most assuredly to the utmost; and yet we shall not turn America into a military camp." The President placed his faith in a volunteer army, a strengthened National Guard, and a strong navy for defense. Anything more than that "would mean that we had lost our self-possession, that we had been thrown off our balance by a war with which we have nothing to do, whose causes cannot touch us, whose very existence affords us opportunities of friendship and disinterested service which should make us ashamed of any thought of hostility or fearful preparation for trouble." He saw no reason for Americans to alter their attitude because "some amongst us are nervous and excited." Make no mistake, he added, the nation had not been negligent in national defense. Wilson's words made a vivid impression upon Kitchin who was in complete accord.[4]

When the U-20 sank the British ocean liner *Lusitania* on the afternoon of May 7, 1915 and sent a shock wave throughout the United States, Kitchin admired Wilson's steadiness of purpose. The incident distressed the President as it did all Americans, but a few days later he reaffirmed his conviction that "America must be the example not merely of peace because it will not fight, but of peace because peace is the healing and elevating influence of the world, and strife is not." It was in this same speech that Wilson uttered his most quoted words, "There is such a thing as a man being too proud to fight. There is such a thing as a nation being so right that it does not need to convince others by force that it is right."[5] Those words sent Theodore Roosevelt into a state of frenzy while they thrilled Kitchin for the reassurance of calm resolve.

Wilson used words skillfully, but they soon took on a different meaning to the astonishment of Kitchin. Both men spoke the same language and used the same vocabulary to express differing viewpoints. Wilson believed in a sound defense, Kitchin believed in a sound defense. Wilson favored a "reasonable" increase in the armed forces. Kitchin favored a "reasonable" increase in the armed forces. Wilson was against huge government expenditures. Kitchin was against huge government expenditures. Both men revered their Jeffersonian heritage. When Wilson said, "The spirit of America is peace," Kitchin agreed.

Despite their common language, there was no common understanding between the two men, and the majority leader soon found himself at odds with the President.

Kitchin favored threatening the British with an embargo on munitions in the interest of easing their continental blockade. It appeared to be an effective way to force the Allies to respect neutral rights. He also thought this would make the Germans more receptive to reason concerning submarine warfare. Wilson, on the other hand, opposed an embargo and made his influence felt in Congress. A more fundamental difference with Wilson, however, became apparent with the issue of preparedness.

By the summer of 1915, Wilson cast aside his repeated public statements that the country was already well defended and initiated a sweeping preparedness program. The "reasonable" increases requested by the President seemed nothing less than stark militarism and "criminally wasteful" to Kitchin. The Congressman did not see the moral, political, or economic need for the abrupt reversal in military policy. He considered the administration's preparedness for peace argument a sham and felt deceived. In the previous year Kitchen had supported an increase in the armed forces and was ready to vote for increases in the coming year. He wondered why the sudden demand for a gigantic five-year program. It flew in the face of any pretense that the United States was working for world peace. He was also acutely aware of the powerful forces behind the program. Among them were the Navy League backed by J. P. Morgan, Elbert Gary of United States Steel, and Ogden Mills of Lackawanna Steel. The National Security League with Theodore Roosevelt and Henry Stimson among its members fought for the expansion of the Army. Kitchin wished he could convince himself that the President was right, but try as he might, he could not. He still believed in the policy that the President had advocated such a short time ago. Now, he said, the administration expected him to "eat my words." Recently, Republicans had presented a similar defense program which he had opposed with the understanding that the White House agreed with him. At that time, Secretary of the Navy Daniels had branded the Republican plan "criminal extravagance and waste." Now, two months later, both the President and Secretary had completely reversed themselves.[6]

By October 1915 the Navy program approved by Wilson called for an expenditure of a half billion dollars over five years to build ten battleships, six battle cruisers, fifty destroyers, and a hundred submarines.

Kitchin, taken back by Wilson's new attitude, wrote to Bryan that it seemed to him that the President, to use his own words, had become "'nervous and excited' and frightened—why and for what purpose I leave to the imagination. Anyway, it seems that the war goblins and jingoes have caught him." The British controlled the seas, not Germany, and he did not know of any intention to go to war against Great Britain. It was Wilson who had changed, not Kitchin. The present stance of the President, so surprising and disappointing, worried him more than anything in his political life. He had seen members of the House throw away their convictions so often to please the President he had no hope that the program could be defeated. John Kern, majority leader of the Senate, was disgusted with "the sickening twaddle of sensationalists" over preparedness, but he followed the President without objection. Kitchin knew that it would be easier and safer to protect his position as leader to go along with the President, but he said, "I ain't built that way."[7]

Wilson stunned Kitchin because they had agreed so recently that there was no threat of attack to the United States by any European nation. The belligerents had their hands full in the present and after the war they would be exhausted militarily and financially, burdened with high taxation and millions of maimed veterans, widows, and orphans. Kitchin saw the War and Navy Department plans geared for an offensive rather than defensive war. In addition, the costs were unprecedented and Kitchin, as chairman of the Ways and Means Committee, had an onerous responsibility for financing such a program.

On November 6, Secretary of War Garrison announced his plan for an increase of about 40 percent in the regular Army and the establishment of a Continental Army of 400,000 men who would serve on active duty two months a year for three years and then become part of a reserve force. Two days later, Wilson conferred with Kitchin at the White House for more than an hour in an attempt to gain his support. Wilson had not sought Kitchin's advice before the program had been formulated. Kitchin, in a similar position to Senator Stone, was called to the White House for assistance, not counsel. The Congressman tried to convince the President that he was ill advised and that his preparedness program was based upon a misconception of facts. Neither man gave way and the meeting ended as it began with opposing minds. According to Kitchin, it was a friendly get together, and the President assured him that his opposition to the program would not affect their cordial relations. Because Wilson was always quick to take personal umbrage, his gracious statement may have been somewhat suspect. Rumors spread that Wilson intended to use his influence to oust Kitchin as majority leader. Nevertheless, the President did not appear to make any move in that direction, possibly because he was aware of Kitchin's popularity in the House. The *New York Times* claimed that Kitchin was virtually divesting himself of the House leadership and that a second leader would be necessary. The *Times* regarded the situation ridiculous and thought Kitchin should resign.[8] The idea of separation of powers seemed to be of little consequence. Kitchin remained in the leadership, but he assured Wilson that he would not speak against his program on the floor of the House as leader, only as an individual. It was a fine distinction. Bryan opposed the preparedness program too, but he was now a private citizen. Kitchin's attack while a leader in Congress was far more embarrassing to Wilson and the Democratic party.

Kitchin was the first member of the House to oppose the War Department plan to build a Continental Army. Soon others lost enthusiasm for an idea that was strongly opposed by the politically powerful National Guard organizations in the states. Privately, many regular Army officers also thought the plan was impractical. Eventually the bill went down to defeat by thirteen votes in the House. Newspapers charged that Kitchin was an extremist in his opposition to preparedness, but that was not true. In keeping with his defensive military mentality, he favored strengthening coastal armament even though he thought it was already the best in the world. When he looked overseas, he noticed that the British had not been able to force their way through the Dardanelles because of coastal defenses. Also, the German navy had not crushed the Russian defenses in the Gulf of Riga to help von Hindenburg's army which had suffered terrible casualties trying to take the city of Riga. This seemed evidence to him that coastal defenses, mines, and submarines plus the present fleet would keep American shores safe.

Kitchin also favored an increase in aircraft, officers in the Army and Navy, and bolstering the National Guard. There was little question that the Army was a small, antiquated organization that required resuscitation. It ranked seventeenth in the world with about 5,800 officers and 122,000 enlisted men, many of them superannuated. Wilson had not given much attention to the condition of the Army before his sudden conversion to preparedness. Despite misrepresentations by the press, Kitchin repeatedly assured constituents that he supported a reasonable program, "but not the hysterical kind and the fabulous increase in appropriations which the President's program contains."[9] He insisted that jingoism had caused the present clamor. The question was: what was reasonable?

Kitchin's chief contention with Wilson was over the navy bill. He was not surprised by the insatiable appetite of admirals for a larger navy, but he was surprised to find Wilson in their company. Big navy advocates had used scare tactics for years. He had seen that game played before. In recent weeks, Rear Admiral Badger had said that ship for ship the United States Navy was as good as any navy in the world except England. Not long after, when preparedness hearings began before the House Committee on Naval Affairs, Assistant Secretary of the Navy Franklin Roosevelt ranked the United States Navy third in power rather than second. Rear Admiral Fiske made more shocking comments that German gunnery was probably superior to both the British and Americans and that it would take five years to recondition the fleet. Still later, the President said that experts ranked the United States Navy fourth in the world. The accounting among high officials was not very precise.

The threat in the Atlantic came from U-boats and Kitchin did not object to building more destroyers and smaller craft to serve on antisubmarine patrols. He had no objection to adding to the submarine force, but the Navy wanted huge appropriations for more big ships. Kitchin was more perceptive than the admirals who still lived under the influence of Captain Alfred Thayer Mahan and the ideas of grand fleet actions. Admiral George Dewey, the hero of another time at Manila Bay, was head of the Navy's General Board and he and his associates did not seem to be exactly in tune with World War I warfare. When the United States entered the war, Navy plans envisioned a fleet action in the Caribbean.

Kitchin had served on the Naval Affairs Committee and had considerable knowledge of the subject. He had supported an increase in the Navy the year before and was certain that the United States Navy was already superior to the German navy. During Kitchin's early years in Congress, Theodore Roosevelt had sponsored a major peacetime shipbuilding program. Naval appropriations jumped almost 40 percent from $85 million to $118 million a year and the United States Navy became the second largest in the world. Since then, Taft, and to a lesser degree Wilson, continued to build the Navy.

Kitchin opposed the request for a five-year program instead of the usual one-year program because seven battleships were under construction and two battleships had been authorized even though not yet let out for contract. There were also a number of destroyers still to be constructed.

Kitchin had the audacity to challenge the official figures of the Navy concerning its comparable strength with other nations. Step by step, he specifically disputed the statistics of the Navy Year Book of 1914 which were misleading. The Navy listed twelve dreadnaughts for the United States, built and building, and twenty in the same category for Germany. He also said that the Navy omitted the *California, Idaho,* and *Mississippi,* which were authorized and under contract before publication of the book. Those three ships, he claimed, were equal to any four German dreadnaughts. Further, two class two dreadnaughts, the *Michigan* and *South Carolina* were reduced to the pre-dreadnaught class even though every other naval authority, including the authoritative *British Naval Annual* and *Jane's Fighting Ships,* listed the two ships as dreadnaughts. It was clear to Kitchin that this was a deliberate attempt by the Navy to create the image of a superior German navy. The tactics appeared evident to him because two years before the "preparedness hysteria" the Navy listed the ships as dreadnaughts. In all, the Navy had failed to count five American dreadnaughts. On the other hand, it was very generous in the count of German dreadnaughts which included the *Nassau, Westfalen, Poxen,* and *Rheinland* which had only eleven-inch guns.

No other nation listed a ship as a dreadnaught unless it had twelve-inch guns, and in addition, *Jane's* described these four ships as defective. Kitchin explained that if they were deleted from the count, Germany had only sixteen dreadnaughts while the United States had seventeen. Since the 1914 Yearbook had been published, Congress had also authorized building two more dreadnaughts which were to be the biggest afloat, while Germany had lost ninety vessels of all classes since the start of the war with a total of three hundred thousand tons.[10]

In the pre-dreadnaught class there were other misleading statements in the Navy Yearbook according to Kitchin. In the list of twenty dreadnaughts, five had been declared not worth repairing by the German Admiralty and had little fighting value. Those five ships were the *Wittelsbach, Zahringen, Wettin, Mecklenburg,* and *Schwaben.* Five other pre-dreadnaughts, *Kaiser Friedrich III, Kaiser Wilhelm II, Kaiser Karl der Grosse, Kaiser Wilhelm der Grosse,* and *Kaiser Barbarossa* were to be repaired, but when work began on two of the ships, the others were

The Majority Leader 119

condemned as of no fighting value, and the repairs were not made. One of these ships became an experimental aviation ship. Despite Kitchin's presentation, the proponents of a larger Navy refused to be convinced that there was any merit in what he had to say. For Kitchin the Navy was guilty of deception to aggrandize the fleet without adding effectiveness.[11]

As the Presidential campaign approached, Kitchin frequently found himself disappointed and discouraged by Wilson's changes in outlook. At times, early in 1916, he felt war was extremely close and said he would not be surprised if hostilities broke out within thirty days if Congress did not pass a resolution warning American citizens against passage on belligerent ships.[12] On February 17, 1916, Representative Jeff:McLemore, a colorful Texas Democrat, who for some unknown reason placed a colon between his first and last names, introduced such a resolution. McLemore had left school at the age of fourteen because of his aversion to teachers and worked as a cowboy, unsuccessful gold prospector, and finally settled down as a newspaperman. He noted with understandable pride in the *Congressional Directory* that he had been elected to the 64th and 65th Congress without campaigning or spending any money. To many Congressmen, perhaps most, McLemore's resolution requesting the President to warn Americans against travel on armed belligerent ships was a sensible idea. Wilson, however, resisted any abridgement of American rights. When McLemore offered his resolution he had no doubt that it represented the wishes of an overwhelming majority of the American people. When he was told that his proposal interfered with administration policy, he agreed that it was his duty to uphold the President when he was right. Nevertheless, he added, "I must know that he is right."[13]

On February 25, Speaker Clark, Congressman Flood, chairman of the House Foreign Affairs Committee, and Kitchin met with Wilson at the White House to tell him of the broad support for the McLemore resolution. Clark thought the resolution would carry two to one and other members thought his estimate was too conservative. The opinion did not budge Wilson from his conviction.

He thought the resolution would encourage all belligerents to "transgress American rights." When Wilson was asked what would happen if a German submarine sank an armed merchant ship with Americans on board, he answered that the United States would sever diplomatic relations and acknowledged that it could lead to war. Kitchin found this mind boggling. How would a U-boat commander know if Americans were on board?

Kitchin left the meeting convinced that Wilson was ready for war. On February 29, he wrote to Charles Nash, a fellow North Carolinian, "*Confidentially*, I think the President is anxious for war with Germany—his sympathies are so strong for the Allies." He feared Wilson would "watch for the first opportunity to strike at Germany and involve this country in a world-wide war."[14] Kitchin, for the life of him, could not understand how it would sacrifice national honor or surrender American rights to warn citizens about travel on belligerent ships. It was especially exasperating to him because there were plenty of neutral ships for them to take passage. It was incredible to Kitchin, as it was to Sherwood, that Wilson could change his mind in such a short time. Kitchin's constituents gave no indication that they favored the President's position. One letter writer noted that every time England assaulted American rights, the administration brought up the *Lusitania*. He told Kitchin that he traveled around the state and spoke to hundreds of people and found that with few exceptions they said, "'Let Americans stay off Ally ships.'" In a Congressional district almost devoid of German-Americans, voters would give Kitchin a strong vote of confidence in the fall election.[15]

Wilson's continued assurance to Congressmen that he intended to avoid war reduced the opposition in the House. There were some subtle and not so subtle pressures from the White House, but mainly politicians were reluctant to defy the President. There were also technical difficulties with the text of the McLemore resolution and Kitchin and others failed to persuade the Rules Committee to provide a direct vote on a clear resolution or the Foreign Affairs Committee to report out a resolution.[16] In the end, Kitchin, and even McLemore, were among those who reluctantly voted to table the resolution. Wilson won the day.

During the summer of 1916, as the Presidential campaign heated up, the naval preparedness bill passed Congress and became law. It dismayed Kitchin who had fought hard for its defeat, but he found that Wilson absolutely dominated Congress. Kitchin called the legislation "outrageous" and looked upon it as a menace to peace even when the war ended. Approval of the program, he said, made the United States "the most militaristic naval nation on earth." It also reinforced an insidious lobby of arms builders who would have a stranglehold on the Treasury that no power in the country could break. At stake were "undreamed of profits." Now that the treasury floodgates were opened, he wondered if the "patriots" who supported the bill would be in the forefront to pay for the expense. He hoped that the sanity of the people and Congress would be restored in the not too distant future so that the program could be modified or repealed. He was curious, too, whether Germany would have a claim for damages against the United States for supplying the Allies war materials. He remembered the damages paid to the United States by the British for building the Confederate ship, *Alabama* and five other commerce destroyers. The basis for the successful claim was that Great Britain had violated the laws of neutrality. Ironically, the only consolation for Kitchin was a touch of internationalism inserted into the navy bill by Walter Hensley of Missouri. His amendment authorized American participation in international conferences on disarmament and judicial settlement of disputes.[17]

Despite Kitchin's anxiety about Wilson's changing attitudes, the country was still at peace, and his interest in the reelection of the President remained strong. Always a party man, the candidacy of Charles Evans Hughes on the Republican ticket was not an alternative for him. Kitchin received hundreds of invitations to speak during the campaign, and he accepted as many as he felt he could physically handle. There was a serious limitation. At the time he suffered from what doctors called neuritis of the head. As far as he was concerned he was simply plagued by a series of severe headaches. Stress and overwork were undoubtedly contributory causes and he needed a rest. Even with this handicap, he made a number of speeches at critical locations in North Carolina and left no uncertainty that he wanted Wilson in the White House for the next four years. He was sure that it would be a close race and every vote counted. Although reservations about Wilson were put aside, he allowed himself a touch of cynicism about the campaign slogan, "He Kept Us Out of War." Kitchin and his friends privately said, "We Kept Him Out of War."[18]

In one of the closest Presidential elections in American history, Kitchin rejoiced when the final results came in from the West to give Wilson a victory. It was, as he suspected, a close call. Kitchin's analysis of the results gave most of the credit to Bryan. Fifteen of the twenty states where Bryan had campaigned went for Wilson. Kitchin wrote to his good friend, Congressman Thomas Reilly of Connecticut, that without the Commoner's influence, Ohio would have been the only state in the North that would have gone for Wilson. Bryan, like Kitchin, had serious doubts about Wilson's policies, but he had thrown himself into the campaign with full force and concentrated his efforts in the critical West. In a little jubilee speech at Scotland Neck, Kitchin said, "I hope now in view of the returns from the West, no friend of the administration will hereafter wish to knock Bryan into a 'cocked hat.'"[19] The reference, of course, was to Wilson's earlier desire to do exactly that to Bryan.

As chairman of the Ways and Means Committee, Kitchin now had a heavy responsibility to develop legislation that would pay for the preparedness program. In his opinion, the Morgans, Fricks, Schwabs, and others of their ilk had been handed everything they wanted. Worse than that, he believed any pretension by the United States in favor of international arbitration would now be nothing more than hypocrisy. Nevertheless, the money had to be found to pay for the expenditures, and he thought increased taxation should be levied against munitions makers in preference to other business. They had been a powerful element in building sentiment for preparedness and increased appropriations and they should help pay the bill.

Kitchin saw the tax battle as part of the war to stem the mad rush to arms. He wrote to Bryan, "I am persuaded to think that when the New York people are thoroughly convinced that the income tax will have to pay for the increase in the army and navy, they will not be one-half so frightened over the future invasion by Germany and that preparedness will not be so popular with them as it is now."[20] That was wishful thinking. DuPont's stock had risen about a thousand percent, and DuPont as well as others had made a hundred percent profit on products sold to the Allies. When Kitchin was instrumental in writing legislation for a tax on munitions, DuPont quickly lodged a protest against such a levy. He was further disillusioned when he found that yachts, perfumes, and other equally nonessential items suddenly became "necessities" when they were vulnerable to taxation as luxuries. While the well-to-do expressed their horror about new taxes, the *Wall Street Journal* suggested lowering tax exempt incomes from $4,000 to $1,000 so that poorer citizens could share in the patriotic privilege of supporting preparedness.

Once again, Kitchin was at odds with the administration. Although the sums of money seem minuscule in the latter part of the twentieth century, the increase in appropriations was, as Kitchin rightfully said, "fabulous." Financially, conservative politicians wanted these new expenses paid for by bonds and additional consumption taxes which, as in the past, would be borne by middle and lower economic classes. As a compromise, Secretary of the Treasury McAdoo presented an increased tax plan instead of a bond issue that would still exempt the rich.

This did not sit well with Kitchin or his constituents who regarded McAdoo's plan grossly unfair.

By July, Kitchin's committee presented a bill to the House that had little resemblance to the President's proposal. The normal tax rose from 1 to 2 percent without any reductions; raised the surtax on incomes over $40,000 to a maximum of 10 percent as compared to a 6 percent maximum in the 1913 law; placed a federal estate tax of 1 to 5 percent on gross profits of munitions manufacturers with a 10 percent or more net profit. Kitchin said every dollar of extra taxes was for the increased preparedness appropriations.

Although there was intense sectional feeling that the South and West had ganged up on northern wealth, the bill passed the House and Kitchin felt the heat of northern bitterness. The *New York Times* pictured him as a narrow minded, vindictive southerner who aimed to place the tax burden on the north and "punish patriotism." He immediately denied the accusation and pointed out that the tax would pay for appropriations chiefly for the benefit of shipyards and munitions makers north of the Mason-Dixon line.[21]

The Senate revenue bill passed in September, and agreed to by the House, actually exceeded the House bill by increasing the surtax on incomes over $20,000 to a maximum of 13 percent; taxed corporation surplus capital and undivided profits; increased the estate tax fee to a top of 10 percent; and increased the tax on gross receipts of munitions makers to 12.5 percent. This progressive measure broke new ground in taxing great wealth in the nation.

The financial situation depressed Kitchin as he reviewed the Report of the Secretary of the Treasury at the end of the year. All other aspects of government had been stinted to pay for defense. Despite these restraints, the Treasury stated that by the end of the fiscal year 1917-1918, there would be a deficit exceeding three hundred million dollars. Kitchin wrote to William Dodd, professor of history at the University of Chicago, "Never since the beginning of Government did such a fiscal situation confront the Treasury."[22]

Kitchin continued to receive his share of sharp criticism and even libel from the press, mainly from the Northeast. He claimed he ignored the abuse, but that was probably a bit of bravado. Later, the editor and publisher, Oswald Garrison Villard, wrote, "If ever a patriot was murdered by the press it was Claude Kitchin."[23] Nevertheless, the greater stress came from the day-to-day meetings in the House with his fellow members. As differences heightened, personal tensions heightened. The one source of encouragement for Kitchin came from the mail that flowed into his office from his district which applauded his views. Even then there were occasionally discordant notes. One read, "Looks to me like Congress is asleep and you are taking a longer nap than anyone. Why is it we can't wake up . . . and have an Army and Navy that is the strongest in the world."[24]

When the bill to arm American merchant ships came before Congress in the New Year, Wilson may have been surprised to find that Kitchin voted for the bill. It certainly surprised his constituents, but the vote was not cast with any assurance. By now, Kitchin was convinced that if the President wanted to go to war he could do so with or without the bill. It seemed almost inconsequential to him. He realized that the Constitution gave the President powers that allowed him to create a situation which could make war the only alternative. He put his trust in Wilson, but the trust was wearing thin. His vote seemed to represent a sense of hopelessness that neither he nor the Congress could do anything to stop the war. He prayed war could be avoided, but he was a realistic politician. In the latter part of February 1917 it appeared certain that there would finally be war with Germany. A weary Kitchin wrote to a friend, "President Wilson delights in having Congress on hand all the time, and there is no telling when we will get a breathing spell." He was tired of Wilson addressing Congress from the Speaker's rostrum and "sending for" recalcitrants. There was, of course, no breathing spell, and soon Kitchin faced the most critical decision of his political life when Wilson asked for a declaration of war.[25]

Congress convened at noon on April 2, 1917 and crowds started to gather early in the day in anticipation of the historic event about to take place. Wilson's speech was scheduled for eight thirty in the evening and by then corridors and galleries were packed. The Cabinet members filed in and sat to the left of the Speaker. Behind them were foreign dignitaries sitting on the floor of the House for the first time. In front of the Speaker were the Justices of the Supreme Court. Congressmen were in their seats when the Senators entered by the center aisle. Many of them were carrying little American flags. The Vice President sat next to the Speaker. When the Clerk of the House announced "The President of the United States" there was a grand ovation. This was the fifth time since the first of the year that Wilson appeared to speak in the Capitol.

Wilson reviewed the events leading up to this moment and asked Congress to consider the activities of the Imperial German Government as war against the people of the United States. The American aim was to fight for the peace of the world which had been given added hope "by the wonderful and heartening things" that were happening in Russia. That nation was now a "fit partner for a League of Honor." The President concluded that the country would fight "for democracy, for the right of those who submit to authority to have a voice in their own Governments, for the rights and liberties of small nations, for a universal dominion of right by such a concert of free peoples as shall bring peace and safety to all nations and make the world at last free." Wilson, always masterful in presenting his views, spoke in a subdued voice and captivated almost everyone in the chamber. It was a brilliant speech, the objectives were clear, and the guiding light was noble.[26]

On April 4, late in the evening, the Senate passed the war resolution by a vote of 82 to 6. On April 5 and 6, the House debated the issue, or more accurately, spoke for the record. There was no question about the outcome.

In this moment of crisis, friends and colleagues sincerely urged Kitchin to go along with the President. Their arguments were persuasive as they warned of the consequences. He knew that other members of Congress had fallen in line against their own judgment and he would be praised for doing the same. As he struggled with his conscience, his wife advised him to follow his own conviction. It was advice that gave him a sense of relief.

During April 5, one Congressman after another spoke in favor of the war resolution. How many spoke against their inner convictions would never be known. Some of their rationalizations seemed strained, but it was true that no one knew what would be the extent of American involvement. Some Congressmen believed an official declaration of war would be sufficient in itself. Others presumed the war would be limited to economic and naval support. William McCulloch of Ohio thought that the United States should withdraw from the war once American grievances were satisfied. Philip Campbell of Kansas was among those who expressed the inevitability of war. "If my vote against this resolution would avert war, I would vote against it. It would not." Therefore, he did not intend to oppose the resolution which could be interpreted as giving comfort to the enemy. It was a nice way to take the responsibility off his own shoulders. Philip Vander Meer, in his study of congressional decision making at the time, wrote that patriotism, Presidential influence, and concern for political survival were elements that led to that sense of inevitability.[27]

Occasionally, a Congressman rose to announce his opposition to the resolution. Their viewpoints differed too. Some were well-established conservative politicians, others were progressives. Some reflected the sentiments of ethnic groups in their constituencies while others voted against what appeared to be the prevailing opinion in their districts. William Mason and Edward King of Illinois opposed the war for religious reasons. Mason said the warring nations had "forgotten to try" Christianity. There were no simple answers for the way Congressmen cast their critical votes. Probably they did not fully comprehend all of the factors that influenced their decisions.[28]

In the allotted ten minutes, Kitchin reviewed the British violation of American rights on the seas and the acceptance of the British war zone. In his judgment, the United States would not sacrifice any more honor if the country kept out of the German war zone than they did by keeping out of the British war zone. He said the people were told that Germany destroyed American lives while the British only destroyed property. "Great Britain destroyed no American lives because this nation kept her ships and her citizens out of her war zone which she sowed with hidden mines." He asked too, if American submarine commanders would permit the shipment of arms and ammunition to enemy ports to use in killing American boys. That was the situation for German U-boat commanders. "Would we demand of our submarine commanders that they give the benefit of the doubt to questions of international law rather than to the safety of our country and the lives of our soldiers?" Kitchin wanted the country to understand that protection of American rights and lives was not the only reason for declaring war. The United States was taking an unprecedented step to make the cause of Great Britain, France, and Russia, right or wrong, its cause. If Kitchin had any doubt, he would have resolved it in favor of the administration. But he had no doubt even though he knew that the "whole yelping pack of defamers and revilers in the Nation will at once be set upon my heels." He was unwilling to throw away "the only remaining compass to which the world can look for guidance in the paths of right and truth, of justice and humanity, and to leave only force and blood to chart hereafter the path of mankind to tread."[29]

Whether or not Kitchin swayed any members in the House when he announced that he would vote against the war resolution is not known. He may have. An early prediction estimated that there would not be more than twelve votes in opposition. When it was learned that Kitchin would speak on the floor against war, the prediction jumped to forty. The final count against the war resolution was fifty.[30]

When Kitchin finished his speech, Congressmen on both sides of the aisle gave him a round of applause. It was a sign of respect for the man. His speech was the most dramatic event of the long night, but it was a severe strain for Kitchin who was near tears at the end.

Next to speak was Heflin of Alabama who attacked Kitchin as a humiliation and called for his resignation. His remarks were greeted with hisses from other members of the House. Heflin shouted in reply, "You may hiss, you who speak for the Kaiser and not for the people of the United States."[31]

Newspapers were not as kind to Kitchin as most of those present in the House. They saw him as nothing more than an obstructionist who lacked a national viewpoint. An editorial in the *New York Times* described the majority leader as a "distressing spectacle." He was a good man gone wrong who "seemed to think himself a martyr for the right when he was only the victim of a delusion." The editorial went on, "Did not Heflin tell the truth?" Two days later, another *Times* editorial claimed Kitchin did not know what the war was all about. He did not know that American ideals were at stake, that democracy was fighting for the right to exist. "All he sees is an incomprehensible brawl, in which his country has gone mad, like the others." It suggested that he resign his leadership before his position became intolerable and led to further mortification.[32]

The condemnation of Kitchin in the northeastern press was not unexpected, but the Congressman received his share of abuse from the North Carolina press too. The *Wilson (N.C.) Daily Times* considered him a disappointment. The *Greenville Reflector* called for his resignation as leader, and the *Rocky Mount Evening Telegram* wrote, "not five per cent of his people hold any such view. Edgcomb has been woefully misrepresented." These comments clashed with the thousands of letters that Kitchin received from his state and around the country. Teutonic names among the letter writers were almost nonexistent. Many writers stressed their British and American heritage. Most of the letters were highly literate and were written in reaction to the unfavorable press comments. Many praised his moral courage and some pleaded that he try to limit American participation in the war. Although the writers were deadly serious, sometimes a light touch appeared. A Virginian wrote, "A dead fish can float with the stream but most assuredly it takes a live one to swim up." A banker from Salisbury, North Carolina wrote,

"Had you thought of it, that the assassin of President Lincoln, was of British ancestry, that the assassin of President Garfield, was a French Canadian, that the assassin of President McKinley was a Russian?" Occasionally, Kitchin received praise from people who disagreed with his vote, but respected his courage. An R. B. Glenn said he would have voted for the war resolution "still I never honored and respected you more" and hoped that he would continue as leader. Among the rare letters of condemnation, one wrote, "You can leave your children the name of a traitor—can you stand the consequences?"[33]

Although Kitchin was too busy to read all the letters, the outpouring of favorable mail must have given him a much needed lift. He believed that his vote against the war resolution probably hurt him in his district, but he told W. A. Finch of Wilson, North Carolina, that it had not hurt him with his colleagues in the House and administration. "They all tell me I stand higher in their estimation than ever. I would like to have voted with the Administration and tried to bring myself to it, but just couldn't...."[34]

True to his word, Kitchin supported the war effort and ably managed the necessary legislation. Contrary to the dire demands in the press, he was never cast aside as majority leader. He, like Stone, retained the respect of the people who worked with him and knew him best. Kitchin never believed that he was mistaken in opposing America's entry into the war.

Chapter 9

The Dissenter

There seemed to be no reason for Norman Thomas, a future Presidential candidate on the Socialist ticket, to become a dissenter. He came from a happy, comfortable Republican family with loving parents and spent his boyhood in a midwestern town that was the epitome of "normalcy." Home was Marion, Ohio, a county seat and railroad center surrounded by prosperous farms. Thomas, a wholesome American boy, had a newspaper route delivering the Marion *Star* edited by Warren Harding, one of the town's conservative citizens. Then Thomas became a devout Princeton man. Princeton, known at the time as "the best country club for boys in America" was about to undergo a change. The year Thomas entered the university, Professor Woodrow Wilson ascended to the presidency and he had definite ideas about raising the academic standards. For Thomas, Princeton was a joy. Studies came easily, he sang in the glee club, played a fair flute in the orchestra, and was an active debater at Whig Hall, the historic secret society. He was also busy in the university YMCA, known as the Philadelphian Society, and was a popular member of the socially acceptable Colonial Club.

Woodrow Wilson, despite his Presidential responsibilities, still taught some select courses in political science, and Thomas was one of his students. Wilson, a gifted speaker and writer, had been and continued to be, a popular professor, and Thomas was among his admirers. He even tried to imitate, or at least utilize, some of his teacher's speaking techniques. Later, looking backward, he was not quite so enthusiastic about Wilson and wondered why he had been so enthralled. He wrote that he had heard him address hostile audiences and move them to cheers even though the conversion was temporary. That, he noted, was a "common experience with orators." By then Thomas was one of the country's ablest speakers, and he realized that his sardonic observation applied to himself as well.

Despite the deep impression that Wilson had made, Thomas held a few reservations about his professor even as a student. He believed that Wilson's political theory, interest, and knowledge were too restricted to the British parliamentary system. Wilson's masters were Burke and Bagehot. He had little to say about Jefferson and Hamilton and nothing about Marx. Countries beyond the English Channel appeared to be unworthy of discussion. The young Princetonian was correct in his appraisal. Wilson once said to his brother-in-law, Stockton Axson, "I have never been in Germany, and I never went to Germany because I have always disliked the German people. I have despised their educational ideas and have distrusted their writers on political science."[1]

At the time, Wilson was a conservative Cleveland Democrat, and Thomas noticed that he gave little attention to economics in relation to politics. He was aware in those days that it was a risky business to disagree with the teacher. Wilson was "inclined to take strong opposition or criticism as a sin against the Holy Ghost."[2] For the friendly Thomas, there was a lack of warmth in Wilson. Later, much later, Thomas doubted that the autocratic Wilson was temperamentally suited for high political office in a democratic society. Nevertheless, Princeton was an important part of Thomas's life. He graduated with high honors in history, jurisprudence and politics, took first prize in history, and was class valedictorian.

Thomas faced the future with the confidence of his generation. There was faith in human progress, goodness, ethical standards, and "the fundamental rationality of life." He knew that society had its problems with ruthless capitalists, corruption, and racial hatred. Nothing was perfect, but there was a certainty that evils could be corrected. Reform was possible, better times were ahead. "It never occurred to us," he once wrote, "that there might be a conflict between liberty and security."[3] Although military rivalries were obvious in Europe, the thought of a large scale war was beyond the imagination. Since the Napoleonic wars, a balance of power had served as a practical restraint. Thomas, with many others, shared the view of H. G. Wells that if a grand war began, the horror would bring wisdom and an abrupt end to the bloodshed. Peace was the wave of the future. People were becoming too civilized. As manifestations of the new world, Carnegie had endowed a peace society and

Nobel had instituted a prestigious peace prize. In America, hope was in the air. The notion that right made might seemed possible.

Perhaps it was foreordained that Thomas, the son and grandson of Presbyterian ministers, would turn to good works. He was an idealistic young man, but he believed that idealism was worthless unless it was put to use. He never experienced a mystical call to the ministry. Instead, he was drawn to the social gospel and the desire for missionary work at home or abroad. After he received his bachelor's degree in 1905, he worked briefly as a social worker at the Presbyterian Spring Street Settlement House in lower Manhattan where he spent much of his time mediating gang wars. This arduous, and not always welcome work, was relieved by a trip around the world. When he returned home his interest in helping to build a better world remained, and he accepted an appointment as assistant minister at Christ Church on West 36th Street near Ninth Avenue close to Hell's Kitchen. It was a poor satellite of the rich and fashionable Brick Presbyterian Church which gave it financial support. At the same time, Thomas entered Union Theological Seminary, a center for the practical application of Christianity which suited Thomas perfectly. There he came under the influence of such modern thinkers as Henry Sloane Coffin and Harry Emerson Fosdick.

While working at Christ Church, Thomas met an attractive young woman who had put her faith to work by establishing a tuberculosis clinic at the church. Her name was Frances Violet Stewart, an unlikely slum worker. She was the daughter of a banker and Princeton trustee—a graduate of the select Brearly School, who was listed in the Social Register and had studied nursing. The match with Thomas was a natural and they were married at Brick Church in 1910, remained devoted to each other all of their lives, and raised a closely knit family with six children. The charming and handsome Thomas mixed with his wife's social friends and family as easily as he did with the toughs in his parish. It would seem that his young wife and her relations might be a conservative influence upon him, but such was not the case. His wife shared his views and was with him every step of the way.

When Thomas graduated from the seminary and became an ordained minister in 1911, he possessed the energy, personality, and intelligence to become one of the future leaders of the church. An assignment at Brick Church or another well-established pulpit, which he could have obtained, would lead to that future. Instead, he became pastor of the East Harlem Presbyterian Church in an immigrant neighborhood, mainly, Italians and Hungarians, which was a center of crime, vice, and poverty with the distinction at the time of the highest homicide rate in the city. Any false illusions that he may have held about the saintliness of mankind dissipated in that atmosphere. If Norman Thomas was a radical, his radicalism was based upon his abiding faith in Christian principles. If he was a contrarion, his contrariness came from his sensitivity to the defects of society. Talking about religious principles, and he was a fascinating talker, was simply insufficient for him. He did not believe that the horrifying, unchristian social conditions that he saw in the city could be altered only by a sense of good will. A plan of action had to bolster humane sentiments to make them work. His deep faith in Christian principles shaped his life and eventually drove him from the church.

During these prewar days socialism was gaining strength as a political force. Thomas, however, was not a socialist. His experiences in the slums and his observation of the needle trade strikes of 1909 and 1910 made him sympathetic to labor and some socialist reforms. Such sympathy by liberal reformers was not unusual at the time. Membership in the party was growing under Eugene Debs, more than a thousand socialists held political offices across the country, and millions outside of the party read Socialist publications with interest. In 1912, Woodrow Wilson said, "When you do socialism justice it is hardly different from the heart of Christianity itself." Nevertheless, Thomas was leery of some of the excesses of socialist propaganda and always independent, he did not wish to become subject to a disciplined organization. Still, he wrote to this mother, "Every Christian must desire a new social order based upon cooperation rather than competition."[4]

When war broke out in Europe in 1914, Thomas was neither a socialist nor a pacifist. In 1912, he had been pleased to vote for Wilson. Since there had not been a major war in Europe for a hundred years, there was a glimmer of hope that the world was moving toward peace. A belief in progress was pervasive. Thomas, like most people, opposed war in a vague, undefined sort of way. Unlike many clergymen, he had not been a member of a peace society before the war, and he held no pacifist convictions based upon either religious or political grounds. In time, however, he became convinced that Christianity and war were "in complete opposition . . . the whole philosophy and ethics of Jesus."[5] His conversion was a gradual process rather than a great awakening. There was also a tie between his desire for peace and helping the underprivileged. It was a belief in the brotherhood of man.

While still working at his East Harlem parish, Thomas became increasingly interested in keeping the United States out of war. The idealist did not disappear, but he opposed the war for reasons beyond religious grounds. There were political, economic, and social arguments against a war that had no meaning for him. He failed to see any "overwhelming margin of virtue on the Allied side."[6] The war in Europe, in his opinion, was a battle between two empires. Always alert to civil liberties, he did not see that the Kaiser's Germany was much more restrictive than France or England. The main risk of war for America, he believed, was economic. It was the "tap root." American trade and loans were linked to the Allies. The sale of arms and ammunition were undeniably making a rich America from the agony of Europe. He cringed when he heard people speak of fighting for national honor. It sounded to him like some sort of "dueling code."[7]

By 1916, Thomas had lost much of his enthusiasm for his former professor. Wilson's imperialistic intervention in Haiti and Mexico had been the beginning of his disillusionment. Then he questioned Wilson's policies toward Germany. After the first battle of the Marne, he believed an opportunity had been lost to bring the war to an end. Nevertheless, like thousands of other Americans, Thomas voted for Wilson in 1916 as the best hope for peace. When all was said and done, "He kept us out of war." It was the perfect slogan to influence those who had doubts.

As the war in Europe went on and the dangers of American involvement gathered momentum, the East Harlem minister stepped up his public activities against that threat. His six foot three height, aristocratic appearance, and powerful musical voice could be seen and heard on street corners above the din as well as on platforms in more dignified surroundings. A thought that ran through the speeches of this idealist was a skepticism about idealists who urged a war for democracy. Day by day he doubted that Wilson's idealism was as lofty as his words. And he sensed an instinct for combat in the country with complex motivations that came under the heading of "patriotism." Nationalism had created patriotism as a new religion that heightened emotions and blocked reasonable attempts to find peace. Christians were willing to kill other Christians. Thomas concluded that it was absurd to claim that the nation was moving toward war because of a love for democracy. The military build-up alone would strengthen autocracy rather than democracy. He also questioned protestations of the American public and press about crimes in Belgium when he thought of their indifference to disgraceful race riots at home. He did not think many men went to war for a cause or to prove their courage. They went to war reluctantly from a sense of duty or fear of public opinion. It was a "characteristic of the crowd mind."[8]

As preparedness became a major issue, Thomas spoke out vociferously in opposition. The making of a mighty military machine would increase suspicion among nations, force the exhausted powers to keep up the race in armaments and delay the possibility for peace. Every nation in the world said it prepared for defense only and was immediately disbelieved by every other nation. War and high mindedness were incompatible. "You cannot conquer war by war; cast out Satan by Satan; or do the enormous evil of war that good may come."[9]

As Thomas became more outspoken against American entry into the war, his old friends and associates began to disappear. He may have been on the side of the angels, but angelic company was scarce. Thomas found himself in an awkward position that was not unlike the aristocratic Wendell Phillips who found that old acquaintances preferred to cross the street rather than speak to him when he fought for the abolition of slavery. Although Thomas was a social reformer in East Harlem, he had been more than welcome in the homes of his wife's Fifth Avenue friends. He was so bright, attractive, and good humored. He may have been angry about the evils of the world, but he had never appeared in their drawing rooms as an angry agitator. Now the personal tensions grew as he expressed his uncommon belief in common Christian virtues. His friends were typical of refined, educated easterners, proud of their British heritage, who looked upon life with a sense of superiority. Their closed culture disdained those outside of their small circle. Shaped by family background, elite private schools, and editorials in the *New York Times,* they created an image of worldliness. They were confident that they knew better than the lower elements in the big cities or the crude provincials to the west. Fortunately for Thomas, his wife was his mainstay as "respectable" friends dropped their platitudes against war and sought intervention.

The social strain distressed Thomas, but the greater disillusion came from the lack of support from those organizations he expected to share his opinions. The general attitude of the Christian church was particularly disturbing as preachers sidestepped the issue. There was also disappointment in prestigious peace societies that had flourished in the United States early in the twentieth century. In peacetime their membership had grown as they issued authoritative studies against war. In wartime, however, their enthusiasm for peace faded. The Carnegie Endowment for International Peace was one example. Founded by the great steel magnate with a grant of ten million dollars, it attracted such heavyweight figures as Nobel Peace Prize winner Elihu Root to their midst. When war broke out in 1914, many of their certainties paled, and they confined themselves to scholarly research. They discouraged mediation and encouraged postwar peace plans, and their prestige influenced other peace organizations. A number of distinguished Americans participated in the newly formed League to Enforce Peace led by former President Taft. It too, looked to the postwar world. Its order of business was to crush Germany first and members had no interest in current anti-war movements.

Thomas believed the church should transcend nationalism. Instead, he found that the conscience of churchmen seemed to take a holiday as the state "takes the place of mankind in general and God." The American Federation of Churches was a special annoyance as it became involved in prowar activities, and the YMCA, for which he held such deep affection, also joined in the military mood. With the Federation of Churches in mind, he was unable to see how the Christian church could advertise its failure by "training of all our young men in the art and philosophy of war and for bringing about war with Germany now in the supposed interests of righteousness." Thomas refused to cooperate when the popular evangelist and former baseball player Billy Sunday brought his revival meeting to New York City. His money making, irreverence, and lack of social message seemed bad enough to Thomas. Worse, as he wrote to a fellow minister, "Billy Sunday, that supposedly great prophet of Christianity, has nothing to say on this subject [war] but the old 'my country right or wrong' stuff and he was quoted as favoring preparedness on a large scale."[10]

If the church failed, it might seem that colleges and universities would become a bastion of peace, but they disappointed Thomas too. There was always a supply of professors ready to rush to Washington to offer their political, economic, or historical opinions as a basis for intervention. Nothing hurt him more than Princetonians who made him an outcast. Princeton was still close to his heart when he attended a class reunion in 1915 and found he was the butt of brutal criticism. Quietly, Thomas resigned from the Philadelphian Society and Colonial Club. When he received an honorary degree from Princeton many years later, he was aware that he had become the university's favorite radical, but he noted "the competition was not very keen."[11]

As war approached, Thomas joined the Fellowship of Reconciliation, a new organization of religious pacifists who strengthened his beliefs. It was founded in England soon after war began as a movement of Christian protest against war. The membership had grown rapidly and came from many nations. Finally, Thomas was a complete pacifist. He wrote to a friend, "I was a long while coming to it but finally became convinced that so far as I could see war and Christianity are incompatible; that you cannot conquer war by war."[12]

Thomas realized at this time that he felt a stronger affinity for the Socialist party even while he remained outside of its membership. The church had failed to overcome nationalism and take a world view, while the socialists struggled against bitterness and scorn to uphold that opinion. Neither Thomas nor the socialists were isolationists in their opposition to war. They were internationalists interested in common humanity who hated to see workers of one country killing workers of another. This was the transcendental belief that the church had forsaken. The East Harlem minister knew that it would be mainly the downtrodden such as his parishioners who would fight and die in the war. It was clear to him that the enemies of peace were aristocratic diplomats, financiers, and big businessmen.

Many of Thomas's misgivings briefly disappeared when he read Wilson's "peace without victory" speech in January 1917. He was thrilled when the President mentioned the service the United States could perform as a neutral to end the war. But the belligerents did not take kindly to the offer. Apparently the President did not realize that it was too late and that too much blood had been spilled to end in a stalemate. In 1915, Wilson had told David Starr Jordan and young Louis Lochner that it was up to him to say when the right moment to act arrived. He had played a waiting game and waited too long.

When Germany unwisely reopened its submarine campaign and indignation swept across the country, Thomas still did not see any reason to abandon Wilson's recently stated position. Thomas had never been pro-German or blind to Germany's moral transgressions, but he knew that war destroyed ideals when a nation fought for its life. The U-boat was a useful weapon that might give Germans a victory. It seemed ridiculous to him to talk of "laws of war" or international law in wartime. Germany's new attack was madness to him. Nevertheless, it was also madness "that bids us conquer this evil result of war by war; to right wrongs by committing new ones." The refrain of "peace through war" was senseless. War and its philosophy was the enemy, not

Germany. He did not believe that any righteous end could be justified by "unholy means." Fighting Germany would force German liberals to become more closely associated with their war party. America at peace could rebuild the world; an America at war could not. It was destruction, hate, conscription, and loss of liberty on one side and reconstruction, love, service, and brotherhood on the other. He wondered which side America would choose; he did not have long to wait.[13]

Thomas had become one of the most active speakers for the American Union Against Militarism (AUAM) which had been founded late in 1915 to oppose Wilson's preparedness program. The objectives of the organization and Thomas were well synchronized. They were against war because it infringed upon liberty, progressive reform, and the elevation of humanity. The AUAM took credit for making a contribution to peace in June 1916 after a shooting took place between Mexican and American soldiers in Chihuahua.

Nine Americans and thirty Mexicans were killed and a number were wounded in the nasty engagement that appeared to make war inevitable. The AUAM promptly countered jingoes by publicizing the provocation by Americans. It also played a part in helping to set up a commission to investigate the situation that provided time for tempers to cool. The AUAM did not believe that the United States could create democracy in Europe by going to war. Instead, the group thought it was wiser to preserve democracy in the western hemisphere by staying out. Thomas found himself in the company of some very able people while working for the AUAM. Among them were Jane Addams and Lillian Wald. He also gained a few admirers and some of them came from unexpected sources. One of them was young James A. Farley, Franklin Roosevelt's future campaign manager and Postmaster General. Farley's antiwar sentiments stemmed from his opposition to Great Britain over the Irish question.

Thomas carried on his speechmaking as the tide of war rushed forward. He may have minimized the political problems in achieving peace, but he was certain that intervention would make matters more complex. War was an illusion that offered a simple solution. When the armed merchant ship bill came before Congress he was sure it would lead to war. He saw it as one more piece of hysterical legislation. Norman Thomas and Woodrow Wilson were now far apart. Wilson grew weary of pacifists who bombarded him with messages urging neutrality. Not long before the declaration of war, he told a convention of the American Federation of Labor, "What I am opposed to is not the feeling of the pacifists, but their stupidity. My heart is with them. I want peace, but I know how to get it and they do not."[14] Convinced of his ability to build a new world, Wilson deceived himself. Thomas had undergone a transformation too. As war approached in the spring of 1917, he was different from the man of 1914. Along the way, working with the Fellowship of Reconciliation and American Union Against Militarism he had moved much more to the left politically.

When war came, Thomas continued to speak his mind. He tired of hearing people talk about sons or friends who died in war as submissive to God's will. If that were the case, he said they should rebel against God. Only a month after the declaration of war he spoke in Philadelphia on "The Christian Patriot" and charged that the United States did not go to war to make the world safe for democracy. The lack of a war referendum, conscription, and the espionage bill that denied the fundamental right of discussion were hardly examples of democracy. He also expressed disbelief that war was the way to stimulate "national regeneration."[15] Such activities did not add to his popularity. Even in his family there were differences. Among his much loved brothers, Evan became a conscientious objector while Arthur joined the Army Air Service, and Ralph became an Army engineer and was seriously wounded in France.

In the fall of 1917, Thomas supported Morris Hillquit, the Socialist candidate for mayor of New York City. He did not join the party, but he worried about how much longer the church would tolerate him for taking such a radical step. He wrote to his mother, "The danger will come from the pressure of respectable church folk with money." And he was quite right. Soon, he was called into Dr. William Brown's office for a talk. Brown was chairman of the Committee on Home Missions of the New York Presbytery. He had a fondness for Thomas, but he told him that a number of substantial contributors had said that Thomas was "contaminating" the poor in his parish and "corrupting its youth." Brown said in a friendly way that it was bad enough to be a pacifist, but to support a socialist was beyond the pale. As Thomas suspected, his actions affected the financial situation of the church as contributions sharply declined. He was not asked to resign, but he saw no alternative.[16] Sadly, he left the church that he had served so diligently for thirteen years. Adding to his injuries, he also lost a part-time job as lecturer at Teacher's College of Columbia University because he was an "embarrassment."

There was little tolerance for men like Thomas. At a Flag Day ceremony, Wilson in his moral righteousness, called for dissenters to be buried "in the dust." Worse was the restriction of constitutional rights and hounding of innocent citizens under the Espionage Act of 1917. The law gave Postmaster General Albert Burleson broad power to block the mailing of any publication considered treasonous, and he wielded his authority to the point of absurdity. When *The Masses* published a cartoon called "Making the World Safer for Capitalism" or *The Freeman's Journal and Catholic Register* reported Thomas Jefferson's opinion that Great Britain should give Ireland independence, Burleson was quick to bar distribution through the mail. Even more ludicrous was the plight of the producer of a motion picture, *The Spirit of '76*, which portrayed atrocities of British soldiers during the American Revolution. He was fined $10,000 and given a ten-year sentence, later reduced to three years, under the Espionage Act. These were not isolated cases, but apparently the President did not think the law was sufficiently tough. The next year he asked Congress for a sterner measure which became the Sedition Act. It made almost any criticism of the Wilson administration illegal and echoed the despised Sedition Act passed during John Adams's Presidency.

The Sedition Act of 1918 used broad language to provide penalties for uttering, writing, or printing "any disloyal, scurrilous, or abusive language" against the government. Few genuine spies or traitors were found, but the law fell upon loyal German-Americans, those ideologically opposed to the war and editors of dubious publications. The restrictive legislation reflected the opinion of a large segment of the population. Popular outcries under the guise of patriotism insisted upon taking down the statue of Frederick the Great in Washington, boycotting German operas, and calling sauerkraut "liberty cabbage." Those who spoke too rashly were often arrested without warrants, held in prison without bail, and sentenced to long terms. The socialist, Eugene Debs, made a speech against the government's war policies and served two and a half years of a ten-year jail sentence. More than one thousand people were convicted under the Espionage and Sedition Acts. The historian Charles Beard wrote that judging by official reports, the aim of the Justice Department was not the apprehension of those giving aid and comfort to the enemy. It seemed to be the "supervision of American citizens suspected of radical opinions about the perfection and perpetuity of the capitalist system of economy at home."[17]

Thomas, almost a pariah, directed his energy toward the production of a new publication for the Fellowship of Reconciliation. It became known as *New World*, later *The World Tomorrow*. He soon ran into trouble with censors and was twice banned from the mail for criticizing the espionage law, objecting to discrimination against black soldiers, and sympathizing with conscientious objectors. His aim was to keep freedom of conscience and dissent alive. As Americans fought for democracy abroad, he saw the danger of losing freedom at home. The Postmaster General was unsympathetic. He said to Thomas, "If I had my way, I'd not only kill your magazine but send you to prison for life." John Nevin Sayre, a friend of Thomas, went to the White House for help. Sayre's brother, Francis, had married Wilson's daughter, Jessie, so there was a friendly connection. Wilson looked over Thomas's magazine which did not look too seditious to him. Nevertheless, he told Sayre, "But you go tell Norman Thomas that an English historian once said, 'There is such a thing as an indecent display of private opinions in public.'"[18]

Such a dual standard did not appeal to Thomas. Nevertheless, the President, under the pressure of war, took the time to write a kindly letter to Postmaster General Albert Burleson about the magazine in question and its editor. "He was once a pupil of mine at Princeton. I have just had a talk with Nevin Sayre. . . . which I hope and believe will alter the policy and, to some extent the point of view of men like Thomas. . . . I know they are absolutely sincere and I would not like to see the publication held up unless there is a very clear case indeed."[19] Wilson's thoughtful gesture was a sharp contrast to his administration policies. Thomas may have appreciated the President's kindness, but he did not alter his ways to any noticeable degree and government agents continued their surveillance of him.

When Thomas looked back on the war years he realized that they had changed his life and work. "I have often asked myself," he wrote, "if it had not been for the war I would have become a Socialist or left the work of the church." Initially, he had expected to return to the ministry, but his experiences concerning the restriction of civil liberties and the brutal treatment of conscientous objectors were among the reasons he changed his mind. "Which was fortunate," he added, "since for many years after the war the church would have none of me."[20]

After the war, Thomas, the internationalist, urged lower tariffs to break down national barriers and supported American participation in a League of Nations. When the United States failed to join the League, however, he did not agree with historians who attempted "to exalt Wilson to a pinnacle of misunderstood greatness, the victim of spite of Henry Cabot Lodge." To him that was a distortion of history. The

Wilson he remembered was the man who intervened in Russian affairs at Archangel and Vladivostok, destroyed the socialist press, jailed Eugene Debs, stood behind Attorney General Mitchell Palmer's red crusade, and persecuted conscientous objectors long after the Armistice. He did not believe that the twenties and thirties would have been different if the United States had joined the League. "The lesson we failed to learn," he said, "went far deeper than that."[21]

In retrospect, Thomas was certain that Wilson had lost his great opportunity to attain peace when he failed to use the nation's moral and economic power after the first battle of the Marne. He felt negotiated terms then could have been more constructive than the results at Versailles. It could be argued that such an achievement would have required superhuman vision, but there were those at the time who pressed Wilson to fulfill that vision. Thomas wrote, "Never since the end of World War I or the Versailles Conference has there been so easy or so clear-cut and dramatic an opportunity to save mankind by the right choice of logical alternatives as both socialists and Woodrow Wilson missed. Their failure paved the way for fascism and communism."[22]

In the years to come, Norman Thomas became the unlikely leader of the Socialist party who spoke eloquently for unpopular causes and continued to horrify respectable people. Although he bore the brunt of name callers and egg throwers, he was neither a very good politician nor a party organizer. Many of the programs he fought for such as low cost housing, unemployment insurance, and minimum wage laws would be taken over by a more astute politician, Franklin D. Roosevelt, in the early days of the New Deal. Essentially, Thomas remained a preacher. As the years passed, he became a national figure and late in life would be called "the conscience of America." Alden Whitman wrote in the *New York Times*, "As with most articulators of conscience, Mr. Thomas knew he was right, but he was denied the pleasure of rectifying the wrongs he saw."[23] The high praise that he received as an elderly man must have pleased him. The outlook of some of his critics probably changed more than he did, but in his good humored way he knew that he received the kind words because he was no longer considered a threat. Through his battles for lost causes, including opposition to Vietnam which he believed was spiritually, morally, and economically bad, he somehow became a success. But the people who threw the bouquets never got the message. The hopeful years of his youth turned into years of moral degeneration. As he approached the end of his life, he wrote, "My deepest concern involves the end of war, all war . . . Will there be interracial fraternity or war?"[24] He never lost faith that peace was possible.

Chapter 10

The Socialist Congressman

Meyer London was a late starter. Born in the Russian-Polish province of Suwalki, he did not arrive in the United States until he was twenty years old. He came with his mother and three brothers. Three years before, in 1888, his father, Ephraim London, and another brother in search of a better life, blazed the trail to the lower east side of New York City where they settled in a shabby tenement house. It was a neighborhood of Jewish immigrants with similar backgrounds, mainly from Poland, Russia, and Rumania. The family was poor, but scholarly. The mother, Rebecca Berson, was the daughter of a rabbi, and the father, a student of the Talmud, became a free thinker who published an anarchist weekly. Meyer seemed to inherit the intellectual attributes of his parents without following the extreme views of his father.

The first objective for Meyer London was to survive in his new surroundings. An insatiable reader, he fortunately found a job in a library, went to night school, and studied law. After seven long years, he was admitted to the bar and began to practice among his neighbors. The next year he married Anna Rosenson and they had one daughter. Never a money maker, he accepted clients without regard for their ability to pay and showed a personal interest in their troubles. Eventually, he became a leader in the trade union movement as the lawyer for the cloakmakers union which had fifty thousand members. A small, trim, friendly man, he was an effectual negotiator with employers and an impressive speaker at union meetings. He skillfully criticized the American Federation of Labor as too conservative, while retaining the respect of its leaders. In 1910, London won the admiration of his community as counsel for cloakmaker unions in a general strike which gained most of their demands.

London's other great interest was politics. Before admission to the bar he was active in the Socialist Labor party led by the militant Daniel DeLeon who wanted a proletarian revolution to bring about the "unconditional surrender of capitalism." London received the party's nomination for the New York Assembly in a losing race, which was a foregone conclusion. In the next few years, however, he became one of the founders of the Socialist party of America as DeLeon became more radical and showed hostility to the labor union movement. Under London's leadership Jewish socialists in the East joined the Social Democracy of America in the West which was led by the popular railway union organizer Eugene Debs.[1]

By 1912, the Socialist party in the United States appeared to be a growing force in the nation. The hectic Presidential election that year with Taft, Roosevelt, and Wilson as candidates was a strong indicator. The fourth candidate was Debs who received almost a million votes out of fifteen million cast. In four years the party showed an increase of 400,000 votes and won more than a thousand state and local elections. Much of its support came from big city immigrants, especially among Jewish voters such as the residents of New York's lower east side. The *Forward,* a daily newspaper published in Yiddish, was a strong influence in building the Socialist party in the city.[2]

When war in Europe began in 1914, the Socialist party in America had a well-defined position on the subject of peace. The executive committee of the party wasted no time in issuing a manifesto in opposition to a war between "crazed monarchs, designing politicians, and scheming capitalists."[3] It was not a war for democracy. That was nothing more than a hollow catch phrase and just as false to them was the German claim that they were fighting for their "culture." The workers of the various nations, they stated, had no quarrel with each other. Their grievances were created by the ruling classes of their own country. The committee called on foreign born workingmen to hold meetings to emphasize their fraternity and solidarity regardless of color, creed, or nationality. This was true Marxist theory; the capitalistic economy had to expand to exist, and that led to imperialism. When two imperialist nations clashed, war ensued. It was clear that the British and Germans were on a collision course commercially. It was also clear that Serbia wanted access to the Adriatic, Russia longed for a warm water port, and Japan, the "England of the east," had a jealous eye on German possessions in China. Essentially, this was the Socialist opinion, but it also recognized other factors that caused war such as nationalism, militarism, race hatred, and religion. Socialists knew that the battles between the Christians and Muslims in the Balkan peninsula had gone on for centuries. They believed, too, that war was a cover-up for a depression in England, a threat of social revolution in France, severe labor problems in Russia, and a rising Social Democratic party in Germany.

As the war went on there would be variations of socialist opinion and splits within the party, but at the outset there was remarkable unity on the question of peace. Socialism was the one great international movement that transcended national boundaries. The Socialist Party of the United States pledged its support to Socialist parties in Europe for any measures that might advance the cause of universal peace and good will. More specifically, it called on the national administration in Washington "to prove the genuineness of its policy of peace by opening immediate negotiations for mediation" to end the conflict. To buttress this request, it cabled socialist leaders in Great Britain, France, Germany, Austria, Belgium, Italy, Holland, Switzerland, Denmark, and Sweden to use their influence with their respective governments to accept mediation by the United States. The wire read, "This can be done without loss of prestige. Conference would be held at The Hague or Washington." There was, of course, no practical result and disillusionment set in among them as socialist workers of one nation fought and died fighting socialist workers of other nations. Nevertheless, they continued to fight for peace.[4]

Meyer London, like many socialists, had an interest in the peace movement long before the outbreak of World War I. He and other socialists showed their good intentions by joining various peace societies that were sprouting up around the country. London joined the New York Peace Society in 1913, but his membership was short lived. The societies had the same objective as he for a peaceful world, but their differences about the causes of war made it an uneasy fellowship. The peace societies consisted mainly of middle class, pro-capitalist members. One socialist claimed that they were "Nothing more or less than schemes whereby certain parasites of the present system amuse themselves or gain a livelihood." It was not a sentiment that built harmony among peace lovers.[5]

By 1914, London was a natural choice to oppose the Democratic candidate for Congress in the Ninth District of New York. His high visibility in the trade union movement, strong advocacy of Jewish rights, and personal popularity in his neighborhood brought him to the forefront. One friendly observer wrote that by temperament he was neither a good fighter nor a good hater, "every blow he struck at his enemies hurt him, but in a world of injustice he was forced to fight, never for himself but for justice for the masses."[6] During the campaign, London fought an uphill battle against entrenched Democrats and found that he had an unexpected ally. It was none other than William Randolph Hearst who happened to be feuding with the Democratic party at the time. Previously, Hearst hurt the Socialist vote in the city when he ran for office as a reformer. His influence was difficult to measure but in a tight race every vote counted. Hearst's *Evening Journal* commented, "To have a few intelligent radicals in Congress, telling unpleasant truths to the conservatives, playing the part of Socrates gadfly, would be an excellent thing."[7]

London's victory at the polls was cause for a grand celebration. It was almost too good to be true. He was the first Socialist elected to Congress from the East and the second in the country to serve as a Representative. His predecessor in the Congress, Victor Berger of Wisconsin, lost reelection and London would be the sole Socialist in the House. The jubilation led to a gathering of 12,000 people at Madison Square Garden to express their delight as a brass band played the "International." Great things were expected of London, but he knew that one Socialist vote in the House of Representatives could accomplish little. At best, he hoped to begin the process of evolution toward social democracy, but London would have a long time to wait before he could take any action at all. The 64th Congress did not convene until December 1915. Meanwhile, he prepared himself for the "war against war" and busied himself with speechmaking. Soon after the election he spoke to a group of reform rabbis on the topic, "Socialism and Religion" and criticized the clergy of all faiths who did not speak out against war. He compared their inactivity to the activity of German Socialists who bravely went to jail for upholding their beliefs.

In April 1915, London was the principal speaker at a Cooper Union meeting of 3,000 men and women organized under the auspices of the Central Federated Union. He had one purpose, to protest the war without favor to any belligerent. His most shocking suggestion was for organized labor to consider a general strike against industries that traded with warring nations. Because international law had failed and the clergy had failed, he wanted the United States government to hear the voice of the people. He did not blame any individual businessmen.

He thought that was worthless because he was sure they would supply hell with fire and brimstone if they had their way. Finally, the meeting broke up when someone ran to the platform and demanded that he speak on behalf of the Belgians who were oppressed by the Germans, and nothing came of his demand for a general strike. In another meeting at Cooper Union for women he sarcastically attacked the National Security League. No one from that organization had answered a question sent to it: Is Europe today your example of peace by preparedness?

A big antiwar meeting was held by Socialists at Cooper Union in June 1915 where enthusiasm was still alive for the new Congressman. London denounced the traffic in arms and said it was not because he favored Germany. "They tell you when you talk like this you are agents of Germany. I have as much use for the German Kaiser as I have for John D. Rockefeller. If the war in Europe were a war of the people against their Governments, then I would be for the war."[8] He was probably carried away with his own words and guilty of rhetorical excess, but these were not the words of a pacifist. His more immediate concern was the destruction of liberty by creating militarism in the United States. He was certain that those who favored building a huge military machine fostered fear in the country by instilling dread of a possible enemy. "Remember," he said, "this is almost the only spot in the world that is free from war and the curse of militarism. . . . the haven of the oppressed, the only place to which the men of Europe can come to escape from military service."[9] He did not want the national and race hatreds in Europe transplanted to the United States. Although there was some admiration for Germany and Austria in his district, the stronger feeling was against Russia, the former home of so many of them. Oppression and hatred had been a part of their personal lives.

During this frustrating period of waiting for Congress to meet, London was heckled by left-wing members of the International Workers of the World. They wanted to know what he was going to do as a Congressman to produce the "Social Revolution." His answer was surprisingly frank and realistic. He said, "I am elected for only two years, and that is too short a time in which to bring about the Social Revolution, so I am going to leave that job until later. I am going to do hardly anything to bring it about. You see I have to be reelected in 1916 and I have to retain some votes in my district."[10] London hoped he could persuade rather than confront.

Despite London's need to play practical politics, he did not wait to combat the war. When Congress finally met in December 1915, the new member promptly presented a resolution calling on the President to convene a congress of neutral nations to mediate among the belligerents. The resolution, offered two days after Congress met, said that a declaration by the national legislature of the greatest neutral in favor of a conference of neutral nations would strengthen the hand of the President in efforts for international peace. It resolved to offer mediation and sit in continuous session until the termination of the war. Obviously the work of Jane Addams and Julia Grace Wales was not lost on London. The experienced labor negotiator saw the practical advantages of such a technique in bringing people together. His resolution went further by suggesting seven basic principles for discussion. They were as follows:

1. Evacuation of invaded territories.
2. Liberation of oppressed nationalities.
3. A plebiscite by the populations of Alsace-Lorraine, Finland, and Poland as to their allegiance or independence.
4. Removal of political and civil disabilities of Jewish people wherever they exist.
5. Freedom of the seas.
6. Gradual concerted disarmament.
7. Establishment of a court of arbitration with commercial boycott as a means of punishment for disobedience.[11]

There was nothing radical in the resolution. Such suggestions had come from other members of Congress. Senator Lane of Oregon presented a similar resolution in the Senate and the influence of the women at The Hague was clear. London was acquainted with Jane Addams and he kept her advised of his progress. He believed that he was working for a consistent, logical method of coping with an international problem. In his mind everything that was worthwhile was international. Nationalism was filled with hatred and prejudice, but the good in life—science, art, music, religion—was international. He wanted members of the House to abandon a narrow conception of patriotism.

London's resolution pleased the National Executive Committee of his party which decided to circulate petitions in its support. It also communicated with Socialist representatives in neutral nations and asked them to submit similar resolutions to their parliaments. A committee was also elected to wait on the President and Congress to urge adoption of the resolution.[12]

When London made a brief maiden speech in the House, he received a friendly welcome. He was something of a curiosity as the only Socialist and the representatives were anxious to hear him. He was also well received because of his courteous manner and mordant sense of humor. Perhaps his heavy foreign accent added a little charm too. In January, he made a more important speech on preparedness and told the House members that he had to force himself to speak because he felt he was imposing upon them. His polite protest had a false ring because he was a natural speaker and never shy about expressing his opinions. He went on to claim that American imperialists had been quick to acquire Puerto Rico and the Philippines and tie a string to Cuba after the Spanish-American War. Now, munitions makers, anxious to protect their capitalistic investments, were responsible for the wild preparedness propaganda which frightened people into believing there was a real danger. The present war was not an accident. It was a clash of economic interests. Preparedness was an artificial issue which clouded the real cause. It was imperative to demand international peace. That was why he had introduced his resolution for a congress of neutral nations in December. He did not believe there was any such thing as offending national honor. National pride led to wars of revenge and he did not want vendetta to become part of moral law.

A week later, January 25, 1916, London, Morris Hillquit, and James Maurer, president of the Pennsylvania State Federation of Labor, and Jane Addams met Wilson at the White House to discuss mediation. London read his resolution to the President who listened carefully. Hillquit thought Wilson appeared weary and preoccupied at first but then became interested as the conversation developed. The President generously gave them an hour to discuss their suggestions. Wilson expressed his distrust of neutrals, but according to Hillquit, he said confidentially that he had a similar plan under consideration and hinted that there was a "possibility of a direct offer of mediation by the government of the United States." His remarks encouraged the visitors and they left, as many before them, with the feeling that they had made substantial progress. Hillquit wrote that Wilson's "sympathies were entirely with us." When they were ready to leave, Maurer, a little more skeptical, undiplomatically said, "Your promises sound good, Mr President, but the trouble with you is that you are surrounded by capitalist and militarist interests who want the war to continue; and I fear you will succumb to their influence." Wilson took the comment well, placed a hand on Maurer's shoulder, and pleasantly replied, "If the truth be known,

I am more often accused of being influenced by radicals and pacifist elements than by the capitalist and militarist interest." There was truth in the President's remark which added to the sense of the Socialists that their meeting had been productive.[13]

London's resolution, however, did not meet with any sympathetic reception by the powers in the House. On February 24, 1916, the House Committee on Foreign Affairs granted a public hearing on House Joint Resolution No. 38. After two days of hearings, the committee took no action and the resolution quietly died. London's influence on war and peace in the house was limited to making speeches, usually without effect. He continued to argue against preparedness, but many other members said the same things. His opposition to preparedness was firm, but he also knew that the threat of war was having a corrosive affect upon the Socialist party. When some Socialists began to show prowar sympathies, he called for latitude on such questions as preparedness for the sake of party harmony.

One of London's most futile suggestions was for his colleagues in Congress to throw away their political ambitions and chances for reelection and join him in the struggle. He emphasized that all Socialists would defend America if it were attacked and that his objection was to excessively large appropriations for defense. War, he said, was no more inevitable than the plague or burning witches. Men burned witches because they were ignorant. Plagues ran rampant because they were not understood. When the cause of a plague was understood, it was eliminated. When men understood the cause of war, it too would be eliminated. The causes of war were, of course, clear to London. Aside from economics, secret diplomacy was a curse. Socialism contended for an international code of morality. When a bill came before the House for an increase in the Army, he cast one of the two negative votes. When passage of the Navy bill became a certainty, he congratulated the Steel Trust. Despite his mild behavior, the *New York Times* reported that one Congressman, unhappy with London's speeches, entertained the idea of a motion to expel the Socialist, but nothing came of the matter.[14]

Meanwhile, London gave his support to legislation that favored the advance of social democracy. He was for measures to abolish labor injunctions, prohibition of child labor, unemployment insurance, and old age pensions, and opposed protective tariffs and restrictions on immigration. One of his particular interests, as a leader of the Jewish labor movement, was the removal of political and civil disabilities against Jewish people everywhere. He revered Jewish culture, but he wanted to see it become a part of the general American culture. He optimistically wrote to a constituent that he was hopeful about Jews in America and he was not worried about "the appearance of a little prejudice here and there. There is prejudice between Catholic and Protestant. There is prejudice of Catholic and Protestant against the Jew, and by the Jews against both. Time will cure all that. The Jew will succeed in America on his merits as a man in proportion to his deserts. More than that he should not ask."[15]

Despite London's optimistic outlook on most subjects, the frustrations of office chipped away at his good nature. The work without satisfactory progress was exhausting and sometimes sent him into depths of gloom. The editor of the *New York Call* wrote to him in a friendly way that some Socialist newspapermen were beginning to believe that he was "getting to be a good bit of a grouch."[16] It was not part of his normal good cheer. London found himself increasingly a target from within his own party from both the right and left wings.

During the 1916 Presidential election, London supported the Socialist party candidate Allan Benson. At the same time, he always tried to help Wilson, when in his opinion, the President worked for social improvement or peace. The Socialist party platform that year repeated many of its usual claims. War was the natural result of the capitalistic system of production. The armed forces were in the hands of the ruling class. Imperialism and militarism plunged Europe into war. Profits in the United States created a frenzy of militarism and preparedness was a cloak for imperialism and industrial tyranny. Socialists called for an international brotherhood of world peace and industrial democracy. The one enemy was the capitalist class. Among the more positive planks were political friendship for Latin America, independence for the Philippines, and a call for a congress of neutral nations; however, the Socialist candidate was not a fierce rival for Wilson. Benson expressed his admiration for the President more than once and said that he was the best second choice in the election. Wilson had always shown respect for the Socialists, listened to them, and frequently earned their assistance in fostering progressive measures.

London faced his own difficult reelection campaign. A coalition in his district backed Judge Leon Sanders, a respected and able Jewish leader, as its candidate on an Independent Democratic ticket. London again counted on backing from the labor movement. Just as London talked about two Germanys, he talked about two east sides of New York. One consisted of the worst elements in the city. They were gangsters, prostitutes, and pool hall habitues who were the result of Tammany Hall. The nobler east side was made up of dreamers, students, and union workers. London campaigned vigorously and spent long hours speaking in the district. He was adept at using humor sometimes and putting on a rough front other times. When Judge Sanders found some incredible reason to attack London's Jewishness, the Congressman retaliated by calling Sanders "Tammany Hall Kosher" and a "Ham sandwich statesman." On election day, he won a very close victory with only 343 more votes than Sanders.

Presidential candidate Benson did not fare as well as London. Droves of Socialists cast their votes for Wilson. The differences within the party, created to a great extent by the war, were becoming evident. The decline in their fortunes as a political party had begun.

After the election, London continued to say kind words about Wilson as he pressed for the United States to act as an arbitrator in the council of nations to end the war. The words arbitration and mediation were frequently confused and used interchangeably. As a labor negotiator, London knew the difference, but either approach was acceptable to him. Mediation was the process of conciliation and discussion to reach an agreement that involved opposing parties. Arbitration, following a hearing, was a judgment concerning the opposing parties which would be binding. London believed that as an arbitrator, the United States, "the one great Republic, the repository of the ideals of democracy and liberty" would be the one neutral nation that could exercise its power for peace.[17] If, however, the United States entered the war, its postwar status would be limited to the extent of its military contribution in relation to the Allies. But it was wishful thinking to believe that Wilson would adopt his viewpoint. Wilson held the opposite opinion. Yet, he would learn at Versailles that America's belligerency was not highly regarded at the peace table.

When the President gave his "peace without victory" speech to the Senate in January 1917, London knew that Wilson was an artist with words and that there were many ways to interpret his remarks. He decided that it was necessary to look at the address as one step in negotiations and an introduction of moral principles into international law. He realized, however, that international law was only concerned with rules of the war game. It did not lay down principles that justified or condemned war. As an example, there was no established principle concerning invasion, and yet big nations had been taking over small, helpless nations for ages. At that moment the United States was in possession of the Philippines and Puerto Rico and the Navy was at Santo Domingo trying to establish a stable government. He would have been more impressed by the President's proclamation to the world about international ethics if the Navy had been withdrawn from the Caribbean as a peace gesture. London favored Wilson's idea of a league of nations, but he was concerned by the President saying that the peace must be "made secure by the organized major force of mankind." London believed that nothing was more dangerous than the United States entering into an international alliance which would involve armed forces. If each member had power to loose military forces, there would be no opportunity for permanent peace. It would only lead to new alliances. And if the United States joined such a league at that time, it would become just one more member of the Allied entente. These were grave concerns, but London welcomed Wilson's message as a move toward peace and an invitation to study the causes of war.[18]

Although London respected Wilson, he feared the President's ability to pressure Congress into the war. This was the time for Congress to be independent and not treat its war powers in a superficial way. As a Socialist he believed the war talk increased because businessmen felt threatened and such talk produced a superabundance of flag wavers within and without Congress. The posturing of politicians irritated London who considered patriotic affectation unnecessary and unhelpful. He thought any fool could act the patriot. "It takes a manly man," he once said, "to live a life of devotion and sacrifice for the best ideals of his country. That is the only kind of patriotism I recognize." When the subject of arming merchant ships came before the House, the chauvinistic hyperbole reached new highs. London tired of these excesses and said on the floor, "We have reached a stage when sentiment rules and reason has been dispensed with when a man finds it necessary to proclaim how deeply he loves his flag and his country, he does not realize that he makes as much of a fool of himself as if he should declare how deeply he loves his wife." He hated professions of loyalty, but he believed he was as deeply in love with the United States as any descendant of the Mayflower.[19]

In a more serious vein, London opposed the concept that American overseas investments carried the right of military protection. American investments in foreign lands were subject to the laws of those countries. Freedom of the seas was also limited by the laws of blockade. He said that with the policy of "protecting property outside of our own territory, and within the war zone, you necessarily carried your Army and Navy with this resolution." London had no intention of voting for armed merchant ships.[20]

When debate began in the house on the war resolution, there was no doubt that London would vote against the declaration, but he had his say. On this momentous occasion he was sorry that he could not force himself to prepare a speech. He said that he had spoken so often on the subject that his mind had stopped creating, and he could not argue with a man who favored an incomprehensible war. Nevertheless, he felt obligated to repeat his position. He had no expectation that he might convert anyone even though the greatest service to democracy would be to reject the request for war. The Congress was the only parliament in the world where the question of war had been submitted. The German Reichstag, British Parliament, French Chamber of Deputies, and the Russian Duma all faced an accomplished fact. In the United States, members of Congress were invited to search their minds and their consciences. "Will they throw away that opportunity? If this representative body endorses the idea of war, then all hope for international peace may as well be abandoned." Members were also invited to fight for rights within a war zone thousands of miles away. It was an invitation to enter into alliances with kings, rulers by divine right. Was Congress simply going to perform a "clerical duty?"[21]

The President said the United States had no war against the German people. London agreed, but he asked how could the country "hurt the Kaiser without striking at the German people." The President also referred favorably to the Russian Revolution, a subject of great interest to London. The socialist did not believe a greater event had taken place in the last hundred years, but he made a shrewd observation: The Russian upheaval had not been created by a foreign military force or an invading army. It was a struggle carried on by the people within the country for the last sixty years.

London said that a member had asked how anyone knew the American people were opposed to war. He knew the people were against the war and "I hate to say I am afraid the President himself doubts whether the people favor war." If there was a certainty where the people stood, there would be no call for compulsory military service. During the Spanish-American War there was a call for volunteers, now no one spoke of recruiting volunteers. The President told the American people on April 2 what they should fight for—for a new idea—not to improve the Republic, not to raise Americans to greater heights. It was to change the forms of government in Turkey, Austria, and Germany. Presumably a foreign military force would accomplish that dream. No wonder Wilson was compelled to recommend conscription. Neither Canada nor Australia had compulsory military service. When the issue was presented to the Australians, they turned it down after two years of war.

London did not see the issue between America and Germany. Just as there were two Germanys, there were also two Americas. One America believed its mission was to influence the world for the better by being a free democracy, by growing into a genuine democracy. The other America believed the United States must follow in the footsteps of European countries and adopt "the jargon of European diplomacy about national honor and national dignity." London admitted his unenviable position, but he could only maintain his self-respect by voting against a declaration of war. He joined forty-nine colleagues in casting his negative vote, the only negative vote cast by a member from the Northeast.[22]

After entrance into the war, London was in an awkward position within his party as well as with Congress. He reluctantly supported the war effort and tried to steer a middle course between the Socialist right and left wings. He understood that neither democracy nor humanity would benefit by defeat of the United States. The result was that he received criticism from both sides. In Congress he voted against the draft and espionage laws, defended civil liberties, and fought war profiteering. Attacks from outside the party for his lack of patriotism were to be expected, but the most brutal attacks came from radicals in his party who later became communists. The *New International*, a left-wing publication wanted to know why London was not expelled from the party. One constituent suggested that London resign because he was disgracing the movement. "You are getting too 'respectable' and 'loyal,'" he wrote, "to fit into a revolutionary workingman's movement."[23] When London subscribed to Liberty loans, he was beyond the pale to many comrades.

Although the Socialist party had not done well in the 1916 election, London believed its philosophy had been making progress. Now, the war tore both the party and its philosophy apart. When Socialists met in an emergency convention in St. Louis soon after the declaration of war and denounced it as a "crime against the people of the United States," many of their most prominent members, including Allan Benson, their Presidential candidate, resigned from the party. London remained with the party in an effort to be a moderating influence.

Aside from self-destruction within the party, Socialists faced attacks from the government and the public. In September 1917, their party headquarters was raided and in February 1918, Adolph Germer, executive secretary, J. Louis Engdahl, editor of *American Socialist,* the party's national publication, William F. Kruse of the Young People's Socialist League, and Irwin St. John Tucker, former head of the party's literature department, were indicted. When the Sedition Act of 1918 strengthened the Espionage Act by providing penalties for saying or printing "any disloyal, scurrilous, or abusive language" the Attorney General and Postmaster General, the thought regulators, had little difficulty finding reasons to indict Socialists across the country. Eugene Debs, the longtime Socialist leader received a ten-year sentence in jail for saying that war was the curse of capitalism. After thirty-two months in prison, President Harding, a man never known for his radical sympathies, gave him a pardon. Others, unknown to the general public, received harsher treatment by the courts.

London regained his seat in Congress in 1920, but lost two years later as a result of gerrymandering his district. He returned to his law practice and remained the poor lawyer personally interested in his clients. In 1926, at the age of fifty-four, he was struck by an automobile while crossing the street at First Avenue and 18th Street. Possibly preoccupied and confused in the traffic, he asked that no charges be placed against the driver before he died. The Republican *New York Herald Tribune* said that the accident removed one of the sanest spokesmen for the Socialist party. The *New York World* said that he disappointed many of his constituents because he was too practical.[24] His death shocked and saddened his neighbors on the east side. Photographs testify to the outpouring of emotion by the enormous crowd estimated to be 50,000 people, that jammed the streets in paying homage.

Meyer London, the practical Socialist and successful negotiator, was never among the powers of Congress, but he was an articulate spokesman for peaceful views that were shared by many non-Socialists. His interest in exploring rational methods to end the bloodshed and keep the United States out of war were no more successful than the attempts of those outside his party. The irony is that the man who appeared to be radical to so many was always ready to listen to reason and negotiate with those who held opposing views.

Chapter 11

The Progressive

Robert La Follette, born in a log cabin in Primrose, Wisconsin, was a descendant of French Huguenots and Scotch-Irish. Two of his great-grandfathers served in the American Revolution, and from the beginning of his political career he seemed to inherit their fighting blood. The year after he worked his way through the University of Wisconsin, he was a member of the bar and District Attorney of Dane County. At the time, the salary of eight hundred dollars a year attracted him as much as any desire to become a prosecutor. When he had hung up his shingle to practice law, he was as poverty stricken as any attorney in the state. Nevertheless, he was ambitious, energetic, and a bundle of nerves and soon found plenty of dragons to slay. Quick to make friends, he was just as quick to make enemies. Short, stocky, and strong, he vibrated with a reformer's zeal and was never at a loss for words. Expressive and effective as a speaker, he was always well prepared, but rarely the light-hearted politician on the platform. He was the serious teacher who appealed to intellect rather than emotion. The local boss was his first target, then the state political machine when he became the youngest member of the legislature.

In 1881, La Follette married bright Belle Case, a former classmate, who was the first woman to graduate from the university law school. She shared his interest in politics and they formed a perfect partnership. La Follette valued her clear, calm advice and throughout his stormy life always called her "the Counselor." They had four children, two girls and two boys. Later, Bob Jr. became United States Senator and Phil, Governor of Wisconsin.

After three terms as a Republican Congressman from 1881 to 1891, La Follette lost reelection and returned to practice law and combat the corrupt party leadership. His rebellion, which he called "the holy war," took ten long years, and he learned the adversity of defeat. Twice he failed to gain the nomination for Governor, but he refused to give up. "Fighting Bob" built his own machine which in his eyes served the people. By 1900, his animating principle of a greater voice in government for the people paid off with election to the Governorship with the largest majority in the state's history. His program, based on fact finding first, stirred a whirlwind of activity. It became known as the "Wisconsin idea" and attracted the envy of progressives throughout the nation. The direct primary to give the people the right to name their candidates became law, the inordinate power of railroads was restricted, corporations paid a larger share of taxes, workers' compensation for industrial accidents went into effect, and forests and water power were conserved. None of the avalanche of reforms was accomplished without bruising battles, but in the process Wisconsin appeared to be a model state, and La Follette became a national figure. His personal goal, the White House, was not merely an idle dream.

La Follette resigned as Governor during his third term to enter the United States Senate. He soon learned that his entrance into that august body was not an occasion for rejoicing among more conservative Senators. He sensed their mistrust, especially among the well-represented millionaires such as Nelson Aldrich, and he kept his distance socially. On the floor of the Senate, however, he was not shy about speaking his mind. He found some colleagues anxious to exhibit a cold shoulder by walking out of the chamber when he spoke for the first time. Undaunted, he said, "I cannot be wholly indifferent to the fact that Senators by their absence at this time indicate their want of interest in what I may have to say about this subject. The public is interested. Unless this important question is rightly settled seats now temporarily vacant may be permanently vacated by those who have a right to occupy them at this time." The gallery showed its approval and Senators began to trickle back to their places.[1]

Although La Follette's independence and liberal views alienated many members of the Republican party, he attracted a large popular following, and his name was placed in nomination for President at the 1908 convention. He was easily defeated, however, by Taft supporters. In the next four years he was frequently at odds with administration policies, and in 1911 he was the driving force in founding the National

Progressive Republican League which opposed the renomination of Taft. During that year, La Follette made great strides toward gaining the Presidential nomination as Taft appeared to be a loser, and Roosevelt denied interest in running again. Progressives in Congress announced their support for him, a progressive convention in Chicago endorsed his candidacy, and widely known leaders that ranged from muckraker Lincoln Steffens to liberal millionaires such as Medill McCormick joined the bandwagon. All went well as La Follette expended his energy on a speechmaking tour across the country that eventually exhausted him. His cause was doomed, however, when Teddy Roosevelt announced in February 1912, "My hat is in the ring." That same month, La Follette, overworked, feeling miserable from intestinal trouble, and worried about a daughter's illness, had harangued publishing executives for two hours at a dinner given by the Periodical Publishers Association in Philadelphia. It was a fatal loss of self-control and an embarrassment that ranked with Andrew Johnson's disastrous Vice Presidential inaugural address. La Follette, not a drinking man, ordered a brandy which confused him. He gave up his carefully prepared speech and rambled on for what seemed an eternity. To make matters worse, Woodrow Wilson, the artful preceding speaker, sat through the entire episode. In the days that followed, newspapers reported La Follette's "mental-breakdown." Many of the stories were flagrant exaggerations or falsehoods that would be repeated for the rest of his life. There was no denying, as La Follette was acutely aware, he had committed a dreadful blunder. He referred to it as his Philadelphia "flunk." Progressives now had an easy excuse to rush to the side of the former President. Louis Brandeis, one of La Follette's more steadfast friends urged Belle to make the Senator take a rest. "When he comes back," he wrote, "we will take up the good fight again together." La Follette failed to gain the Republican nomination, but he did not surrender. He wrote, "There won't be any funeral unless it's a real one with music and flowers."[2]

La Follette was a Republican and had never wanted to destroy the party or himself by joining another movement. His differences with Taft were within the party. Now he had an additional stimulus to remain a Republican when Roosevelt received the third-party nomination as a Progressive. The feeling was personal as well as political. The two men had always been wary of each other and La Follette considered Roosevelt an opportunist and suspect progressive. Although La Follette remained a Republican, he did not vote for a Presidential candidate. It was a backhanded assist for Wilson who carried Wisconsin, and

La Follette left no doubt that he would support Wilson's policies if they were progressive.

As President-elect, Wilson signaled his friendship when he said of La Follette, "He is strong because he studies every angle of every question. When he gets up to speak, he knows what he is talking about. When he has finished speaking, it is difficult for a man to vote against him and give any convincing reason for doing so because La Follette has presented the case from the standpoint of the man who knows. The only way a man can justify voting against La Follette is to know more about the subject than La Follette knows." It was true that La Follette's opinions matured from careful study and brooding. When the Payne-Aldrich Tariff bill came before the Senate he buried himself in rate schedules, reports, and production costs. It took a van to deliver all the books he ordered from the Library of Congress to consult. That was his normal procedure. One writer said he worked like a "hod carrier."

During the Wilson administration, La Follette continued to go his own way. He found fault with the income tax bill of 1913 because he believed it did not equalize tax burdens. Eventually he helped to amend the rate for incomes over a hundred thousand dollars a year from about 4 percent to 7 percent. He was also critical of the highly acclaimed Federal Reserve Act which he regarded as a "big bankers bill" that legalized the concentration of capital. Nevertheless, the President, intent upon implementing a progressive program, recognized La Follette's potential value because Democrats had only a narrow margin in the Senate. In another public bouquet, he once said, "I take off my cap to Bob La Follette . . . Taunted, laughed at, called back, going steadfastly on . . . I love these lonely figures." And the Senator was helpful. At times it seemed as though the Republican Senator would become an adviser to the Democratic President. He was delighted with the tariff lobby investigation and gave his support to the Underwood bill which lowered tariffs. Wilson, in turn, finally decided in favor of La Follette's Seamen's Bill to improve working conditions. The Senator noted in 1915 that Wilson urged him to "talk with him about legislation from time to time without waiting to be called, as he believed we had much the same point of view and desires regarding service to the public."[3]

During the Mexican troubles, La Follette agreed with Wilson's call for Americans to leave Mexico and his embargo on shipping munitions to that country. He also hailed the President's declaration of neutrality as "high statesmanship" when war broke out in Europe. One of Wilson's first steps related to the war was to propose a government shipping corporation to carry on foreign trade. Unlike Republicans Henry Cabot Lodge and Elihu Root, who raised the specter of socialism and feared the purchase of available German ships, La Follette backed the measure as a believer in a strong merchant marine. An editorial in the *New York Times* complained that the bill was unconstitutional and aside from the President and the Secretary of the Treasury, the only support came from socialists and others such as La Follette who it inaccurately categorized as a "near socialist." Although the bill failed to pass Congress, La Follette showed that there were times when he could cooperate with the administration.

La Follette appreciated Wilson's early efforts to keep the United States out of war which he saw as a threat to progressive reforms in America even more keenly than the President. When Senator Hitchcock of Nebraska attempted to place an embargo on the shipment of munitions overseas, La Follette stood with him. La Follette also offered a joint peace resolution in February 1915. He had always had his own ideas to put forth in a constructive way and had never been simply a naysayer. His resolution called for a conference of neutral nations to foster mediation in the hope of attaining an early peace. Others had similar thoughts, but he wanted Congress to formally support the President to strengthen his mediation efforts. He had no objection to working for international cooperation even if it meant building a permanent organization. To his surprise, however, his resolution received no encouragement from Wilson and was buried in the Foreign Relations Committee. Nevertheless, La Follette gave his moral support to the President during the *Lusitania* crisis when others attacked his "too proud to fight" attitude. The Senator wrote to a constituent that Wilson was meeting his responsibility with firmness and wisdom as he protected American rights and honor. "At the same time I am confident that he will save us from the dire consequences which befall us . . . if we were involved in this awful slaughter."[4]

As 1915 wore on, however, La Follette worried about the administration policy change that allowed loans to the Allies through J. P. Morgan and Company. The Anglo-French Financial Commission received a half billion dollar loan and the bonds were sold to Americans. In the early days of the war, the business press warned of the danger of poor credit that could create a depression after the war. Now, most of the business press favored loans to belligerents. The *Wall Street Journal* did not see the loan as support for the war. Instead, they saw it as a means to finance American trade. La Follette saw it as the end of genuine neutrality and the ability of the United States to serve as a disinterested party in attaining peace. The country was no longer "neutral in fact as well as in name," Wilson's original objective.[5] The President's reversal on preparedness also alarmed the Senator. He, like Kitchin, favored a strong Navy and National Guard, but he was against extreme expansion which would lead to war. He believed too that ordinary citizens agreed with him. Not long ago, the President, in his annual message to Congress of December 8, 1914, had also agreed. This new push for preparedness appeared to La Follette as the work of war profiteers and propagandists. Sarcastically, he said the new "Patriots" were the Morgans, Rockefellers, Schwabs, Garys, DuPonts and others like them who gained most from war orders. He called it "financial imperialism."

In the New Year, La Follette joined others in Congress who favored legislation to warn Americans against sailing on belligerent ships. He saw no sense in risking war over an abstraction related to freedom of the seas. When Wilson had warned Americans to leave Mexico to avoid dangerous incidents, he agreed. What was the difference now? Wilson, opposed to such measures, irked him by calling for free discussion and then using a variety of private pressures to block debate. La Follette saw a Constitutional issue that went beyond any tactical maneuvers. Wilson had written in his book, *Constitutional Government in the United States*, "The initiative in foreign affairs, which the President possesses without any restriction whatsoever, is virtually the power to control them absolutely." No one disagreed with this principle which denied the will of the people more than La Follette. He said, "If the President is clothed with such unlimited power, if in conducting foreign affairs he can go unhindered of Congress to the limit of making war inevitable, and if Congress has no alternative but to accept and sanction his course, then we have become a one-man power, then the President has authority to make war as absolutely as though he were Czar of Russia." La Follette did not believe that was the intent of the founding fathers. He was certain that Congress had a right to have a say in foreign policy.[6]

Throughout the year, La Follette, considered by so many as nothing more than a midwestern isolationist, continued to call for a conference of neutral nations and the formation of an international organization to settle disputes. Mediation by neutrals appealed to him as much as to Stone and Kitchin who were hardheaded politicians. As experienced legislators they knew the frustrations and pitfalls in trying to move a political body, but they were willing to make the attempt. Each of them had spent long hours in conferences coping with policy differences, personality clashes, and intractable problems resistant to change. Each of them had faced threats, roadblocks, and special interests. Each of them had been scarred in the battle of making laws. They had suffered defeats and scored tough victories. When they, and other members of Congress, spoke in favor of mediation, they spoke as veteran negotiators. That was their business, and they were aware of both the perils and opportunities. Far from naive, they believed it was one of the few avenues to peace that might gather sufficient force to influence the belligerents. Neither dreamers nor eccentrics, they saw a possibility for peace, not a guarantee. In May 1916, Wilson outlined a postwar plan in a speech to the League to Enforce Peace. The *Brooklyn Times* observed that while the President could not do the slightest thing to end this war, "he can lay down a formula to prevent all future wars!"[7]

La Follette searched for ways to reduce the war fever. He favored government production of munitions to remove skyrocketing profits which were an incentive to war, but he received no help from the White House. He also introduced a bill for an advisory war referendum if the President broke diplomatic relations with Germany. It was consistent with his belief that the people's voice should be heard. The plan evolved from his service on the Committee on Census and did not seem radical to the man who had pioneered direct democracy. If one percent of qualified electors of twenty-five states filed petitions with the Bureau of Census calling for a popular vote, an advisory referendum would be held through the mail and the results reported to Congress. The bill was sidetracked and never voted upon. Nevertheless, it illustrated the different philosophies of Wilson and La Follette. Wilson believed the people had to be directed by an enlightened leader. Years ago, he had expressed the view that the people were "as clay in the hands of a consummate leader." La Follette believed that democratic control was essential for peace and that Wilson's attempts to silence Congress were unprecedented.

When the Republican national convention met in 1916, the Wisconsin delegation, under the influence of La Follette, offered a platform. It included a proposal for a neutral nations peace effort, government manufacture of munitions, and an excess profits tax on munitions. All were rejected. The *Chicago Tribune* accused La Follette of acting like a German because there was a large German electorate in his state. "He is also acting like a Democrat to make trouble for the Republican party. La Follette, in his disappointed ambitions, is a Democrat. He is not a Republican." There was some cause for the *Tribune's* impression of the

Senator's behavior, but the *New York Times*, an exponent of free speech, went to extremes in its vilification. The paper claimed, "Wisconsin has one American Senator. She needs another. Mr. La Follette beside his multifarious crankeries and orotundities, has not spoken or voted as an American."[8]

Although La Follette had much to say about international affairs, he would have preferred to concentrate on domestic affairs. He wrote to a friend, "There is enough to do here—real things too outside of the Mexican and European affairs—It is open season for Big Graft-Armor Plate-Enlarged Navy-Greater Army etc."[9] There was also a political campaign to conduct. Wilson and La Follette were both candidates for reelection. La Follette, with his customary intensity, made seven or eight long speeches a day during his Senate campaign with his usual independence. Nominally a Republican, he did not have substantial support from any party. He could not even count on a phalanx of people who considered themselves progressives. Some historians have claimed that progressives favored participation in the war. Progressive opinion was actually split just as Wilson, Roosevelt, and La Follette were divided.

John J. Hannan, La Follette's secretary, wrote that a large number of Republicans were ready to "knife" the Senator. So La Follette played his own hand. "We told them," Hannan wrote, "you can go dog or you can go bear and there you are." La Follette remained silent about both Wilson and Hughes and many interpreted this aloofness as approval of Wilson. They were probably correct, but it did not help his own campaign. The State Central Committee and every county Republican committee brought pressure upon him to support Hughes and his resistance was costly. Many Scandinavians in the state voted for Wilson because "He Kept Us Out of War," but many German-Americans intended to vote for Hughes. There were so many crosscurrents in the state, the outcome was impossible to predict.[10]

Shortly after the election, Hannan wrote to Louis Brandeis that La Follette had lost at least 30,000 votes by withholding support for Hughes. Nonetheless, he carried the state with a plurality of 100,000 on election day against all odds. Wilson, on the other hand, lost the state because the Democrats did not hold their vote in the heavily populated German counties. The German-American agricultural communities were opposed to Wilson "by a blind unreasoning antagonism." That was not true in Milwaukee where German-Americans were more tolerant of Wilson. Ironically, Republican counties gave Wilson a big vote. His strength in Wisconsin, according to Hannan, came from progressive Republicans and labor unions. La Follette's victory was the only cause for celebration for Hannan. "You can certainly feel joyful," he wrote Brandeis, "over that because without your practical assistance even that might not have been possible."[11]

La Follette, tired but happy, looked upon his reelection as a mandate to keep out of war. Jingoism had received a setback and the plain people had spoken. The unofficial, unspoken cooperation with Wilson was approaching its high point.

With the election won, Wilson tried once again to initiate a negotiated peace. His timing had failed earlier in the year. Now he believed the people in the belligerent countries were tired of war and that his chances for success would be better. At the moment, however, Germany was in a stronger military position. In a bloody battle at the Somme which would cost another half million lives before it was over, the Germans had blocked the British offensive. Again, the Germans claimed they were interested in a peace conference. On December 18, 1915, President Wilson sent his peace note to the belligerents. Mainly, he wanted to obtain a definition of terms which could be the basis for an end to the fighting. He did not propose peace or offer mediation, but he was searching for a place to begin negotiations.

Wilson's peace note attracted a lukewarm reception at best. Lansing tried to undercut the President's initiative because he feared it would be linked to the German peace feeler and lacked sufficient sympathy for the Allies. Colonel House was unhappy because Wilson likened the war aims of the Allies and Central Powers. The President had mentioned that the war aims on both sides were "virtually the same," but La Follette was not one of the critics. He was delighted with Wilson's action. Nevertheless, the Allies suffering from heavy military losses, were offended by the note and embittered by the reference to similar war aims. They replied by offering conditions for a peace conference which were purposely over-demanding to prevent serious consideration. The Germans courteously agreed that there was a need for a direct exchange of views. They also expressed a willingness to cooperate in the prevention of future wars at the end of the present conflict. Privately, German officials had no interest in American meddling at that time. Soon their all-out U-boat campaign would begin.

When an undeterred Wilson made his proposal for "peace without victory" before the Senate in January 1917, La Follette was the first to applaud. He said, "We have just passed through a very important hour in the life of the world."[12] When Wilson spoke of the rights of small nations, self-determination, the consent of the governed, freedom of seas, and moderation of arms, La Follette enthusiastically voiced his agreement. Nonetheless, he was still concerned about Wilson's departure from true neutrality and his strenuous efforts to manage Congress. Their differences, for the moment, seemed to be over means rather than ends.

On February 2, 1917, La Follette wrote to his family at home in Wisconsin that he could not "shake off the feeling that an awful crisis is impending." He thought he should try to "break through & see Wilson—But it is given out that he is 'locked up alone' and seeing no one." Meanwhile, newspapers were more "blatant" than ever for war to begin. "You can only stand and grimly wait for a chance to fight the devils off." He was thwarted by the lack of information from either the White House or State Department which were "sealed up tight as a drum." No one had a hunch where they were headed. "The Democrats are saying little—just waiting for orders."[13]

The next day La Follette found that he had not suffered from empty fears. Word arrived that von Bernstorff, the German ambassador, had been handed his passport and Wilson would address Congress that afternoon. When Wilson announced the severance with Germany because of its intention to sink American ships in its declared war zone, most of Congress applauded. La Follette, however, thought the progressive Republicans and Democrats were sick at heart. It was hard for La Follette to sit out the President's speech, and when it was over, he went to his office to be alone. He did not want to see anybody. A depressed Bryan phoned and wanted to get together with him at the Lafayette Hotel that evening. La Follette joined him and they discussed what, if anything, could be done. Bryan favored a mass meeting which did not strike the Senator as a great idea. Nevertheless, La Follette agreed to check with progressives while Bryan conferred with Democrats. Nothing came of the plan. La Follette wrote to his family, "And all the while there is the danger the 'Maine will be blown up'—and we be carried into a declaration of war—by jingoes in spite of everything." Other neutral nations had issued diplomatic protests against unrestricted submarine activity, but they had not broken diplomatic relations. The European and Latin American neutrals had not considered it necessary to assuage their honor and dignity by such a step. He wondered why the powerful United States could not endure a few tribulations for "the sake of saving the world from being drawn into this dire catastrophe."[14]

While Wilson leaned heavily on Congress to follow his direction, he continued to keep it in ignorance. La Follette wrote, "I don't think the President consulted a Senator or Rep.—till he had everything fixed for today's program & that he never changed a thing—after he did see a few of them."[15] The next day La Follette wrote to his family that if he were home he would feel that he was missing what was happening in Washington. "But you don't." He hoped against hope that the "fool business" would blow over. If he were President, he would not permit a ship to leave for Europe, "in 60 days the war would be over & the cost of living would be reduced 40%." The passage of time seemed to be the only possible cure. He counted every day that passed without incident a gain. In the meantime, he tried to stir up some groups that might influence "this flock of Congressional sheep." He found the farmers' Equity, the farmers' Union, the Grange, and labor organizations ready to respond. As a politician, he stayed away from extreme pacifists who could produce a boomerang effect against the cause of peace.[16]

Senator Stone disappointed La Follette when he introduced a resolution approving the President's break in diplomatic relations with Germany. He thought it was another unnecessary tactic. He could not vote for it and felt certain that many Senators preferred to avoid the resolution. A number of them who spoke on the resolution said it had no business before the Senate, but they were obligated to sustain the President so that foreign governments would know they were united. Their "right or wrong for our country" attitude irritated La Follette. Giving up an abstract right in connection with citizens traveling on belligerent ships did not seem of much importance to him. "We have surrendered our rights to England already." His mind again turned to Mexico when the administration pressured Americans to abandon their property rights in that country where lives had been lost. It was folly to him for citizens to insist upon sailing into the European war zone.

He dreaded what might happen if an American ship was sunk and lives lost, especially without "warning." La Follette remained in a state of tension and the lack of information continued to exasperate him. No one in Congress knew what the President's plans were and La Follette believed he would "pursue his policy of telling Congress—*afterwards* and not before." All he knew was what he read in the papers and he missed talking things over with Belle. She was at home tending to the family.[17]

On February 12, 1917, as time grew short, La Follette introduced another resolution that led nowhere. His objective was to make it unlawful for armed merchant ships of the United States to depart from American ports in time of peace. He was aware of the hopelessness of the situation, but he felt he had to make an effort. He had an ominous sense that the President would make another announcement soon and feared the result. It all made him tired, depressed, and lonesome. He was weary of jingo papers that maligned anyone who did not "shout for war." He suspected that some newspapers were subsidized by war interests but he had no proof. He also felt the invective of Theodore Roosevelt and his followers who could scarcely wait for war to begin. Roosevelt, in a private letter to Henry Cabot Lodge, wrote that La Follette was a type "considerably inferior in morality and capacity, to Robespierre." The strain obviously affected the former Rough Rider too. His vitriol became so extreme it seemed as though he had lost all balance. Despite the slings that came his way, La Follette, always tough and stubborn, did not intend to quit. He wrote to "Mamma & Kiddies—Lets have peace if we have to fight all Hell to preserve it."[18]

The real fight was about to begin. On February 26, 1917, Wilson called for arming merchant ships as the Congressional session was near an end. To La Follette it was a call to war and a violation of the warmaking powers of Congress. He was ready to resist and as usual he was well prepared. A friend said to him if he defeated the bill, "they'll crucify you." He simply replied, "I know it."[19] La Follette, Norris, and a few other Senators planned to block action by talking the measure to death. La Follette was to make the concluding speech.

During the debate, La Follette, ever intense, became increasingly worked up when he realized that the presiding officer would deny him the right to speak. In the cloakroom there was talk of violence as anger seethed on both sides. The atmosphere was so taut, "Young Bob," watching the proceedings, thought a riot would break out. His father sent him for a traveling bag which he knew contained a gun. The son went for the bag, but wisely took out the gun. He became so concerned about his father's excited state he sent him a note, "Please, Please be calm—you know what the Press will do—remember Mother." A little later, he sent another note, "You cannot afford to get into a physical argument or be arrested by the Serg[eant] at Arms for misconduct. For God's sake make your protest & prevent passage of the bill but if previous question is made and sustained do not try to fight Senate physically . . . I am about crazy with strain. B."[20]

When Norris realized that the filibuster would succeed in blocking the bill, he told La Follette not to do anything to upset the outcome. It was a deep disappointment that he did not speak. He wanted his views on the record, but there was no doubt where he stood. The temporary tactical victory was very costly to the Senators whom Wilson condemned as "the willful men." La Follette was sneered at in street cars, spat upon, and colleagues went out of their way to avoid him. In Wisconsin, usually pictured as a bastion of German-Americans, he was treated with equal severity. The *Milwaukee Journal* considered him a humiliation, and other papers across the state shared the same view. The personal venom expressed in Madison hurt the most where old friends suddenly became enemies. The censure of La Follette, a national figure, extended from coast to coast. Rollin Kirby, the talented political cartoonist for the *New York World* portrayed La Follette at the head of a line of "willful men" receiving an Iron Cross from an armored hand. It was called, "The Only Adequate Reward." Many years later, after La Follette died, Kirby wrote a letter of apology for his malignant work. Other comments and cartoons, however, were filled with as much hatred. Yet amid the abuse, La Follette received an avalanche of telegrams and letters from around the nation commending his stand. Within the next few weeks thousands of messages poured into his office and an estimated 90 percent were favorable to him.

La Follette deceived himself in thinking that Wilson had been defeated in his attempt to arm merchant ships. He also believed that the war-making powers of Congress had not been surrendered to the President. He wrote to his family that Wilson would not dare to arm merchant ships now without congressional authority even though the State Department assumed he had that right. He thought the President could convoy ships that did not carry contraband, but the British had declared almost everything contraband. Soon, Wilson proved him wrong when he armed merchant ships on his executive authority.

La Follette's delaying actions in the hope of gaining time for reconsideration were ineffective. He wrote to his son, Phil, on March 27, "No one knows just what the President will ask Congress to do . . . The lid is kept screwed down and no one knows what form of action will be proposed—He may spring some new sensation—as in the Zimmerman letter."[21]

The country was already taking on a warlike air. In New York City, young and old, men and women, exhibited their military instincts. Members of The American Women's League for Self-Defense drilled under an army officer on Governor's Island. Men of the Home Defense League, organized to protect water works and other public property, were "whipped into shape" at the Sixty-ninth Regiment Armory by a policeman. On Ward's Island, naval militiamen practiced bayonet charges. In Central Park, Boy Scouts mobilized for service in field hospital units.

On the evening of April 2, 1917, Wilson unscrewed the lid. He set out for the Capitol with a cavalry escort to deliver his war message. Anticipation, tension, and patriotism permeated the packed House chamber. Most Senators displayed a small American flag, but La Follette was an exception. He was in no mood for chauvinism. Neither hyperpatriotic displays nor the rousing welcome the President received matched his frame of mind.

A subdued Wilson stated that the new German submarine policy was "warfare against mankind." He had called the Congress into extraordinary session because there were serious choices of policy to make "which it was neither right nor Constitutionally permissible that I should assume the responsibility of making." He was right about the limits of his authority and personally he had always sought the endorsement of Congress for his decisions even when he avoided its advice.[22]

The President surprised La Follette when he admitted that armed neutrality was "worse than ineffectual" because it would draw the country into war without the rights of belligerents. That had been La Follette's opinion as one of the "willful men." Wilson asked Congress for a declaration of war because the nation would not take the path of submission. The object was to vindicate the principles of peace and justice against autocratic power. There was no quarrel with the German people. They had been deceived by their government. In a democracy such as the United States that was "happily impossible where public opinion commands and insists upon full information concerning all the nation's affairs." Peace would require a partnership of democratic nations which would be a "league of honor, a partnership of opinion." The Russians, "always in fact democratic at heart" were now a fit partner for this league since they had shaken off their autocratic government. At that early date, there was little reason to place Russia in such exalted company. Little more than two weeks had passed since the Tsar had abdicated. Prince George Lvov headed a fragile Provisional Government on the brink of defeat by the Germans. Although the Bolsheviks, with Lenin in the background, were not yet in power, they talked openly of signing an early peace treaty. No one could foretell the outcome for that troubled land. Nevertheless, Wilson hastily accepted

Russia into the band of civilized nations that would make the world safe for democracy.[22]

Wilson concluded, "with the pride of those who know that the day has come when America is privileged to spend her blood and her might for the principles that gave her birth and happiness and the peace which she has treasured. God helping her, she can do no other." The end of the moving speech brought a cheering, standing ovation. The Chief Justice of the Supreme Court of the United States, Edward D. White, behaved as though he was the cheer leader of the impassioned crowd. For La Follette, it was a dark moment. There was nothing to celebrate. He stood quietly with his arms folded in front of him.

The next day, Senator Hitchcock introduced the war resolution and asked for immediate consideration. La Follette was not about to oblige. He insisted, in accordance with Senate rules, that it go over a day for study. That night a Columbia University professor compared La Follette with Benedict Arnold and Judas Iscariot. Students at the Massachusetts Institute of Technology burned an effigy of La Follette for Bostonians to see on the shore of the Charles River. And soon the Madison [Wisconsin] *Democrat* asked, "Is La Follette mad?"[23]

On April 4, Senator Vardaman of Mississippi was the first to speak against the war resolution. He suppressed his talent as a southern orator of the old school for florid statements, and in a relatively few words expressed his opinion. Ultimately, with the help of Wilson, his conviction that day would cost him his Senate seat. Stone spoke next. He had made his position clear during the armed ship debate and now confined his remarks to less than five minutes. Norris of Nebraska savagely charged, "I feel we are about to put the dollar sign upon the American flag."[24] Gronna of North Dakota, stolid, sincere, said he intended to vote against war because "it would have been possible to maintain an honorable peace." Lane of Oregon, a dying man, voted against war, but he did not speak.

It was almost four o'clock in the afternoon when La Follette's turn to speak came. Although he had a mass of material to support his case, there had been little time to pull it into shape since Wilson's address. He worked frantically with the help of Belle, Bob Jr., John Hannan, and Gilbert Roe, his former law partner. Because he had been denied the right to speak during the armed ship battle, he intended to have his say now. And he had much to say. He spoke from his desk in the first row of the center aisle, and the excitability that he had recently exhibited in the chamber had disappeared. Calm and sure of himself, he settled down to his arguments and spoke from a manuscript. Never a man of a few words, he took until six forty-five in the evening to make his case which was essentially the grand summation in a lost cause. The Senators, in their places, listened intently and there were few interruptions.[25]

La Follette announced at the start that he supposed it was the duty of Senators to vote according to their convictions. Recently, he said ,newspapers had put forth a new doctrine, "standing back of the President" whether he was right or wrong. He did not intend to subscribe to that idea. He reminded his fellow Senators that Wilson said he was not contemplating war when he proposed arming merchant ships. Now, not much more than a month later, he asked for a declaration of war when there was no change in the situation between the United States and Germany.

In recent days, La Follette received 15,000 letters and telegrams from forty-four states and nine out of ten opposed war with Germany. He also reported the results of some polls that had been taken. Among them was one in Monroe, Wisconsin, that indicated 954 for peace, 95 for war. In Massachusetts, a 20,000 postcard referendum showed 60 percent of the respondents against war. He recited other results that convinced him that most Americans still opposed entry into the war. A few messages from individuals were also read. A telegram from Philadelphia said, "President Wilson said German people were not consulted about entering war. Were we?" It was signed "Common People." A case could be made that La Follette spoke for the people because no one really knew the opinion of the majority of Americans.

Since the President admitted that he was wrong about the effectiveness of arming merchant ships in February, he could be wrong about declaring war in April. La Follette wanted his listeners to examine the President's address. He questioned Wilson's accuracy about the German government's promise concerning submarine warfare. La Follette read from an official statement of the German government which made the promise of restraint and freedom of the seas on the condition that England obey international law in naval warfare. And, he said, no one contended that England observed international law. Germany, in contrast to Wilson's implication, had not made an unconditional promise that had been dishonorably violated.

The President condemned Germany for inhumane practices in conducting U-boat warfare. La Follette said it was England that had refused to follow the humane Declaration of London while Germany had offered to abide by it. Wilson also charged that German warfare was against mankind, yet no other neutral nation considered Germany's conduct a cause for entering the war. La Follette thought the Scandinavian nations, Spain, and Switzerland, among others, had a better right to express grievances to mankind since they had not sold war materials to either side and were not suspected of war profiteering. Neutral nations were asking if the United States was seizing upon the war to extend an imperialistic policy.

La Follette continued to dissect the President's speech. Wilson said there was no quarrel with the German people while he added that the United States would cooperate with the Allies. That meant, the Senator said, joining in starving the young and old, sick and maimed of Germany. It was idle to talk of a war against only a government. Cooperation with the Allies was an endorsement of their violations of international law, shameful methods of warfare, and ancient animosities. "If we can not resist now the pressure she is exerting to carry us into the war, how can we resist, then, the thousandfold greater pressure she will exert to bend us to her purposes and compel compliance with her demands?"

The President said that this was a war for democracy and that the United States could never be friends with "Prussian autocracy." Yet the United States had been friends with a militaristic Germany when war broke out in 1914. Wilson did not suggest that Great Britain, with her hereditary land system, limited suffrage, and grinding industrial conditions, grant home rule to Ireland, Egypt, or India before Americans rally to her side. "Are the people of this country being so well represented in this war movement that we need to go abroad to give other people control of their governments? Will the President and the supporters of this war bill submit it to a vote of the people before the declaration of war goes into effect?" He wondered who had registered the approval of the American people. The espionage bills, conscription bills, and military measures under preparation restricting the rights of citizens were proof to him that the war had no popular support.

La Follette turned to the original causes of the war which were outside the realm of American responsibility. He believed the causes were created by a small group of men in each government who saw war as an opportunity for profit and power. He had been sure for a long time that financial imperialism was behind every modern war. Great Britain wanted to suppress commercial competition and Germany feared commercial isolation. (Wilson said in a speech in St. Louis in 1919, "The real reason that the war we have just finished took place was that Germany was afraid her commercial rivals were going to get the better of her, and the reason why some nations went into war against Germany was that they thought that Germany would get the commercial advantages of them.")

As the war continued, the British scrapped the principles of the Declaration of London which limited blockade to ports and coasts of the enemy, free access to neutral ports, and a clear definition of contraband. The British, La Follette explained, shifted the classification of free goods to conditional contraband and ignored American rights on the high seas. Soon, scarcely an article of commerce with neutrals was free from seizure by England. While Germany yielded to American protests, the British had only given way for a brief time in the case of cotton. In the interests of time, he said he would not dwell on the relatively minor violations of British seizure of mail, violations of the use of a neutral flag, seizing goods without warrants, and seizing American ships and placing them into their service. He wanted to move on to the more important subject of war zones.

Only three months after war began, Britain on three days' notice, created the North Sea war zone which stretched from Scotland to Iceland to bar neutral commerce by mining the area. The British government made no pretense that it was legal. Its justification was necessity. This violation of international law took place without a word of protest from the United States. The loss of ships in the zone was minimal because America submitted to British dictation. Germany waited three months for the United States to protest. When that did not happen, Germany in retaliation, established a war zone around the British Isles. This, according to La Follette, was the heart of the trouble between the United States and Germany. "It is for this, and this only, that we are urged to make war." Germany's assertion of this right was what the British were doing with American consent. He had read the diplomatic correspondence and found the note warning that Germany would be held to "strict accountability" for violation of neutral rights; however, he searched in vain for a copy of the British order-in-council mining the North Sea.

"We acquiesced in England's action without protest. It is proposed that we now go to war with Germany for identically the same action upon her part." This was the fatal mistake the administration had made. Its policy enforced the principles of international law against one belligerent and not the other. "That thing no nation can do without losing its character as a neutral nation and without losing the rights that go with strict and absolute neutrality." This was not a new principle. Thomas Jefferson had said the same thing when he asserted that the United States could not permit one warring nation to curtail our neutral rights if we were not ready to allow the enemy the same privilege. La Follette cited the case of *Resolution* in the Federal Court of Appeals in 1781 which said that the concept of a neutral nation "implies two nations at war and a third in friendship with both." John Quincy Adams, Secretary of State, said in 1818, "By the usual principles of international law the state of neutrality recognizes the cause of both parties to the contest as *just*—that is, it avoids all consideration of the merits of the contest."

In closing, La Follette said, "We should not seek to hide our blunder behind the smoke of battle, to inflame the mind of our people by half truths into the frenzy of war, in order that they may never appreciate the real cause of it until it is too late. I do not believe that our national honor is served by such a course. The right way is the honorable way." He saw two alternatives. The United States could admit its mistake and enforce its neutral rights against both belligerents or withdraw American commerce from both.

La Follette held the attention of his colleagues and the gallery through the long hours, but he did not change any votes. He tried to focus on the "fatal mistake" which was futile. The administration and press had minimized the government policy of abiding by one war zone and ignoring the other, and the inconsistency remained unrecognized by the average citizen. German U-boats sinking American ships inflamed the public beyond judicious thought. The Senator had devoted his life to giving the people a voice in government, but the people, struggling to make a living, uninformed, misled, confused, could only respond to their emotions.[23]

One may wonder whether or not any of La Follette's fellow Senators admired his courage for speaking out against Wilson and war when it would only bring ignominy upon himself. Senator Williams of Mississippi was certainly not a secret admirer. A member of the Board of Trustees of the Carnegie Endowment for International Peace, he could scarcely wait for the speech to end and the war to begin. As soon as La Follette finished, Williams was on his feet to denounce the Wisconsin Senator. "Mr. President," he said, "If immortality could be attained by verbal eternity, the Senator from Wisconsin would have approximated immortality. We have waited and have heard a speech from him which would have better become Herr Bethmann-Hollweg . . . I have heard from him a speech which was pro-German, pretty nearly pro-Goth, and pro-Vandal, which was anti-American President and anti-American Congress, and anti-American people."[26] He continued to arraign his colleague for a considerable time, but La Follette had not remained in the chamber long after his speech. He was on hand later, however, to cast his negative vote against the war resolution which passed, 82 to 6 at a little after eleven o'clock in the evening.

La Follette spoke his mind throughout the war, especially in trying to place a greater share of the tax burden on war profiteers. The greatest threat to him as a Senator came from a false Associated Press report that quoted him as saying in a speech in St. Paul that the United States had "no grievances" against Germany. On the basis of the report, the Minnesota Commission of Public Safety petitioned the Senate to expel La Follette for disloyalty and seditious statements. This led to a public outcry, more burning of effigies, and two Madison newspapers charging him with treason. When La Follette began a libel action, the papers apologized. Nevertheless, the Senate Committee of Privileges and Elections pondered a decision about the accusation even after the Associated Press admitted its error and retracted its report.

Alice Brandeis, wife of the Supreme Court Justice, wrote to Mrs. La Follette, "I can't tell you how shocked we are & outraged too, by these recent attacks on the Senator—it is almost incredible that such things should come to pass—his long, long years of utmost service, his loyalty, his devotion all forgotten. It makes my blood boil, Belle & I can't at the same time feel aught but very sad we should have reached such a stage as this." Unfortunately, the country had reached such a stage.[27]

It was not until long after the Armistice, in January 1919, that the Senate committee declared no action against La Follette was justified, and a majority in the Senate concurred. Still later, in 1921, the Senate approved a payment of $5,000 to La Follette for expenses he had incurred in defending himself.

In the postwar world, La Follette gained new respect as the country had second thoughts about the war. Although it was a conservative Coolidge era, he ran for President in 1924 on a Progressive ticket. He received almost five million votes, about one-sixth of the total, carried his home state with thirteen electoral votes, and made a strong showing in twelve western states where he ran ahead of John W. Davis, the Democratic candidate. Thirty-three years later, a Senate committee selected five "outstanding" Senators whose portraits were to hang in the Senate reception room. La Follette was one of the five who took his place with Henry Clay and Daniel Webster.

Chapter 12

Conclusion

At the outbreak of World War I, Woodrow Wilson told the nation to be neutral in thought as well as in action. Those who followed his advice, found to their surprise, that they were eventually cast in the role of villains. Few words seemed strong enough to convey the scorn of the people. The American people, quick to praise and quick to condemn, were also quick to categorize right and wrong, but they were not completely to blame. Average citizens did not have the time or resources to study national and international affairs. Those interested in the European war from 1914 to 1917 reached their conclusions in haphazard ways just as we do today. Their opinions, usually of necessity, were created by flash impressions rather than facts. Labels became the guideposts for discussion. Unfortunately, artificial classifications, especially about internationalism did not explain complexities, ambiguities, and conditions. Misconceptions abounded as false images were formed that became more important than truth. Appearance became reality.

Wilson, like all Presidents, was never short of advice or criticism. While some fought to remain neutral, others were equally adamant about intervention. A spirit of righteousness prevailed on both sides and the President, as he pondered the issues, had his own high sense of morality. The decisions that he faced were mammoth, if not insuperable, and the greatest responsibility rested with him. Lack of sympathy for his decisions should not deny sympathy for his cares in the office of the Presidency.

Those who fought to keep America out of the European war were frequently misunderstood in their own time. Perhaps worse, there is a reluctance to give up some of the glib ideas about internationalism and intervention that were current then. The terms are not absolute, but the thought persists that intervention is synonymous with internationalism. Even hindsight, the great helpmate of historians, can be blind when too much emphasis is placed upon the path taken rather than the possibilities of the path not taken. Historians tend to cling to standard heroes and ignore other voices.

A multitude of prewar pacifists who had spoken in such glowing terms about world peace faded when the shooting began. Clergymen and professors who had been pillars of the peace societies ran to their private foxholes when critics aimed harsh words their way. They walked away from the greatest challenge of the century and confined themselves to sermons and scholarly studies about peace in a distant postwar era. Religion, in a time of tension, as Norman Thomas discovered, did not transcend nationalism. The battle to stop the spread of bloodshed fell upon the kind of people in this book who did not regard themselves as pacifists. They presented the other side of the argument and had the courage to withstand withering criticism for their belief that the time had come to stand up and be counted. Neither naive nor Utopian, they lived in the real world and had no desire for martyrdom as they struggled with specific issues that they believed were leading the country into the maelstrom. Any illusions that they entertained were no more improbable than those of their critics. Although ignored by the President, who once appeared to be one of their own, they presented a case despite their diversity that deserved greater consideration then as it does now.

Those who opposed America's entry into the war understood some elementary truths that escaped more sophisticated minds. Their most obvious and often repeated insight was that war leads to war, not peace. Foresight, not hindsight, told them and they in turn told Wilson, that it was not a war to end all wars. World War II may be looked upon as the "good war," but it might have been an unnecessary war if it had not been for the disastrous results of World War I. Yet the adage that war is for the sake of peace is commonplace today and widely accepted. When the first crisis in the Persian Gulf developed, President Bush declared time and again that the nation fought for peace and a new world order just as President Wilson pronounced in 1917. We have grown so accustomed to equating military action with peace we fail to recognize the irony.

The opponents of war were also aware that there is no such thing as half-way neutrality. Partiality was not the way to serve as a mighty mediator or moral arbiter. President Wilson failed to follow his own advice as his British inclinations became more evident. Munitions and loans to the Allies, American passage on Allied ships, and military preparedness with only one possible enemy were not the acts of a neutral nation. Claude Kitchin believed that excess preparedness reinforced an insidious lobby of arms makers and was a menace to peace. In his opinion the new militarism made any pretension by the United States to favor an international settlement nothing more than hypocrisy. Anyone with the slightest acquaintance with conflict resolution knows that a mediator cannot take sides. The mediator's job, as Julia Grace Wales explained, was to study causes, analyze problems, and bring them to the conference table in the hope that it might lead to a solution. Continuous mediation was a slow, grinding process that required time and inordinate patience if there was to be the slightest possibility for success. A peaceful end to such a climactic event as World War I could not be achieved by brief visits of special emissaries. It was the belligerents themselves who would have to settle their differences. The loss of absolute neutrality meant the dilution of any chance to serve as an effective mediator for the benefit of "mankind," one of Wilson's favorite words.

Despite the handicap of partial neutrality, those who expected their country to set an example for the world diligently pursued mediation to end hostilities. It was the plea that ran through the years. It began with Bryan who realized that it was necessary to end the war quickly before nationalistic hatreds hardened. Others sought mediation even when they were aware that the opportune time had passed. Wilson, the sponsor of a league of nations, distrusted the neutral nations and dismissed the idea of a neutral conference as impractical. His distrust stemmed from the danger that the neutrals might not agree with his views. At Princeton or elsewhere, Wilson was never known for open-mindedness in negotiation. The proponents of such a conference were called ingenuous. Yet when we look at those who favored a mediation effort in concert with other nations, we see tough legislators like Stone, Kitchin, La Follette, and a seasoned labor negotiator in Meyer London. All had extensive experience working with opposing parties. They did not minimize the difficulties and consequences, but they were not afraid to embrace continuous mediation as presented by the women at The Hague while Wilson preferred to act alone. He thought he knew when the right time would arrive, but if there was a right time, it passed him by. As Emily Balch wrote, "He doubtless felt that he could act better alone when the time came, but when it came he was no longer a neutral but completely involved in the power politics of the Allies."[1]

Negotiations did not have to mean "appeasement," a word that fills Americans with dread. A failed attempt was a small loss in an effort to stop a war that caused more than eight million battlefield deaths. A success, possible or not, remained to be seen, but it might have achieved a peace without victory, saved countless lives, and formed a sounder basis for a postwar world. A conference of neutral nations might have failed, and Wilson's image might have been marred, but his real failure as an internationalist was that he did not try before it was too late. Ford, with his many deficiencies, took a brutal beating in his attempt at unofficial mediation. He tried and despite failure even found sympathy at the polls.

In domestic politics, there was nothing radical in opposing false neutrality. To the contrary, opposition to favorite nations, privileged trade policies, war profiteering, and large military establishments were traditional in 1914. Admittedly there had been danger in upholding such rational views. George Washington recognized that "real patriots" who resisted the intrigues of a favorite nation were liable to be "suspected and odious" while "tools and dupes" were applauded. False patriotism, often found attractive, has played havoc since the earliest days of the republic. La Follette understood that if the United States could not withstand Allied pressure to take the country into war, there would be little chance to withstand far greater pressures later.

Woodrow Wilson frankly admitted after the war that commercial rivalries were a cause of the war in 1914, but minimized them as a factor during the war. His opponents did not all agree with the Socialists that capitalism caused the war, but conservatives as well as liberals urged economic restraints in America. Their suggestions for higher taxes for arms makers, government manufacture of weapons, or an embargo on overseas sales of munitions to curb the treacherous influence of excess profits were ignored.

Wilson had his own ironic ideas about leadership in a democracy. The Presidential election of 1916 appeared to be a mandate to keep the country out of war. It was the popular referendum that some people wanted. Yet Wilson, with his preconceived notions, preferred to lead the people to peace his way not their way. Inflexible self-righteousness, individual or national, was bound to lead to trouble. Jane Addams concluded that the President overrated his own leadership. Did he have the right to rate his moral leadership so high that he could consider the

Conclusion

sacrifice of his young countrymen a necessity? It raises another question that is relevant today. Should war be entered into by the whim of one man? That was the disturbing question that nagged Stone. It was not a new problem. Because many members of Congress defer to the President as a matter of politics or weakness, they contradict the intent of the Constitution. It was conceivable, as Justice Story wrote, that a President could force Congress to declare war. Justice Story recognized the danger and believed that Congress should be kept fully informed. Strangely, Wilson, who appeared before Congress so frequently, did not maintain close communications between the executive and legislative branches as the threat of war loomed. He simply sought endorsement for his ideas.

World War I was to be the war for democracy that would create the new order. Peace, as Wilson said, would be built upon a partnership of democratic governments. Russia had discarded its autocracy. Next, the Central Powers—Germany, Austria-Hungary, Turkey—would overhaul their governments and presumably that would take place immediately after the war. He failed to realize that profound government changes had to come from the people and took time. True democracy could not be superimposed by a foreign power. It had to evolve from within.

Arthur Link, the outstanding Wilson scholar, has written that in his opinion, the most important reason for Wilson's decision to enter the war was the hope for an early peace and reconstruction of the international community. As a belligerent the United States would have more influence with the Allies and some bargaining power with Germany. It went back to Wilson's remark to Jane Addams that "if he remained the representative of a neutral country he could at best only 'call through a crack in the door.'"[2] U-boat warfare which inflamed the American people, was not uppermost in his reasoning. Meyer London's foresight was clearer than the President's. He saw the United States limited to its military contribution in relation to the Allies. At the peace table the Allies did not show their gratitude to a late arriving belligerent when their casualties were counted in the millions. Wilson's error was the expectation of favors from nation to nation.

World War I has been overshadowed by World War II. Nevertheless, World War I was the line of departure for America. The second World War has clouded our perspective concerning those, especially internationalists, who preferred to stay out of the first war. They deserved better because we know that democracy did not take root in Europe, and democracy took some heavy blows in the United States. The individuals in this book may have been exasperating, but were they so wrong? The war did not lead to a new world of peace and decency, and out of the ashes came Hitler, Mussolini, and Stalin. The new order needed a long process of development uncomplicated by war and its disastrous ramifications.

Today, without a superpower enemy, the opportunities for American participation in wars around the world are staggering. The Middle East, Central Europe, Central America, and the Caribbean offer great temptations. The Wilsonian desire to impose our image upon the rest of the world remains. History does more than parallel the past. It builds and enhances the mistakes of the past. The same shibboleths are repeated for the benefit of the public. We heard them during the Grenada, Panama, and Iraq wars and will hear them again. Internationalism will require intervention, dissenters will be called isolationists, and war will supposedly bring peace.

Meanwhile, domestic politics, complicated by special interests, block progress for real peace. Those who have opinions that vary from the mass are still maligned, and some new touches have been added. Television makes war, as someone said, a spectator sport; women fight to serve in combat; and covert imbroglios and air strikes are accepted as normal behavior.

No one knows whether the majority of Americans favored entry into the war by April 1917. War hysteria, however, was rampant by then and abetted by a large part of the press. The major newspapers, except those controlled by Hearst, who was never a model of virtue, generally beat the war drums. Selective editing, especially in the Northeast, continually prevented access to facts that could have been the basis for calmer reasoning. Editorials often fueled the flames. Newspapers, always ready to defend their rights, did not mind condemning to oblivion those who disagreed with them. Freedom of the press was not always sympathetic to freedom of speech. This was an old problem that remains with us today. When Thomas Jefferson was asked how a newspaper should be conducted to be most useful, he answered "by restraining it to true facts and sound principles only," but he feared that such a paper would have few subscribers. In his opinion, nothing could be believed in newspapers, and he felt sorry for citizens who read papers and thought they knew something of the world in their time. General facts, he said, could be gathered but details could not be relied on. And, according to Jefferson, defamation of character was becoming a necessity of life. His words could have been written in 1917 or today. Certainly the American people did not understand Wilson's intentions or policies that unwittingly or not led step by step to war. The public will probably never completely understand its political leaders, but the press added confusion as much as clarification. Wilson, not always forthcoming, exaggerated when he said that in a democracy the public insisted upon complete information concerning the nation's business. Enlightened public opinion has a long way to go and new forms of media do not make the job easier.

Few people in the total population, unlike Sherwood, know anything about the horrors of war from first-hand experience. The thought lingers, as it did with Colonel House, that there is such a thing as civilized warfare. Will we ever learn? The idea of peace as Emily Balch wrote, is "so powerless before the vast physical force of the military masses today." She had to remind herself that it was only ideas that created force. "Let that force once be disbelieved and that force melts into nothing." The hope for a more peaceful world remains, but we need a new frame of mind that can seriously consider possible alternatives to force. The British historian, George Macaulay Trevelyan, once wrote, "if all historians . . . had condemned aggressive wars, including those begun by their own kings and countrymen, we should not be where we are today."[3] Attitudes can change. In our history we have seen opinions once believed to be carved in granite erode and eventually vanish. As a starter, pundits could stop writing about some future peace and concentrate on conflict resolution in the present, and Presidents could mediate with less self-righteousness before shooting. Otherwise we will become a nation perpetually at war.

Notes

Chapter 2 The Secretary of State

1. Arthur S. Link, *Wilson, The Road to the White House* (Princeton: Princeton Univ. Press, 1947), 25, 96.
2. *Ibid.* 117–120; Louis W. Koenig, *A Political Biography of William Jennings Bryan* (New York: G. P. Putnam's Sons, 1971), 476.
3. Link, *Wilson, Road to the White House*, 316, 353, 356.
4. Arthur S. Link, *Wilson, The New Freedom* (Princeton: Princeton Univ. Press, 1956), 7.
5. Charles S. Seymour, ed., *The Intimate Papers of Colonel House*, 4 vols. (Boston: Houghton Mifflin, 1926–1928), 1:88; John Milton Cooper, Jr. *Walter Hines Page, The Southerner as American, 1855–1918* (Chapel Hill: The Univ. of North Carolina Press, 1977), 247, Koenig, *Bryan*, 500.
6. n.a. "The Ten Best Secretaries of State—and the Five Worst," *American Heritage*, Vol. 33, no. 1, December 1981, 78–80.
7. Seymour, *House Papers*, 1:268, 279, 282; Arthur S. Link, ed., *The Papers of Woodrow Wilson* (Princeton: Princeton Univ. Press, 68 vols., 1967–1993), 30:327.
8. Koenig, *Bryan*, 534.
9. Arthur S. Link, *Wilson, The Struggle for Neutrality, 1914–1915* (Princeton: Princeton Univ. Press, 1960), 133n.
10. Link, ed., *Wilson Papers*, 32:10, Diary of Nancy Saunders Toy, Jan. 3, 1915.
11. Bryan to Wilson, Aug. 28, 1914, Bryan Papers, National Archives.
12. Link, ed. *Wilson Papers*, 31:56, 57; 55n3; Bryan to Wilson, Dec. 1, 1914, Bryan Papers, NA.
13. Paolo E. Coletta, *William Jennings Bryan*, 3 vols. (Lincoln: Univ. of Nebraska Press, 1964–1969), 3:30.
14. Bryan to Wilson, Dec. 1, 1914, Bryan Papers, NA.
15. Oscar Straus to Bryan, Sept. 16, 1914, Bryan Papers, Library of Congress; Cyrus Adler, *Jacob H. Schiff, His Life and Letters*, 2 vols. (Garden City: Doubleday, Doran, 1929), 2:182–193.
16. Wilson to Bryan, Oct. 8, 1914, Bryan Papers, NA.

17. James Gerard to Bryan, Feb. 11, 1915, Bryan Papers, LC; Ray Stannard Baker, *Woodrow Wilson, Life and Letters*, 8 vols. (Garden City: Doubleday, Doran, 1937), 5:309.
18. Link, ed., *Wilson Papers*, 31:384.
19. *Ibid*, 31:354–356.
20. Link, *Wilson, The New Freedom*, 111–113; Anne W. Lane and Louise Herrick Wall, eds., *The Letters of Franklin K. Lane, Personal and Political* (Boston:Houghton Mifflin, 1922), 167; William C. Redfield, *With Congress and Cabinet* (Garden City: Doubleday, Page, 1924), 102.
21. Robert Lansing, *War Memoirs of Robert Lansing, Secretary of State* (Indianapolis: The Bobbs-Merrill Co., 1935), 26.
22. Link, ed., *Wilson Papers*, 31:384; House Diary, Dec. 3, 1914; 32:117, Jan 24.,1915.
23. Wilson to Bryan, Mar. 18, 1915, Bryan Papers, LC.
24. Bryan to Wilson, Apr. 19, 1915, Bryan Papers, LC; Paolo E. Coletta, "A Question of Alternatives: Wilson, Bryan, Lansing and America's Intervention in World War I," *Nebraska History* 63, no. 1 (1982): 33–53.
25. Bryan to Wilson, April 23, 1915, Bryan Papers, LC.
26. Link, ed., *Wilson Papers*, 33:85; William Jennings Bryan and Mary Baird Bryan, *The Memoirs of William Jennings Bryan*, 2 vols. 1925. Reprint. (Port Washington: Kennikat Press, 1971) 2:420, 421; Page Smith, *America Enters the World* (New York: McGraw-Hill, 1985), 470.
27. Coletta, *Bryan*, 2:258.
28. Burton J. Hendrick, *The Life and Letters of Walter Hines Page* 3 vols. (Garden City: Doubleday, Page, 1926), 2:170.
29. Koenig, *Bryan*, 541.
30. Bryan to Wilson, May 9, 1915, Bryan Papers, LC.
31. Link, ed., *Wilson Papers*, 33:134.
32. Bryan to Wilson, May 12, 1915, Bryan Papers, LC.
33. Wilson to Bryan, June 2, 1915, Bryan Papers, NA.
34. Merle Curti, *Bryan and World Peace* 1931. Reprint. (New York: Octagon Books, 1969), 208; Bryan, *Memoirs*, 2:421.
35. Wilson to Bryan, June 5, 1915, Bryan Papers, LC.
36. Koenig, *Bryan*, 548.
37. *Ibid*, 549.
38. For correspondence between Wilson and Galt see Edwin Tribble, ed., *President in Love, The Courtship of Woodrow Wilson and Edith Bolling Galt* (Boston: Houghton Mifflin, 1981), 53, 54, 67, 125, 131–33; Edwin A. Weinstein, *Woodrow Wilson: A Medical and Psychological Biography* (Princeton: Princeton Univ. Press, 1981), 287.
39. Belmont Phillips to Bryan, 1915, Bryan Papers, LC.
40. Link, *Struggle for Neutrality*, 427; *NYT,* June 10, 1915; John Milton Cooper, Jr., *The Vanity of Power, American Isolationism and the First World War 1914–1917* (Westport: Greenwood Publishing, 1969), 41.

41. Ernest May, *The World and American Isolation* (Cambridge: Harvard Univ. Press, 1959), 436.

Chapter 3   The Chairman

1. Ruth Warner Towne, *Senator William J. Stone and the Politics of Compromise* (Port Washington: Kennikat Press, 1979), 132.
2. *NYT,* Jan. 24, 1915.
3. Link, ed., *Wilson Papers,* 32:134.
4. *Ibid,* 32:289–291.
5. John A. Garraty, *Henry Cabot Lodge, A Biography* (New York: Alfred A. Knopf, 1953), 120, 319; Towne, *Stone,* 193.
6. Link, ed., *Wilson Papers,* 35:352.
7. *Ibid,* 35:374.
8. Arthur S. Link, *Wilson, Confusion and Crises, 1915 –1916* (Princeton: Princeton Univ. Press, 1964), 169.
9. Link, ed., *Wilson Papers,* 36:209–211, 213.
10. *Ibid,* 36:225, 226.
11. Link, *Confusion and Crises,* 171.
12. *Current Opinion,* Feb. 1916, 91, 92.
13. Link, *Confusion and Crises,* 135. Quotes House-Grey memorandum from copy in House Papers initiated by Grey in Foreign Office, Feb. 22, 1916.
14. Link, ed., *Wilson Papers,* 36:517.
15. *Ibid,* 38:277, 278, 318.
16. *Ibid,* 40:533–539.
17. John Clark Crighton, *Missouri and the World War, 1914 –1917, A Study in Public Opinion* (Columbia: Univ. of Missouri, 1947), University of Missouri Studies, Vol. 21, no. 3, 92, 130, 131.
18. Belle and Fola La Follette, *Robert M. La Follette,* 2 vols. (New York: Macmillan, 1953), 1:593.
19. *NYT,* Feb. 4, 1917.
20. Link, ed., *Wilson Papers,* 41:283 –287; Thomas Ryley, *A Little Group of Willful Men* (Port Washington: Kennikat Press, 1975), 11.
21. Stone's speech against arming merchant ships referred to in following paragraphs is in *Cong. Record,* 64th Cong., 2nd Sess., 4877–4893.
22. Alan P. Gilmer to Desha Breckinridge, editor, The Lexington (Kentucky) *Herald,* Feb. 22, 1917, Stone Papers, Western Historical Manuscript Collection, University of Missouri-Columbia.
23. Thomas Woodrow Wilson, *Congressional Government: A Study in American Politics.* Reprint. (Baltimore: The Johns Hopkins Univ. Press, 1981), 201.

24. Arthur S. Link, *Wilson, Campaigns for Progressivism and Peace 1916–1917* (Princeton: Princeton Univ. Press, 1965), 361–363.
25. *NYT*, Mar. 9, 1917.
26. Newspaper collection, Western Historical Manuscript Collection, University of Missouri-Columbia; *Literary Digest*, Mar. 24, 1917, 803,804, quotes St. Louis *Post–Dispatch* and Kansas City *Star*.
27. *Literary Digest*, Mar. 24, 1917, 803, 804.
28. A. J. Fitzsimmons to W. J. Stone, Mar. 8, 1917, Stone Papers, Western Historical Manuscript Collection; Link, *Campaign for Progressivism and Peace*, 365.
29. *William Joel Stone: Memorial Addresses Delivered in the Senate*, 1919, 74.
30. Link, *Confusion and Crises*, 398. Quotes House Diary, Mar. 19, 1917.
31. *NYT*, Apr. 5, 1917.
32. Belle and Fola La Follette, *La Follette*, 1:654.
33. Thomas Marshall, *Recollections of Thomas R. Marshall* (Indianapolis: The Bobbs-Merrill Company, 1925), 305–309.
34. *NYT*, May 11, 1915; Sandra R. Herman, *Eleven Against War: Studies in American International Thought, 1898–1921* (Stanford: Hoover Institution Press, 1969), 194.

Chapter 4 The Publisher

1. Oliver Carlson and Ernest Sutherland Bates, *Hearst, Lord of San Simeon* (New York: The Viking Press, 1936), 178.
2. *Ibid*, 182.
3. Anne W. Lane and Louise Herrick Wall, eds. *The Letters of Franklin K. Lane* (Boston: Houghton Mifflin, 1922), 39, 40, 51, 52, 142.
4. Oliver Carlson, *Brisbane, A Candid Biography* (New York: Stackpole Sons, 1937), 216.
5. H.C. Peterson, *Propaganda for War, The Campaign Against American Neutrality* Reprint. Univ. of Oklahoma Press, 1939. (Port Washington: Kennikat Press, 1968), 165–166n.
6. W. A. Swanberg, *Citizen Hearst, A Biography of William Randolph Hearst* (New York: Charles Scribner's Sons, 1961), 301.
7. Martin Gilbert, *Winston S. Churchill, The Challenge of War, 1914–1916* 8 vols. (Boston: Houghton Mifflin, 1971), 3:141–143; Oliver Carlson, *Brisbane, A Candid Biography* (New York: Stackpole Sons, 1937), 217.
8. Edward Coblentz, ed., *William Randolph Hearst, A Portrait in His Own Words* (New York: Simon & Schuster, 1952), 83; New York *Evening Journal*, Oct. 12, Nov. 16, 1916; New York *American*, Oct. 15, 1916; Swanberg, *Hearst*, 301.
9. Arthur S. Link, *Wilson: Campaigns for Progressivism and Peace, 1916–1917* (Princeton: Princeton Univ. Press, 1965), 104, 105.

Notes

10. New York *American,* Oct. 1, 1916.
11. Coblentz, ed., *Hearst,* 38, 39.
12. John K. Winkler, *W. R. Hearst, An American Phenomenon* (New York: Simon & Schuster, 1928), 272.
13. New York *Evening Journal,* Mar. 22, 1917; Edward S. Martin, *The Life of Joseph Hodges Choate.* 2 vols. (New York: Scribner's, 1920), 1:240, 241.
14. John Milton Cooper, Jr., *The Vanity of Power, American Isolationism and the First World War 1914–1917* (Westport: Greenwood Publishing, 1969), 159. Cites New York *American,* Jan. 29, 1917.
15. Winkler, *W. R. Hearst,* 281. Refers to *New York Tribune* without specific date.
16. Swanberg, *Hearst,* 308–309; Coblentz, ed., *Hearst, Portrait In Own Words,* 91.
17. William Randolph Hearst, *Selections from the Writings and Speeches of William Randolph Hearst* (San Francisco: Published privately, 1948), 410.

Chapter 5 The War Hero

1. See Isaac R. Sherwood, *Memories of War* (Toledo: The H. J. Chittenden Co., 1923); Virginia E. McCormick, "The Talented Sherwoods: Poets and Politicians," *Northwest Ohio Quarterly,* Summer 1980, 52, no. 3; Francis P. Weisenburger, "General Isaac R. Sherwood," *Quarterly Bulletin,* (*Northwest Ohio Quarterly*), April 1942, 14, no. 2.
2. James M. McPherson, *Battle Cry of Freedom, The Civil War Era* (New York: Oxford Univ. Press, 1988), 812, 813.
3. Harvey Scribner, *Memoirs of Lucas County and the City of Toledo,* 1910, 2 vols., 2:18, 19. From the collection of the Toledo-Lucas County Public Library, Toledo, Ohio.
4. *Congressional Record,* 65th Cong., 1st Sess., Washington, 1917, 337.
5. Champ Clark, *My Quarter Century of American Politics,* 2 vols. (New York: Harper & Brothers, 1920), 2:379.
6. Weisenburger, "Sherwood," 44.
7. *Ibid,* 45; Sherwood, *Memories of War,* 235; Weisenburger, "Sherwood," 47.
8. *Cong. Record,* 64th Cong., 1st Sess., 456–463.
9. *Ibid.,* 461.
10. *Ibid.,* 463.
11. *NYT,* Mar. 8, July 11, 1916; Link, ed. *Wilson Papers,* 37:395n.
12. *Cong. Record,* 65th Cong., 1st Sess., 336–337.
13. *Cong. Record,* 65th Cong., 1st Sess., 316–318; Philip R. Vander Meer, "Congressional Decision Making and World War I: A Case Study of Illinois Congressional Opponents," *Congressional Studies, A Journal of the Congress,* 8, no. 2, 59–79. Published by the U.S. Capitol Historical Society, 1981.
14. *Toledo Times,* Oct. 10, 16, 1925. Toledo-Lucas County Public Library.

Chapter 6   The Women at the Hague

1. Olga S. Opfell, *The Lady Laureates, Women Who Have Won the Nobel Prize* (Metuchen: The Scarecrow Press, 1986) 28; *NYHT*, May 22, 1935.
2. Anne Fior, "Saint Jane and the Ward Boss," *American Heritage* 12, no. 1 (1960): 12–17, 94–99.
3. Page Smith, *America Enters the World* (McGraw-Hill, 1985), 332.
4. Allen F. Davis, ed. *Jane Addams on Peace, War and International Understanding 1899–1932* (New York: Garland, 1976). Quotes from *Unity* 43, May 4, 1899.
5. *Ibid.* Quotes St. Louis *Post-Dispatch*, Feb. 18, 1900.
6. Allen F. Davis, *American Heroine, The Life and Legend of Jane Addams* (New York: Oxford Univ. Press, 1973), 141.
7. Smith, *America Enters the World*, 334.
8. Davis, *American Heroine*, 216.
9. Charles Chatfield with Robert Kleidman, *The American Peace Movement, Idealism and Activism* (New York: Twayne, 1992), 32.
10. Carrie Chapman Catt to Jane Addams, Nov. 12, 1915, Addams Papers, Swarthmore College Peace Collection.
11. Rosika Schwimmer to Jane Addams, Feb. 16, 1915, Addams Papers, Swarthmore.
12. Woodrow Wilson to Jane Addams, Mar. 8, 1915, Addams Papers, Swarthmore.
13. Jane Addams to Lillian Wald, Mar. 6, 1915, Addams Papers, Swarthmore.
14. Jane Addams to Emily Balch, Mar. 26, 1915, Addams Papers, Swarthmore.
15. Mercedes M. Randall, *Improper Bostonian, Emily Greene Balch, Nobel Peace Laureate, 1946* (New York: Twayne, 1964) 15.
16. Emily Balch to Jane Addams, Feb. 27, 1915, Addams Papers, Swarthmore.
17. John A. Garraty and Mark C. Carnes eds., *Dictionary of American Biography,* Supplement Eight, 1966–1970 (New York: Charles Scribner's Sons, 1988), 241, 242; Barbara Sicherman, *Alice Hamilton, A Life in Letters* (Cambridge: Harvard Univ. Press, 1984).
18. James Weber Linn, *Jane Addams, A Biography* Reprint. (New York: Greenwood Press, 1968), 300; *NYT,* Apr. 29, 1915; George Banschbach to Jane Addams, 1915, Addams Papers, Swarthmore.
19. Jane Addams to David Starr Jordan, Apr. 9, 1915; Addams to Ray Stannard Baker, Mar. 26, 1915, Addams Papers, Swarthmore; *NYT,* Apr. 23, 1915.
20. *NYT,* Apr. 21, 1915.
21. Addams to Lillian Wald, Apr. 6, 1915; Alice Hamilton to Mary Rozet Smith, Apr. 2, 1915, Addams Papers, Swarthmore; Sicherman, *Hamilton,* 185.
22. Randall, *Improper Bostonian,* 151.
23. Jane Addams, Emily G. Balch, Alice Hamilton, *Women at The Hague, The International Congress of Women and Its Results* (New York: Macmillan, 1915), 18.
24. Randall, *Improper Bostonian,* 159.

Notes

25. Addams, Balch, Hamilton, *Women at The Hague*, 22– 81; Randall, *Improper Bostonian*, 166 –192.
26. Eric Drummond for Viscount Grey to Addams, May 12, 1915, Addams Papers.
27. Louis Lochner to Woodrow Wilson, June 2, 1915, Addams Papers.
28. Edward Marshall, "Jane Addams Points Way to Peace," *New York Times Magazine*, 4, 5, July 11, 1915.
29. Randall, *Improper Bostonian*, 172, 173.
30. Bertrand Russell to Lucy Martin, July 13, 1915, Addams Papers.
31. Emily Balch to Louis Lochner, June 1, 1915, Addams Papers.
32. Addams to Balch, Aug. 3, 1915, Addams Papers; Linn, *Addams*, 315.
33. *The Survey*, July 17, 1915, in Lillian Wald Papers, New York Public Library; Davis, *American Heroine*, 224–230.
34. Addams, Balch, Hamilton, *Women at The Hague*, 61.
35. Seymour, *House Papers*, 2:22.
36. Julia Grace Wales to Addams, July 24, 1915, Addams Papers.
37. Ray Stannard Baker, *Woodrow Wilson, Life and Letters*, 8 vols. (Garden City: Doubleday, Doran, 1937), 6:125n.
38. Emily Balch to Addams, Aug. 19, 1915, Addams Papers; David S. Patterson, "Woodrow Wilson and the Mediation Movement, 1914 –1917," *The Historian* 33, no. 4 (1971) 535 –556; Randall, *Improper Bostonian*, 210.
39. Randall, *Improper Bostonian*, 196, 197.
40. *Ibid*, 194, 199; Baker, *Wilson*, 6:122, 123.
41. Seymour, ed. *House Papers*, 2:96.
42. O. P. Williams to Addams, Oct. 1915, Addams Papers.
43. Linn, *Addams*, 312.
44. Thomas J. Knock, *To End All Wars, Woodrow Wilson and the Quest for the New World Order* (New York: Oxford Univ. Press, 1992), viii.
45. Davis, ed., *Jane Addams on Peace*, 143. Quotes Jane Addams in "Women, War and Suffrage," *The Survey*, Nov. 6, 1915; H. C. Peterson and Gilbert C. Fite, *Opponents of War, 1917–1918* (Madison: The Univ. of Wisconsin Press, 1957), 14. Quotes *NYT*, Feb. 2, 1917.
46. Davis, ed., *Jane Addams on Peace*, 142.
47. Linn, *Addams*, 324.
48. Link, *Wilson*, 5:414.
49. Jane Addams, *Peace and Bread in Time of War* (New York: Macmillan, 1922), 47, 64; Knock, *War to End All Wars*, 120.
50. Daniel Levine, *Jane Addams and the Liberal Tradition* (Madison: State Historical Society of Wisconsin, 1971), 222; Page Smith, *America Enters the World* (New York: McGraw-Hill, 1985), 555.
51. Levine, *Jane Addams and the Liberal Tradition*, 223.
52. Randall, *Improper Bostonian*, 263.
53. Linn, *Addams*, 380, 390, 391.
54. *NYT*, Nov. 16, 1946; Randall, *Improper Bostonian*, 422.

Chapter 7   The Tycoon

1. *NYT*, Apr. 11, 1915.
2. *Ibid.*
3. Henry Ford with Samuel Crowther, *My Life and Work* (Garden City: Doubleday, Page, 1925), 240; Keith Seward, *The Legend of Henry Ford* (New York: Rinehart, 1948), 84; Barbara S. Kraft, *The Peace Ship, Henry Ford's Pacifist Adventure in the First World War* (New York: Macmillan, 1978), 50.
4. *NYT*, Aug. 23, 1915.
5. *NYT*, Aug. 24, 1915.
6. Allan Nevins and Frank Ernest Hill, *Ford, Expansion and Challenge, 1915–1933* (New York: Charles Scribner's Sons, 1957), 24.
7. Nevins and Hill, *Ford*, 26.
8. *NYT*, Dec. 1, 1915.
9. Nevins and Hill, *Ford*, 26; Kraft, *Peace Ship*, 65.
10. Nevins and Hill, *Ford*, 29.
11. *Ibid.*
12. *Ibid*, 36; *NYT*, Dec. 1, 1915.
13. Burnet Hershey, *The Odyssey of Henry Ford and the Great Peace Ship* (New York: Taplinger Publishing Co., 1967), 60.
14. Ford Peace Plans, Library of Congress.
15. Randall, *Improper Bostonian*, 207.
16. Arthur S. Link, *Confusion and Crises, 1915–1916* (Princeton: Princeton Univ. Press, 1964), 107n18.
17. Kraft, *The Peace Ship*, 85.
18. Samuel S. Marquis, *Henry Ford, An Interpretation* (Boston: Little, Brown, 1923), 19.
19. Marquis, *Henry Ford*, 49; Louis Lochner, *America's Don Quixote, Henry Ford's Attempt to Save Europe* (London: Kegan Paul, Trench, Trubner & Co., 1924), xxi.
20. Kraft, *Peace Ship*, 155; Walter Millis, *Road to War, America 1914–1917*. Reprint. (New York: Howard Fertig, 1970), 245; Nevins and Hill, *Ford*, 42; Ford Peace Plans, LC, Ford to Woodrow Wilson, Dec. 5, 1915.
21. Kraft, *Peace Ship*, 90.
22. Ford Peace Plans, LC.
23. Nevins and Hill, *Ford*, 53.
24. John Milton Cooper and Charles E. Neu, eds., *The Wilson Era-Essays in Honor of Arthur S. Link* (Arlington Heights: Harlan Davidson, 1991), 313.
25. Kraft, *Peace Ship*, 50; *NYT*, Feb. 23, 1916.
26. *NYT*, Feb. 24, 1916.
27. *New York American*, Nov. 5, 1916. Ford advertisement in support of Wilson for President.

28. *NYT,* Sept. 28, 1916.
29. Ford, *My Life and Work,* 281.

Chapter 8   The Majority Leader

1. *Cong. Record,* 65th Cong. 1st Sess., Apr. 6, 1917, 332, 333.
2. Champ Clark, *My Quarter Century of American Politics,* 2:339; *The World's Work,* Dec. 1915, 136–140.
3. *Dictionary of American Biography,* 10:439, 440. Quotes *News and Observer,* June 1, 1923.
4. Link, ed., *Wilson Papers,* 31: 414 – 424.
5. *Ibid,* 33:147–149.
6. Kitchin to J. W. Davenport, Feb. 10, 1916; Kitchin to Brevard Nixon, Feb. 18, 1916 Kitchin Papers, University of North Carolina; Alex Matthews Arnett, *Claude Kitchin and the Wilson War Policies,* Reprint. (New York: Russell & Russell, 1971), 49–53; Oswald Garrison Villard, *Fighting Years, Memoirs of a Liberal Editor* (New York: Harcourt, Brace, 1939), 308; *NYT,* Aug. 16, 1915.
7. Arnett, *Kitchin,* 68, 69; Cooper, *Vanity of Power,* 95.
8. *NYT,* Nov. 16, 1915.
9. Kitchin to H. S. Overman, Mar. 13, 1916, Kitchin Papers, UNC; *NYT,* May 30, 1916.
10. Kitchin to G. W. Norris, Apr. 25, 1916, Kitchin Papers, UNC.
11. *Ibid.*
12. Item 406, #123, Feb. 26, 1916, Kitchin Papers, UNC.
13. Page Smith, *America Enters the World,* 480.
14. Kitchin to Rev. Charles H. Nash, Feb. 29, 1916, Kitchin Papers, UNC.
15. Kitchin to O. L. Spock, Mar. 4, 1916; Kitchin to Dr. H. Q. Alexander, Mar. 9, 1916; Rev. J. M. Millard to Kitchin, Apr. 19, 1916, Kitchin Papers, UNC.
16. Kitchin to Jas. K. Risk, Mar. 4, 1916, Kitchin Papers, UNC; *NYT,* Mar. 9, 1916.
17. Kitchin to Chas. F. Dole, Aug. 5, 1916; Kitchin to Secretary of State, Aug. 14, 1916; Kitchin to John Wales, Aug. 19, 1916; Kitchin Papers, UNC; *NYT,* Aug. 16, 1916; Arnett, *Kitchin,* 63 – 65.
18. Arnett, *Kitchin,* 192.
19. Kitchin to Thomas Reilly, Nov. 11, 1916; Kitchin to Leonidas Stone, Nov. 17, 1916, Kitchin Papers, UNC.
20. David M. Kennedy, *Over Here, The First World War and American Society* (New York: Oxford Univ. Press, 1980), 16.
21. Kitchin to Editor, The Florida *Times-Union,* Feb. 24, 1917, Kitchin Papers, UNC.
22. Kitchin to William Dodd, Dec. 16, 1916, Kitchin Papers, UNC.
23. Villard, *Fighting Years,* 308.

24. Arthur Harris to Kitchin, May 29, 1916, Kitchin Papers, UNC.
25. Kitchin handwritten comments, Feb. or Mar. 1917; Kitchin to Hon. Wm. M. Howard, Mar. 26, 1917.
26. Ray S. Baker and William E. Dodd eds., *The Public Papers of Woodrow Wilson*, 2 vols. (New York: Harper Brothers, 1927), 1:6 –16.
27. Philip R. Vander Meer, "Congressional Decision-Making and World War I: A Case Study of Illinois Congressional Opponents," *Congressional Studies, A Journal of the Congress*, Vol. 8, no. 2, 59–79. Published by the U.S. Capitol Historical Society, 1981.
28. *Ibid.*, 64 – 68.
29. *Cong. Record*, 65th Cong. 1st Sess., Apr. 6, 1917, 332, 333.
30. Link, ed., *Wilson Papers*, 41:550. Diary of T. W. Brahany, Apr. 15, 1917.
31. *Cong. Record*, 65th Cong. 1st Sess., Apr. 6, 1917, 333; *NYT*, Apr. 6, 1917.
32. *NYT*, Apr. 7, 1917.
33. Letter from Virginia to Kitchin, Apr. 7, 1917; R. B. Glenn to Kitchin, Apr. 6, 1917; letter from a banker, Salisbury, N.C. to Kitchin, Apr. 6, 1917; Kitchin Papers, UNC.
34. Kitchin to W. A. Finch, Apr. 18, 1917, Kitchin Papers, UNC.

Chapter 9   The Dissenter

1. Unpublished autobiography, 31, 32, Thomas Papers, New York Public Library; Arthur S. Link, John Little, Kathleen Arnon and Nancy Plum, eds., *"Brother Woodrow."* A memoir by Stockton Axson (Princeton: Princeton Univ. Press, 1993), 55.
2. Murray B. Seidler, *Norman Thomas, Respectable Rebel* (Syracuse: Syracuse Univ. Press, 1967), 11.
3. Norman Thomas, *A Socialist's Faith*. Reprint. (Port Washington: Kennikat Press, 1971), 10.
4. Thomas J. Knock, *To End All Wars, Woodrow Wilson and the Quest for a New World Order* (New York: Oxford Univ. Press, 1992), 18; Seidler, *Thomas*, 25.
5. Thomas, Unpublished autobiography, 65–66, Thomas Papers, NYPL.
6. *Ibid*, 67.
7. Handwritten comments, Feb. 18, 1917, Thomas Papers, NYPL.
8. W. A. Swanberg, *Norman Thomas, The Last Idealist* (New York: Charles Scribner's Sons, 1976), 55.
9. Thomas to unknown, Oct. 1916, Thomas Papers, NYPL; Bernard K. Johnpoll, *Pacifist's progress, Norman Thomas and the decline of American Socialism* [sic] (Chicago: Quadrangle Books, 1970), 22.
10. Thomas to Dr. Laidlaw, Mar. 15, 1917, Thomas Papers, NYPL; James C. Duram, "In Defense of Conscience: Norman Thomas as an Exponent of

Christian Pacifism During World War I," *Journal of Presbyterian History*, 52:1, Spring 1974, 19–32.
11. Thomas, Unpublished autobiography, 36, Thomas Papers, NYPL.
12. *Ibid*, 66; Duram, "In Defense of Conscience," 24.
13. Handwritten comments, Feb. 18, 1917, Thomas Papers, NYPL.
14. Patterson, "Woodrow Wilson and the Mediation Movement, 1914–1917," *Historian*, 33, no. 4. (1971), 555.
15. Harry Fleichman, *Norman Thomas, A Biography: 1884–1968* (New York: W. W. Norton, 1969), 59; Thomas to "Dear Jack," Mar. 30, 1917, Thomas Papers, NYPL.
16. Swanberg, *Thomas*, 57–59.
17. Charles A. Beard and Mary A. Beard, *The Rise of American Civilization*. 2 vols. in one. Revised. (New York: Macmillan, 1939), 2:642.
18. Swanberg, *Thomas*, 63; Norman Thomas, *A Socialist's Faith* Reprint. (Port Washington: Kennikat Press, 1971), 312.
19. Thomas J. Knock, *To End All Wars*, 159; Swanberg, *Thomas*, 63.
20. Thomas, Unpublished autobiography, 68, 77. Thomas Papers, NYPL.
21. *Ibid*, 74, 75.
22. Thomas, *A Socialist's Faith*, 34, 35.
23. *NYT*, Dec. 22, 1968.
24. Johnpoll, *Pacifist's progress*, 293.

Chapter 10 The Socialist Congressman

1. See Harry Rogoff, *An East Side Epic, The Life and Work of Meyer London* (New York: The Vanguard Press, 1930); William Freiburger, "The Lone Socialist Vote: A Political Study of Meyer London," Ph.D. diss., Univ. Microfilm Intl., 1980; *Dictionary of American Biography*, Vol. 6, Pt. 1, 372–374.
2. Donald Drew Egbert and Stow Persons, eds., *Socialism and American Life* (Princeton: Princeton Univ. Press, 1952), 1:310.
3. Rogoff, *An East Side Epic*, 62.
4. William English Walling, ed., *The Socialists and the War, A Documentary Statement of the Position of the Socialists of All Countries; With Special Reference to Their Peace Policy* (New York: Henry Holt & Co., 1915), 212, 405.
5. C. Roland Marchand, *The American Peace Movement and Social Reform, 1898–1918* (Princeton: Princeton Univ. Press, 1972), 269n6.
6. *The Outlook*, June 23, 1926, 270.
7. Freiburger, *Lone Socialist Vote*, 119.
8. *Ibid*, 134.
9. *NYT*, June 22, 1915.
10. David Shannon, *The Socialist Party of America, A History*. Reprint. (Chicago: Quadrangle Publications, 1967), 11, 12.
11. Rogoff, *East Side Epic*, 67, 68.

12. Alexander Trachtenberg, *The American Socialists and the War*. Reprint. (New York: Garland Publishing, 1973), 22.
13. Knock, *To End All Wars*, 54, 55.
14. James Waldo Fawcett to London, May 6, 1916, London Papers, Tamiment Institute Coll., New York University.
15. London to Mr. Bernstein, Apr. 5, 1916, London Papers, NYU.
16. Charles Wright to London, Apr. 30, 1916, London Papers, NYU.
17. Freiburger, "Lone Socialist Vote," 209.
18. *Cong. Record*, Appendix, 64th Cong. 2nd Sess., Jan. 27, 1917, 390, 391.
19. Rogoff, *East Side Epic*, 73; *NYT*, Mar. 2, 1917.
20. Freiburger, "Lone Socialist Vote," 214.
21. *Cong. Record*, 65th Cong. 1st Sess., Apr. 5, 1917, 329, 330.
22. *Ibid.*
23. L. Lipschitz to London, Apr. 21, 1917, London Papers, NYU.
24. Rogoff, *East Side Epic*, 310.

Chapter 11 The Progressive

1. Page Smith, *America Enters the World* (New York: McGraw-Hill, 1985), 294; Edward N. Doan, *The La Follettes and the Wisconsin Idea* (New York: Rinehart, 1947), 45.
2. Link, *Road to the White House*, 395n15; Oswald Garrison Villard, *Fighting Years, Memoirs of a Liberal Editor* (New York: Harcourt, Brace, 1939), 227. Belle and Fola La Follette, *Robert M. La Follette*, 2 vols. (New York: Macmillan, 1953), 1:406, 414.
3. Belle and Fola La Follette, *La Follette* [short title] 460; Arthur S. Link, *Wilson, The Road to the White House* (Princeton: Princeton Univ. Press, 1947), 272n 114; Link, ed., *Wilson Papers*, 32:61n2; Millis, *Road to War*, 412.
4. La Follette to Henry Lockney, May 17, 1915, La Follette Papers, LC; Belle and Fola La Follette, *La Follette* [short title] 1:519; Doan, *La Follettes*, 78.
5. Belle and Fola La Follette, *La Follette*, 1:549.
6. *Cong. Record*, 64th Cong., 1st Sess., 53:3886, Mar. 8, 1916. Woodrow Wilson, *Constitutional Government in the United States* (New York: Columbia Univ. Press, 1908), 77.
7. *Literary Digest*, June 10, 1916. Quotes Brooklyn *Times*, May 27, 1916.
8. Doan, *La Follettes*, 81, 82.
9. La Follette to "My dear Gil," Mar. 16, 1916, La Follette Papers, LC.
10. John J. Hannan to Hon. Francis J. Henry, Oct. 13, 1916; C. H. Crownhart to Henry Felling, Oct. 23, 1916; J. J. Hannan to E. C. Barnhart, Nov. 7, 1916, La Follette Papers, LC.
11. John J. Hannan to Justice Brandeis, Nov. 10, 1916, La Follette Papers, LC.
12. *NYT*, Jan. 23, 1917.
13. La Follette to "Dear Ones All," Feb. 2, 1917, La Follette Papers, LC.

14. La Follette to "Beloved Ones," Feb. 3, 1917, La Follette Papers, LC.
15. *Ibid.*
16. La Follette to "Dearest Ones," Feb. 4, 1917; La Follette to "Dear Hearts," Feb. 6, 1917, La Follette Papers, LC.
17. La Follette to "Dear Hearts," Feb. 6, 1917; La Follette to "My dear ones," Feb. 8, 1917; La Follette to "Dear Mama & Kiddies," Feb. 13, 1917, La Follette Papers, LC.
18. La Follette to "Dear Ones," Feb. 15, 1917, La Follette Papers, LC; La Follette to "Mama & Kiddies," Feb. 18, 1917, La Follette Papers, LC: Belle and Fola La Follette, *La Follette*, 1:596.
19. Belle and Fola La Follette, *La Follette*, 1:625.
20. *Ibid*, 1:623.
21. La Follette to "my dear Phil," Mar. 27, 1917, La Follette Papers, LC.
22. Link, *Wilson, Campaigns for Progressivism and Peace*, 423–426. Quotations from Wilson's speech to Congress which are included in the following paragraphs.
23. Madison (Wisconsin) *Democrat* quoted in Belle and Fola La Follette, *La Follette*, 651.
24. Link, *Wilson, Campaigns for Progressivism and Peace*, 430.
25. *Cong. Record,* Vol. 55, Pt. 1, 65th Cong. 1st Sess. Apr. 4, 1917, 223–234. Quotations from La Follette's speech are included in the following paragraphs.
26. *Ibid*, 234–236.
27. Melvin I. Urofsky and Daniel W. Levy, ed., *Letters of Louis D. Brandeis.* 5 vols. (Albany: State University of New York Press, 1975), 4:314n.

Conclusion

1. Mercedes M. Randall, *Improper Bostonian, Emily Greene Balch, Nobel Peace Laureate* (New York: Twayne Publishers, 1964), 210.
2. Arthur S. Link, *Wilson, Campaigns for Progressivism and Peace, 1916–1917* (Princeton: Princeton Univ. Press, 1965), 414.
3. David Cannadine, *G. M. Trevelyan, A Life in History* (New York: W. W. Norton, 1993), 199.

Bibliography

Manuscript Collections

Addams, Jane. Papers. Swarthmore College Peace Collection.
Bryan, William Jennings. Papers. Manuscript Division, Library of Congress.
Papers. National Archives.
Ford, Henry. Peace Plans. Library of Congress.
Kitchin, Claude. Papers. University of North Carolina, Chapel Hill.
La Follette, Robert. Papers. Library of Congress.
London, Meyer. Papers. Tamiment Institute Collection, New York University Library.
Stone, William J. Papers. Western Historical Manuscript Collection, University of Missouri.
Thomas, Norman. Papers. New York Public Library.
Wald, Lillian. Papers. New York Public Library.

Public Documents

Congressional Record, 1914–1917.
Congressional Directory, 64th–66th Cong.

Newspapers

Joplin (Missouri) *Globe*
Joplin (Missouri) *News Herald*
Lamar Democrat (Missouri)
Nevada (Missouri) *Post*
New York American
New York Herald Tribune
New York Evening Journal
New York Times
News Bee (Missouri)

The *Republic* (Missouri)
St. Louis Globe Democrat
Times Bee (Missouri)

Chapter 2   The Secretary of State

Adler, Cyrus. *Jacob H. Schiff: His Life and Letters.* 2 vols. Garden City: Doubleday, Doran, 1929.
Baker, Ray Stannard. *Woodrow Wilson, Life and Letters.* 8 vols., Garden City: Doubleday, Page, and Doubleday, Doran, 1927–1939
Bryan, William J. and Mary Baird Bryan. *The Memoirs of William Jennings Bryan.* 2 vols. 1925. Reprint. Port Washington: Kennikat Press, 1971.
Clements, Kendrick A. *William Jennings Bryan, Missionary Isolationist.* Knoxville: Univ. of Tennessee Press, 1982.
Coletta, Paolo E. *William Jennings Bryan.* 3 vols. Lincoln: Univ. of Nebraska Press, 1964–1969.
Cooper, John Milton Jr. *Walter Hines Page: The Southerner as American, 1855–1918.* Chapel Hill: Univ. of North Carolina Press, 1977.
Curti, Merle E. *Bryan and World Peace.* 1931. Reprint. New York: Octagon Books, 1969.
Hendrick, Burton J. *The Life and Letters of Walter H. Page.* 3 vols. Garden City: Doubleday, Page, 1926.
Johnson, Claudius O. *Borah of Idaho.* New York: Longmans, Green, 1936.
Koenig, Louis W. *Bryan: A Political Biography of William Jennings Bryan.* New York: G. P. Putnam's Sons, 1971.
Lane, Anne W. and Louise H. Wall. eds. *The Letters of Franklin K. Lane: Personal and Political.* Boston: Houghton, Mifflin, 1922.
Lansing, Robert. *War Memoirs of Robert Lansing.* Indianapolis: Bobbs Merrill, 1935.
Levine, Laurence W. *Defender of the Faith, William Jennings Bryan: The Last Decade, 1915–1925.* New York: Oxford Univ. Press.
Link, Arthur S. *Wilson: The Road to the White House,* Princeton: Princeton Univ. Press, 1947.
Link, Arthur S. *Wilson: The Struggle for Neutrality, 1914–1915,* Princeton: Princeton Univ. Press, 1960.
   Wilson: Campaigns for Progressivism and Peace, 1916–1917. Princeton: Princeton Univ. Press, 1965.
   Wilson: Confusions and Crises, 1915–1916. Princeton: Princeton Univ. Press, 1964.
Link, Arthur S. ed. *Papers of Woodrow Wilson.* 68 vols. Princeton: Princeton Univ. Press, 1967–1993.
May, Ernest. *The World and American Isolation.* Cambridge: Harvard Univ. Press, 1959.

Bibliography

Redfield, William C. *With Congress and Cabinet.* Garden City: Doubleday, Page, 1924.
Seymour, Charles. ed. *The Intimate Papers of Colonel House.* 4 vols. Boston: Houghton, Mifflin, 1926.
Smith, Page. *America Enters the World.* New York: McGraw-Hill, 1985.
Tansill, C. C. *America Goes to War.* Boston: Little, Brown, 1938 and 1942.
Tribble, Edwin. ed. *President in Love, the Courtship Letters of Woodrow Wilson and Edith Bolling Galt.* Boston: Houghton, Mifflin, 1981.
Wall, Joseph Frazier. *Henry Watterson: Reconstructed Rebel.* New York: Oxford Univ. Press, 1956.
Weinstein, Edwin A. *Woodrow Wilson: A Medical and Psychological Biography,* Princeton: Princeton Univ. Press, 1981.
Williams, Wayne C. *William Jennings Bryan.* New York: G. P. Putnam's Sons, 1936.

Articles

Coletta, Paolo. "A Question of Alternatives: Wilson, Bryan, Lansing, and American Intervention in World War I." *Nebraska History* 63, no. 1 (1982) 33–53.
n.a. "The Ten Best Secretaries of State—and the Five Worst". *American Heritage,* 33, no. 1 (1981) 78–80.

Chapter 2   The Chairman

Crighton, John Clark. *Missouri and the World War: 1914–1917.* Columbia: Univ. of Missouri Studies, Vol. XXI, No. 3.
Garraty, John A. *Henry Cabot Lodge: A Biography.* New York: Alfred A. Knopf, 1953.
Herman, Sandra R. *Eleven Against War: Studies in American* International Thought, 1898–1921. Stanford: Hoover Institution Press, 1969.
La Follette, Belle and Fola La Follette. *Robert M. La Follette.* 2 vols. New York: Macmillan, 1953.
Link, Arthur S. *Wilson: Confusions and Crises, 1915–1916.* Princeton: Princeton Univ. Press, 1964.
Link, Arthur S. ed. *Papers of Woodrow Wilson.* 68 vols. Princeton: Princeton Univ. Press, 1967–1993.
McReynolds, Edwin C. *Missouri: A History of the Crossroads State.* Norman: Univ. of Oklahoma Press, 1962.
Marshall, Thomas R. *Recollections of Thomas R. Marshall.* Indianapolis: Bobbs-Merrill, 1925.
Millis, Walter. *Road to War: America 1914–1917.* Boston: Houghton Mifflin, 1935.
Neuberger, Richard L. and Stephen B. Kahn. *Integrity: The Life of George Norris.* New York: Vanguard Press, 1937.
Schriftgeisser, Karl. *The Gentleman from Massachusetts: Henry Cabot Lodge.* Boston: Little, Brown, 1944.

Towne, Ruth Warner. *Senator William J. Stone and the Politics of Compromise.* Port Washington: Kennikat Press, 1979.

Workers of the Writers Program of the Works Progress Administration. *Missouri: A Guide to the "Show Me" State.* Duell, Sloane and Pearce, 1941.

Ryley, Thomas W. *A Little Group of Willful Men: A Study of Congressional-Presidential Authority.* Port Washington: Kennikat Press, 1975.

Wilson, Thomas Woodrow, *Congressional Government: A Study in American Politics.* Reprint. Baltimore: The Johns Hopkins Univ. Press, 1981.

Dissertation

Phillips, W. W. "The Life of Asle J. Gronna, A Self-Made Man of the Prairie." Doctoral dissertation, Univ. of Missouri-Columbia, 1958.

Articles

McDonald, Timothy G. "The Gore-McLemore Resolutions: Democratic Revolt Against Wilson's Submarine Policy." *The Historian* 26, Nov. 1963, 50–74.

n.a. "Old School Bourbon Democrat." *Current Opinion*, Feb. 1916.

Chapter 4   The Publisher

Carlson, Oliver and Ernest Sutherland Bates. *Hearst: Lord of San Simeon.* New York: The Viking Press, 1936.

Carlson, Oliver. *Brisbane: A Candid Biography.* New York: The Viking Press, 1937.

Coblentz, Edward D. ed. *William Randolph Hearst: A Portrait In His Own Words.* New York: Simon & Schuster, 1952.

Cooper, John Milton Jr. *The Vanity of Power: American Isolationism and the First World War 1914–1917.* Westport: Greenwood, 1969.

Hearst, William Randolph. *Selections from the Writings and Speeches of William Randolph Hearst.* San Francisco: Privately Published, 1948.

Lundberg, Ferdinand. *Imperial Hearst: A Social Biography.* Reprint. New York: Arno and The New York Times, 1970.

Peterson, H. C. *Propaganda for War: The Campaign Against American Neutrality, 1914–1917.* 1939. Reprint. Port Washington: Kennikat Press, 1968.

Swanberg, W. A. *Citizen Hearst.* New York: Charles Scribner's Sons, 1961.

Tebbel, John. *The Life and Good Times of William Randolph Hearst.* New York: E. P. Dutton, 1952.

Winkler, John K. *W. R. Hearst: An American Phenomenon.* New York: Simon & Schuster, 1928.

Chapter 5   The War Hero

Clark, Champ. *My Quarter Century of American Politics.* 2 vols. New York: Harper & Brothers, 1920.

Bibliography

Link, Arthur S. ed., *Papers of Woodrow Wilson*. 68 vols. Princeton: Princeton Univ. Press, 1967–1993.
McPherson, James M. *Battle Cry of Freedom, The Civil War Era*. New York: Oxford Univ. Press, 1988.
Scribner, Harvey. *Memories of Lucas County and the City of Toledo*. 2 vols. Toledo: Published 1910. [Citation provided by Toledo Public Library. No other information.]
Sherwood, Isaac. *Memories of War*. Toledo: H. J. Chittenden Co., 1923.

Articles

McCormick, Virginia E. "The Talented Sherwoods: Poets and Politicians," *Northwest Ohio Quarterly*, Summer 1980, 52, no. 3.
Vander Meer, Philip R. "Congressional Decision Making and World War I: A Case Study of Illinois Congressional Opponents." *Congressional Studies, A Journal of Congress* 8, no. 2, 59–79. Published by the U.S. Capitol Historical Society, 1981.
Weisenburger, Francis P. "General Isaac R. Sherwood." *Quarterly Bulletin*, Historical Society of Northwest Ohio. 14 (1942): no. 2.

Chapter 6   The Women at The Hague

Addams, Jane. *Peace and Bread In Time of War*. New York: Macmillan, 1922.
Addams, Jane and Emily G. Balch and Alice Hamilton. *Women at The Hague: The International Congress of Women and its Results*. New York: Macmillan, 1915.
Baker, Ray Stannard. *Woodrow Wilson: Life and Letters*. 8 vols. Garden City: Doubleday, Doran, 1937.
Chatfield, Charles. *The American Peace Movement: Ideas and Activism*. New York: Twayne, 1992.
Cooper, John Milton and Thomas J. Knock, eds. *The Wilson Era: Essays in Honor of Arthur S. Link*. Arlington Heights: Harlan Davidson, 1991.
Coss, Clare. ed. *Lillian D. Wald: Progressive Activist*. New York: The Feminist Press at City Univ. of New York, 1989.
Davis, Allen F. *American Heroine: The Life and Legend of Jane Addams*. New York: Oxford Univ. Press, 1973.
Davis, Allen. ed. *Jane Addams on Peace, War, and International Understanding: 1899–1932*. New York: Garland, 1976.
Farrell, John C. *Beloved Lady: A History of Jane Addams' Ideas on Reform and Peace*. Baltimore: Johns Hopkins Press, 1967.
Grattan, C. Hartley. *Why We Fought*. New York: Vanguard Press, 1929.
Herman, Sandra R. *Eleven Against War: Studies in American International Thought, 1898–1921*. Stanford: Hoover Institution Press, 1969.
Knock, Thomas J. *To End All Wars, Woodrow Wilson and the Quest for the New World Order*. New York: Oxford Univ. Press, 1992.

Levine, Daniel. *Jane Addams and the Liberal Tradition*. Madison: State Historical Society of Wisconsin, 1971.

Linn, James Weber. *Jane Addams, A Biography*. Reprint. New York: Greenwood Press, 1968.

Opfell, Olga S. *The Lady Laureates: Women Who Have Won the Nobel Prize*. Metuchen: Scarecrow Press, 1986.

Randall, Mercedes M. *Improper Bostonian: Emily Greene Balch, Nobel Peace Laureate*. New York: Twayne, 1964.

Seymour, Charles. ed. *The Intimate Papers of Colonel House*. 4 vols. Boston: Houghton, Mifflin, 1926.

Sicherman, Barbara. *Alice Hamilton: A Life in Letters*. Cambridge: Harvard Univ. Press, 1984.

Smith, Page. *America Enters the World*. New York: McGraw-Hill, 1985.

Villard, Oswald G. *Fighting Years: Memories of a Liberal Editor*. New York: Harcourt, Brace, 1939.

Articles

Marshall, Edward. "Jane Addams Points Way to Peace." *New York Times Magazine*, July 11, 1915, 4, 5.

Patterson, David S. "Woodrow Wilson and the Mediation Movement, 1914–1917." "The Historian" 33 (1971) 535–556.

Scott, Anne Fior. "Saint Jane and the Ward Boss." *American Heritage* 12, no. 1 (1960) 12–17, 94–99.

n.a. *Literary Digest*, May 1, Nov. 20, 1915.

n.a. *The Survey*, July 17, 1915.

n.a. *Unity*, July 15, 1935.

Chapter 7 The Tycoon

Cooper, John Milton and Charles E. Neu, eds. *The Wilson Era-Essays in Honor of Arthur S. Link*. Arlington Heights: Harlan Davidson, 1991.

Curti, Merle. *Peace or War: The American Struggle, 1636–1936*. Boston: J. S. Canner, 1959.

Ford, Henry and Samuel Crowther. *My Life and Work*. Garden City: Doubleday, Page, 1925.

Gelderman, Carol. *Henry Ford: The Wayward Capitalist*. New York: Dial Press, 1981.

Hershey, Burnet. *The Odyssey of Henry Ford and the Great Peace Ship*. New York: Taplinger, 1967.

Kraft, Barbara S. *The Peace Ship: Henry Ford's Pacifist Adventure in the First World War*. New York: Macmillan, 1978.

Lochner, Louis. *America's Don Quixote: Henry Ford's Attempt to Save Europe*. London: Kegan Paul, Trench, Trubner & Co., Ltd., 1924.

Marquis, Samuel S. *Henry Ford: An Interpretation*. Boston: Little, Brown, 1923.

Millis, Walter. *Road to War, America 1914–1917.* Reprint. New York: Howard Fertig, 1970.
Nevins, Allan and Frank Ernest Hill. *Ford.* 2 vols. Charles Scribner's Sons, 1957–1962.
Peterson, H. C. and Gilbert C. Fite. *Opponents of War: 1917–1918.* Madison: Univ. of Wisconsin Press, 1957.
Randall, Mercedes M. *Improper Bostonian: Emily Greene Balch, Nobel Peace Laureate.* New York: Twayne, 1964.
Seward, Keith. *The Legend of Henry Ford.* New York: Rinehart, 1948.

Chapter 8   The Majority Leader

Arnett, Alex Matthews. *Claude Kitchin and the Wilson War Policies.* 1937. Reprint. New York: Russell & Russell, 1971.
Clark, Champ. *My Quarter Century of American Politics.* 2 vols. New York: Harper & Brothers, 1920.
Kennedy, David M. *Over Here, The First World War and American Society.* New York: Oxford Univ. Press, 1980.
Link, Arthur. ed. *Papers of Woodrow Wilson.* 68 vols. Princeton: Princeton Univ. Press, 1967–1993.
Villard, Garrison. *Fighting Years, Memoirs of a Liberal Editor.* New York: Harcourt, Brace, 1939.

Articles

n.a. *The Outlook*, June 13, 161.
n.a. *Literary Digest*, February 10, 1917, 326; April 7, 1917.
Hendrick, Burton J. "The New Democratic Leader in Congress." *The World's Work*, December 1915, 136–140.
Vander Meer, Philip R. "Congressional Decision Making and World War I: A Case Study of Illinois Congressional Opponents." *Congressional Studies, A Journal of Congress* 8, no. 2, 59–79.

Chapter 9   The Dissenter

Beard, Charles A. and Mary A. Beard. *The Rise of American Civilization*, 2 vols. New York: Macmillan, 1939.
Fleischman, Harry. *Norman Thomas: A Biography, 1884–1968.* New York: W. W. Norton, 1969.
Johnpoll, Bernard K. *Pacifist's Progress: Norman Thomas and the Decline of American Socialism* [sic]. Chicago: Quadrangle Books, 1970.
Knock, Thomas J. *To End All Wars, Woodrow Wilson and the Quest for a New World Order.* New York: Oxford Univ. Press, 1992.

Link, Arthur S. and John Little, Kathleen Arnon, and Nancy Plum, eds. *"Brother Woodrow"*. Princeton: Princeton Univ. Press, 1993.
Seidler, Murray B. *Norman Thomas: Respectable Rebel*. Syracuse: Syracuse Univ. Press, 1967.
Swanberg, W. A. *Norman Thomas: The Last Idealist*. New York: Charles Scribner's Sons, 1976.
Thomas, Norman. *A Socialist's Faith*. 1951. Reprint. Port Washington: Kennikat Press, 1971.

Articles

Duram, James C. "In Defense of Conscience: Norman Thomas as an Exponent of Christian Pacifism During World War I." *Journal of Presbyterian History*, 52, no. 1 (1974) 19–32.
Patterson, David S. "Woodrow Wilson and the Mediation Movement, 1914–17." *The Historian*, 33, no. 4 (1971) 525–556.

Chapter 10 The Socialist Congressman

Draper, Theodore. *The Roots of American Communism*. New York: Viking Press, 1957.
Egbert, Donald Drew and Stow Persons. *Socialism and American Life*. Princeton: Princeton Univ. Press, 1952.
Marchand, C. Roland. *The American Peace Movement and Social Reform, 1898–1918*. Princeton: Princeton Univ. Press, 1972.
Kissin, S. F. *War and the Marxists: Socialist Theory and Practice in Capitalist Wars*. Boulder: Westview Press, 1988.
Livermore, Seward W. *Politics Is Adjourned: Woodrow Wilson and the War Congress, 1916–1918*. Middletown: Wesleyan Univ. Press, 1966.
Rogoff, Harry. *An East Side Epic: The Life of Meyer London*. New York: Vanguard Press, 1930.
Shannon, David. *The Socialist Party of America*. 1955. Reprint. Chicago: Quadrangle Publications, 1967.
Trachtenberg, Alexander. *The American Socialists and the War*. 1917. Reprint. Garland, 1973.
Walling, William English. ed. *The Socialists and the War*. New York: Henry Holt, 1915.
Weinstein, James. *The Decline of Socialism in America*. New York: Monthly Review Press, 1967.

Dissertation

Freiburger, William. "The Lone Socialist Vote: A Political Study of Meyer London." Ph.D. diss. Univ. of Cincinnati, 1980.

Chapter 11 The Progressive

Doan, Edward N. *The La Follettes and the Wisconsin Idea.* New York: Rinehart, 1947.
La Follette, Belle and Fola La Follette. *Robert M. La Follette.* 2 vols. New York: Macmillan, 1953.
Link, Arthur S. *Wilson, The Road to the White House.* Princeton: Princeton Univ. Press, 1947.
Campaigns for Progressivism and Peace, 1916–1917. Princeton: Princeton Univ. Press, 1964.
Millis, Walter. *Road to War, America 1914–1917.* Reprint. New York: Howard Fertig, 1970.
Smith, Page. *America Enters the World.* New York: McGraw-Hill, 1988.
Urofsky, Melvin I. and David W. Levy. eds. *Letters of Louis D. Brandeis.* 5 vols. Albany: State Univ. of New York Press, 1975.
Wilson, Woodrow. *Constitutional Government in the United States.* New York: Columbia Univ. Press, 1908.
Young, Donald. *Adventure in Politics: The Memoirs of Philip La Follette.* New York: Holt, Rinehart, & Winston, 1970.

Articles
Sutton, Walter A. "Bryan, La Follette, Norris: Three Mid-Western Politicians." *Journal of the West,* Oct. 1969, 613–629.
Trattner, Walter I. "Progressivism and World War I: A Reappraisal." *Mid-America* 44, no. 3 (1962) 131–139.

Conclusion

Randall, Mercedes M. *Improper Bostonian, Emily Greene Balch, Nobel Peace Laureate.* New York: Twayne Publishers, 1964.
Link, Arthur S. *Wilson, Campaigns for Progressivism and Peace, 1916–1917.* Princeton: Princeton Univ. Press, 1965.
Cannadine, David. *G. M. Trevelyan, A Life in History.* New York: 1993.

Index

Abeles, Henry, 36
Adams, John Quincy, 8, 175
Addams, Jane, 4, 69–79, 81–95, 103, 137, 148, 149, 180, 181
Addams, John, 70
Addams, Sarah Weber, 70
Adriatic, 144
Aisne River, 121
Alabama, CS, 121
Aldrich, Nelson, 158
Allies, 9, 12, 19, 20, 28, 33, 34, 37, 45, 46, 54, 58, 83, 85, 86, 88, 91, 94, 114, 120–122, 133, 161, 165, 173, 179, 180, 181
Alsace-Lorraine, 148
American (magazine), 70
American Federation of Churches, 135
American Federation of Labor, 137, 143
American Heritage (magazine), 8
American Peace Society, 71
American Press Resumé, 53
American Red Cross, 57
American Socialist, 156
American Truth Society, 55
American Union Against Militarism, 137, 138
American Women's League for Self-Defense, 169
Amerika, 36
Anglo-French Financial Commission, 161

Antioch College, 59
Archangel, 141
Argonne (battle), 94
Arizona, 39
Armed Ship Bill, 38–45, 124, 168, 169
Army, U.S., 114, 116, 150
Asquith, Herbert, 9, 33
Associated Press, 78, 176
Association of College Editors, 58
Atlantic campaign (battle), 59
Atlanta Journal, 44
Atlantic (magazine), 70
Audacious, HMS, 54
Australia, 155
Austria, 79, 84, 145, 147, 154
Austria-Hungary, 11, 181
Axson, Stockton, 130

Bagehot, Walter, 130
Baker, Ray Stannard, 78
Balch, Emily, 75, 76, 79, 80, 81, 83, 86, 87, 90, 91, 104, 179, 183
Balfour, Arthur, 32
Balkan Peninsula, 145
Balkan War, 81
Battle Cry of Freedom, 61
Beard, Charles, 139
Belgium, 12, 79, 83, 88, 133, 145
Belmont, Perry, 108
Benedict XV, Pope, 85
Benson, Allan, 151, 152, 155
Benton, Thomas Hart, 25

Berger, Victor, 146
Berlin, 41, 83, 84, 87
Bernstorff, Johann von, 33, 84, 166
Bethmann-Hollweg, Theobald von, 33, 84, 175
Bismarck, Otto von, 65
Boer War, 51
Boston, 42
Boston Club, 58
Brandeis, Alice, 176
Brandeis, Louis, 103, 159, 164
Brearly School, 131
Breckinridge, Sophonisba, 77
Briand, Aristide, 33
Brick Presbyterian Church, 131
British-American, 64
British Foreign Office, 53
British Isles, 37
British Naval Annual, 118
British Parliament, 154
British war zone, 45
Britten, Fred, 68
Brooklyn Times, 163
Brown, John, 60
Brown, William, 138
Brownlee, Katharine Margaret, 60
Bryan, Mary, 18
Bryan, William Jennings, 5–24, 29, 30, 36, 52, 71, 93, 105, 108, 112, 115, 116, 121, 122, 166, 179
Bryce, James (Lord), 10
Budapest, 85
Bureau of Census, 163
Burián, Count, 85
Burke, Edmund, 130
Burnside, Ambrose, 60, 61
Burroughs, John, 101, 105
Bush, George, 178
Butler, Nicholas Murray, 72, 95

California, 49
California, USS, 118
Cambon, Jules, 33
Campbell, Philip, 125

Campbell's Station (battle), 61
Canada, 42, 55, 79, 155
Cannon, Joseph, 39
Canton News-Democrat, 61
Caribbean, 182
Carnegie, Andrew, 130
Carnegie Endowment for International Peace, 135, 175
Carolina, USS, 41
Carpenter, Alice, 77
Carrick's Ford (battle), 60
Carter, Jimmy, 2
Catt, Carrie Chapman, 73, 74
Cedarville, Illinois, 70
Central America, 182
Central Europe, 182
Central Federated Union, 146
Central Labor Union of Toledo, 63
Central Powers, 28, 90, 165, 181
Chamberlain, Neville, 15
Chamber of Deputies, France, 154
Chattanoga News, 105
Chesterton, G. K., 53
Chicago, 69, 70, 74
Chicago Evening Post, 44
Chicago Tribune, 163
Chihuahua, 137
China, 145
Christ Church, New York City, 131
Christians, 145
Churchill, Winston, 54
City of Memphis, 45
Civil War, 2, 57, 59, 62, 67, 70, 98
Clapp, Moses, 42
Clark, Champ, 26, 31, 51, 62, 112, 119
Clay, Henry, 176
Cleveland Leader, 61
Cobden, Richard, 51
Coffin, Henry Sloane, 131
Cold Harbor (battle), 61
Collier's (magazine), 32
Columbia University, 95, 171
Committee of Privileges and Elections, U.S. Senate, 176

Index 211

Committee on Census, 163
Committee on Home Missions of the New York Presbytery, 138
Committee on Military Affairs, New York Assembly, 78
Commoner, The, 7
Confederates, 61
Congress, U.S., 43rd, 61; 64th, 43, 119, 146; 65th, 119
Congressional Directory, 119
Congressional Government, 29, 43
Constitution, U.S., war making powers, 40, 68
Constitutional Government in the United States, 162
Continental Army, 115
Cooper Union, 146, 147
Copenhagen, 86
Corwin, Tom, 43
Cossacks, 88
Couzens, James, 100
Cristiana, 87
Cuba, 50, 64, 149
Current Opinion (magazine), 32

Dane County (Wisconsin), 157
Daniels, Josephus, 23, 114
Dardanelles, 64, 116
Darrow, Clarence, 5, 103
Davies, Marion, 53, 54
d'Avignon, Belgian Minister of Foreign Affairs, 86
Davis, John W., 176
Debs, Eugene, 132, 139, 141, 144, 156
Declaration of London of 1909, 10, 172, 174
Delavigne, Theodore, 99
Delcassé, Théophile, 86
De Leon, Daniel, 144
Democratic National Convention, 1896, 5
Democrats, 116, 146, 164, 166
Deneen, Charles, 77
Denmark, 79, 145

de Scovines, Danish Minister of Foreign Affairs, 86
Devlin, Lord (Patrick), 17
Dewey, George, 117
Dodd, William, 123
Doty, Madeleine, 77
Duluth News-Tribune, 44
DuPont, 66, 122, 162

East Harlem Presbyterian Church, 131
East Prussia, 88
East Tennessee, 60
Ecole Normale, 26
Edison, Thomas, 105
Eliot, Charles, 48
Emergency Peace Federation, 93
Emperor of India, 46
Emperor of Japan, 46
Engdahl, J. Louis, 156
England, 41, 55, 67, 73, 83, 84, 86, 120, 133, 136, 145, 172, 174
Espionage Act of 1917, 139, 156
Europe, 66, 67, 73, 77, 88, 106, 107, 133, 147, 151

Falaba, 16, 17
Fall, Albert, 23
Farley, James A., 137
Farmer's Alliance, 26
Farmer's Equity, 167
Farmer's Union, 167
Fatherland, 36
Federal Reserve Act (1913), 160
Fellowship of Reconciliation, 136, 138
Finch, W. A., 128
First Amendment, 56, 58
Fiske, Rear Admiral, 117
Ford, Clara Bryant, 98, 104, 106
Ford, Henry, 63, 97–109, 180
Ford, Mary, 98
Ford Motor Company, 97
Ford, William, 98
Foreign Affairs Committee, U.S.H.R., 30, 31, 119, 120, 150

Foreign Relations Committee, U.S. Senate, 27, 28, 39, 47, 161
Forsyth Post of Grand Army of the Republic, 66, 68
Fort Sumter, 60
Forward, The, 144
Fosdick, Harry Emerson, 131
Fourteenth Ohio Infantry, 60
France, 11, 37, 79, 126, 133, 145
Frankfurter, Felix, 77
Franklin (battle), 61
Freeman's Journal and Catholic Register, The, 139
Frick, Henry Clay, 57, 122
Fuehr, Albert, 54

Garfield, James, 128
Garrison, Lindley M., 115
Garrison, William Lloyd, 73
Gary, Elbert, 114, 162
Gasparre, Cardinal, 85
Genomi, Rose, 82
George, Lloyd, 33
Gerard, James, 13, 41, 84
German-American, 14, 30, 36, 62, 67, 139, 164, 169
German-American Catholic Societies, 36
Germania Life Insurance Company, 36
German war zone, 42, 45, 174
Germany, 10, 12, 16, 17, 19, 20, 21, 31, 34, 37, 42, 44, 53, 56, 58, 64, 65, 79, 80, 83, 84, 86, 115, 118, 120, 121, 124, 126, 130, 133, 135–137, 145, 147, 151, 154, 155, 163, 165, 167, 172, 173
Germer, Adolph, 156
Gettysburg (battle), 98
Glenn, R. B., 128
Gore resolution, 30, 32
Governor's Island, 169
Grange (Wisconsin), 167
Grayson, Cary, 44

Great Britain, 9–11, 17, 20, 21, 29, 30, 42, 53, 66, 79, 80, 83, 115, 121, 126, 137, 139, 145, 173
Greenfield Township, Wayne County, Michigan, 98
Greenville Reflector (North Carolina), 127
Grenada, 1, 182
Grey, Sir Edward (later Viscount), 11, 16, 18, 32, 33, 81, 83, 87, 89–91, 93
Gronna, Asle J., 37, 38, 44, 47, 171
Guam, 68

Haakon VII (king of Norway), 87
Hague, The, 57, 72, 75, 76, 78, 82, 83, 86, 93, 100, 145, 148
Haiti, 9, 133
Hale, William Bayard, 53
Halifax, 42
Halifax County, (North Carolina), 112
Hamilton, Alexander, 130
Hamilton, Alice, 71, 76, 78–80, 82
Hannan, John J., 164, 165, 171
Harding, Warren, 129, 156
Harper's Ferry, 60
Harris, J. J., 55
Harrison, Benjamin, 41
Harvard Law School, 26
Harvard Medical School, 71
Harvard University, 49, 78
Hawaiian Islands, 68
Hearst, George, 49
Hearst, Phoebe, 49
Hearst, William Randolph, 49–58, 105, 146, 182
Heflin, J. Thomas, 127
Heinz, H. J., 103
Hempel, John Wilhelm, 106
Henry Street Settlement, 75
Hensley, Walter, 121
Hibben, John, 102, 105, 108
Hillquit, Morris, 138, 149
Hitchcock, Gilbert M., 28, 39, 161, 171
Hitler, Adolph, 15, 24

Index 213

Hoboken, New Jersey, 105
Hoffman, Swiss Foreign Minister, 85
Holland (The Netherlands), 145
Holston River, 60
Holy Alliance, 57
Hood, John B., 61
Hoover, Herbert, 94
House, Edward M., 7, 9, 11, 13, 15, 16, 18, 19, 22, 23, 25, 32–34, 37, 46, 55, 89–91, 93, 97, 103, 165, 183
House-Grey Memorandum, 33, 34
How The Other Half Lives, 76
Hughes, Charles Evans, 108, 121, 164
Hull House, 69–71, 77, 92
Hungary, 73, 79, 85

Iceland, 174
Idaho, USS, 118
Ideals of Peace, 72
Illinois, 67, 68, 126
Illinois (steamship), 45
Illinois College, 10
Imperial German Government, 54
Income tax bill of 1913, 160
Industrial Poisons in the United States, 77
International Committee of Women for Permanent Peace (later known as The Women's International League for Peace and Freedom), 82
International Congress of Women, 75, 79, 80, 89, 92, 100, 107
International Mercantile Marine, 41
International News Service, 55
International Workers of the World, 147
Invalid Pensions Committee, U.S.H.R., 62
Ipswich, England, 59
Iraq, 1, 182
Italy, 37, 79, 82, 145

J. P. Morgan & Company, 41, 161
Jagow, Gottlieb von, 84, 87, 89
Jahn, Gunnar, 95
James, Ollie M., 40
Jane's Fighting Ships, 118
Japan, 52, 57, 65, 68, 91, 144
Java, 68
Jefferson, Thomas, 8, 51, 105, 130, 139, 175, 182
Jefferson City, 26
Johnson, Andrew, 159
Joplin News-Herald, 44
Jordan, David Starr, 78, 103, 136
Joy, Henry, 108
Judiciary Committee, U.S. Senate, 95
Justice Department, 58, 139

Kaiser Barbarossa, (German pre-dreadnaught), 118
Kaiser Friedrich III (German pre-dreadnaught), 118
Kaiser Karl der Grosse (German pre-dreadnaught), 118
Kaiser Wilhelm II (German pre-dreadnaught), 118
Kaiser Wilhelm der Grosse (German pre-dreadnaught), 118
Kansas, 125
Kansas City Star, 44
Keller, Helen, 103
Kelley, Florence, 71, 87
Kentucky, 60
Kentucky State Senate, 45
King, Edward, 67, 126
Kern, John 30, 115
King of England, 46
King of Italy, 46
King of Montenegro, 46
King of Rumania, 46
King of Serbia, 46
Kipling, Rudyard, 53
Kirby, Rollin, 169
Kitchener, Horatio Herbert, 80
Kitchin, Claude, 111–128, 162, 179

Kitchin, Kate Mills, 112
Kitchin, William, 112
Knock, Thomas J., 92
Knoxville, 60
Knudsen, Prime Minister, Norway, 87
Koenig, Louis, 8
Koht, Halvan, 95
Kruse, William F., 156

Lackawanna Steel, 114
Ladies Home Journal, 70
Lafayette Hotel, Washington, D.C., 166
La Follette, Belle Case, 73, 157, 167, 171
La Follette, Philip, 157, 169
La Follette, Robert, 37, 38, 46, 47, 95, 157–180
La Follette, Robert Jr., 157, 168, 171
Lane, Franklin, 14, 52
Lane, Harry, 40, 47, 148, 171
Lansing, Robert, 11, 14, 22, 23, 29, 30, 40, 46, 91
Laurel Mountain (battle), 60
Lawrence, Andrew, 51
Lawrence, David, 18
League of Nations, 109, 140
League to Enforce Peace, 135, 163
Legal Tender - A Study in American Monetary History, 77
Le Havre, 86
Leipzig, 77
Lenin, Nicholas, 170
Lewis, J. Hamilton, 37
Lewis, Lucy Biddle, 77
Lexington (Kentucky) *Herald*, 43
Library of Congress, 160
Lincoln, Abraham, 60, 61, 70, 128
Lindsey, Ben, 105
Link, Arthur, 181
Lippmann, Walter, 69
Literary Digest, 47
Liverpool, England, 42
Livingston, William, 104

Lochner, Louis, 83, 100, 101, 103–106, 136
Lodge, Henry Cabot, 27–29, 38, 41, 140, 161, 168
London, Anna Rosenson, 143
London, Ephraim, 143
London, Meyer, 143–156, 179, 181
London, Rebecca Berson, 143
London Daily Telegraph, 53
London Times, 51, 53
Longstreet, James, 60
Los Angeles, 58
Louisville Courier, 23
Lucas County, (Ohio), 62
Lusitania, 18–20, 28, 29, 48, 52, 54, 83, 113, 120, 161
Lvov, Prince George, 170

Macmillan, Chrystal, 83, 86, 87
Madison, Wisconsin, 169
Madison (Wisconsin) *Democrat*, 171
Madison Square Garden, 146
Mahan, Alfred Thayer, 117
Maine, USS, 50
Mann, Horace, 59
Marion, Ohio, 129
Marion Star, 129
Marne (battle), 12, 133
Marquis, Samuel, 104, 107
Marshall, Thomas, 47
Marx, Karl, 130
Maryland, 67
Mason, William, 126
Massachusetts, 172
Massachusetts Institute of Technology, 171
Masses, The, 139
Maurer, James, 149
May, Ernest R., 24
McAdoo, William, 21, 122, 123
McAlpin Hotel, 100
McCay, Winsor, 56
McClellan, George, 61
McCormick, Medill, 159

Index

McCulloch, William, 125
McKinley, William, 128
McLemore Jeff:, 119, 120
McLemore resolution, 30–32, 66, 119, 120
McPherson, James, 61
Mecklenberg (German dreadnaught), 118
Men of the Home Defense League, 169
Meuse Valley, 33
Mexican War, 2, 43
Mexico, 39, 46, 52, 64, 133, 160, 162, 167
Michigan, 98, 108, 109
Michigan, USS, 118
Middle East, 182
Military Affairs Committee, U.S.H.R., 62, 92
Military Intelligence Bureau, 95
Mill, John Stuart, 51
Mills, Ogden, 114
Milton, George Fort, 105
Milwaukee Journal, 169
Minnesota Commission of Public Safety, 176
Mississippi, USS, 118
Missouri, 44, 67
Monroe, James, 66
Monroe (Wisconsin), 172
Monroe Doctrine, 66
Montana, 67
Morgan, J. P., 41, 99, 114, 122, 162
Mott, John, 95
Motta, President (Switzerland), 85
Munich, 77
Muslims, 145
My Life and Work, 109

Nash, Charles, 120
Nashville (battle), 61
Nassau (German dreadnaught), 118
National Democratic Club, 6
National Guard, 65, 113, 116, 162

National Peace Congress, 72
National Progressive Republican League, 159
National Security League, 57, 114, 147
Naval Affairs Committee, U.S.H.R., 117
Navy General Board, U.S., 117
Navy League, 108, 114
Navy, U.S., 114, 117–119, 153, 162
Navy Yearbook, 118
Nebraska, 43, 161
Netherlands, The, 75, 79, 83, 107
Neutral Conference for Continuous Mediation, 106
Nevada (Missouri), 25
Newburyport (Massachusetts), 76
New Deal, 141
New International, 155
New Jersey, 50
New Mexico, 39
New Republic, 14
New Willard Hotel, 73, 82
New World, 139
New York American, 53, 56, 57, 105
New York Assembly, 144
New York Call, 52, 151
New York City, 59, 75, 78, 135, 138, 143, 169
New Yorker *Staats-Zeitung*, 36
New York Evening Journal, 146
New York Herald Tribune, 156
New York Journal, 50, 53, 55
New York Peace Society, 145
New York Sun, 76
New York Times, 36, 37, 44, 46, 63, 80, 95, 100, 108, 116, 123, 127, 134, 141
New York Tribune, 58
New York World, 14, 23, 44, 50, 106, 156, 169
New Zealand, 42
Niagara Falls, 41
Nicaragua, 9
Nineteenth Amendment, 67, 72

Ninth Congressional District, New York, 145
Ninth Congressional District, Ohio, 62
Nobel Institute, 87
Nobel Peace Prize, 95
Noordam (steamship), 78
Norris, George W., 40, 43, 46, 47, 168, 171
North Carolina, 112, 121
Northcliffe, Lord, 53
Norway, 79, 87, 107
Noyes, Ellen Maria, 76

Ohio, 43, 125
Ohio Law College, 59
O'Leary, Jeremiah, 55
One hundred eleventh Ohio Infantry, 60, 62
O'Neill, Joseph Jefferson, 106
Oscar II (steamship), 101, 104, 105

Pacific Ocean, 65
Page, Walter Hines, 9, 11, 18, 23, 33, 83
Palmer, A. Mitchell, 141
Palmstierna, Ellen, 87
Panama, 1, 182
Paris, 77, 85
Paris *Temps*, 80
Parker, Alton B., 102
Pasteur Institute, 77
Payne-Aldrich Tariff Bill, 160
Peace and Bread, 94
Pearl Harbor, 62, 68
Pennsylvania State Federation of Labor, 149
Periodical Publishers Association, 159
Pethick-Laurence, Mrs. Emmeline, 73, 80
Philadelphia, 159, 172
Philadelphia North American, 44
Philippi (battle), 60

Philippine Insurrection, 2, 64
Philippine Islands, 65, 68, 149, 151, 153
Phillips, Wendell, 134
Phillips, William, 22
Poland, 143, 148
Powers, Johnny, 70
Poxen (German dreadnaught), 118
Presbyterian, 63
Presbyterian Spring Street Settlement House, 131
Primrose (Wisconsin), 157
Princeton, 10, 129, 130, 135, 179
Progressive Party, 72, 159, 176
Puck (magazine), 74
Puerto Rico, 149, 153
Pulitzer, Joseph, 50
Putnam, Mrs. William Lowell, 77

Quakers, 63, 70

Radcliffe, 76
Ramondt-Hirschmann, Madame, 83, 86, 87
Randall Mercedes, 76
Rankin, Jeannette, 67
Redfield, William C., 14
Reed, James, 45, 47
Reichstag, 154
Reilly, Thomas, 121
Republicans, 114, 121, 129, 158, 159, 165, 166
Republican national convention, 1916, 163
Republican State Central Committee (Wisconsin), 164
Resaca (battle), 61
Resolution, Federal Court of Appeals, 1781, 175
Rheinland (German dreadnaught), 118
Ridder, Victor F., 36
Riis, Jacob, 76
Rockefeller, John D., 147, 162

Index 217

Rockford Seminary, 70
Rocky Mount Evening Telegram, 127
Roe, Gilbert, 171
Rome, 85
Roosevelt, Franklin D., 23, 141
Roosevelt, Theodore, 6, 9, 18, 26–28, 58, 62, 63, 72, 77, 91, 102, 108, 113, 114, 117, 144, 159, 164, 168
Root, Elihu, 57, 72, 135, 161
Rublee, Mrs. George, 77
Rules Committee, U.S.H.R., 120
Rumania, 143
Russell, Bertrand, 86
Russia, 11, 46, 54, 71, 79, 83, 91, 125, 126, 143–145, 147, 170, 181
Russian Duma, 154
Russian Revolution, 46, 154

Saint George's Channel, 16
St. Louis, 26, 37, 155, 173
St. Louis Post-Dispatch, 44
Salandra, Prime Minister, Italy, 85
Salisbury, North Carolina, 127
Sanders, Leon, 151, 152
San Francisco Examiner, 50
Santiago harbor, 50
Sasanov, Russian Foreign Minister, 87
Sayre, John Nevin, 140
Scandinavians, 164, 173
Schiff, Jacob, 12
Schwab, Charles, 122, 162
Schwaben (German dreadnaught), 118
Schwimmer, Rosika, 73, 74, 81, 82, 83, 87, 91, 100, 106
Scotland, 59, 174
Scotland Neck, North Carolina, 112, 122
Seabury, Samuel, 58
Seamen's Bill, 160
Sedition Act of 1918, 139, 156
Serbia, 144
Seven Days (battle), 61
Shaw, George Bernard, 53, 74, 86

Sherman, John, 61
Sherwood, Aaron, 59
Sherwood, Isaac, 59–68, 120, 183
Sherwood, Maria Yeomans, 59
Sherwood, Thomas, 59
Shoreham Hotel, 18
Sixty-ninth Regiment Armory, New York, 170
Sixth Congressional District, Ohio, 61
Smith, Alden, 108
Social Democracy of America, 144
Social Democratic party (Germany), 145
Socialist, 129, 136, 141, 144–147, 149, 150, 151, 155, 156
Socialist Labor Party, 144
Society of Friends, 63
Somme (battle), 165
Sonino, Foreign Minister, Italy, 85
Sons of the Revolution, 66, 68
South Africa, 42
South Carolina, USS, 118
Spain, 173
Spalding, Roland, 103
Spanish-American War, 2, 8, 50, 64, 71, 149, 154
Spirit of 76, The, 139
Spring-Rice, Cecil, 16
Standard Oil Company, 75
Stanford University, 78
Stanton (Duchess County, N.Y.), 59
Starr, Ellen, 70, 85
State Grange of Ohio, 63
Steffens, Lincoln, 159
Steinmetz, Charles, 103
Stewart, Frances Violet, 131
Stimson, Henry, 114
Stockholm, 87, 106
Stone, Kimbrough, 26
Stone, Mabel, 26
Stone, Mildred, 26
Stone, Sarah Louise Winston, 26
Stone, William Joel, 25–47, 93, 115, 128, 162, 167, 171, 179

Story, Joseph, 31, 40, 181
Straus, Oscar, 12
Strawberry Plains (battle), 60
Stürgkh, von, Austrian Prime Minister, 84, 85
Sumner, Charles, 47, 76
Sunday, Billy, 102, 135
Sussex (steamship), 34, 37
Suwalki, 143
Swarthmore College, 77
Sweden, 79, 107, 145
Switzerland, 85, 107, 145, 173

Taft, William Howard, 6, 8, 26, 62, 72, 108, 117, 135, 144, 158
Tammany Hall, 152
Tarbell, Ida, 75
Teacher's College, Columbia University, 138
Teapot Dome, 23
Texas, 39
Third Nebraska Volunteer Regiment, 8
Thrasher, Leon, 16
Thomas, Arthur, 138
Thomas, Evan, 138
Thomas, Norman, 129–141, 178
Thomas, Ralph, 138
Tisza, Count, Hungarian Prime Minister, 85
Toledo Commercial, 61
Toledo Journal, 61
Tolstoy, Leo, 71
Toynbee Hall, London, 70
Treaty of Versailles, 15
Tucker, Irwin, St. John, 156
Tumulty, Joseph, 36, 44, 101
Turkey, 84, 154, 181

Underwood Bill, 160
Union Theological Seminary, 131
United Nations, 95
United States, 14, 17, 24, 41–43, 53, 55–57, 63–65, 68, 73, 79, 81, 83, 86, 88, 90, 91, 113–115, 119, 126, 134, 145–147, 152, 166, 170, 173–176
United States Children's Bureau, 71
United States Steel, 7
University of Berlin, 76
University of California, 49
University of Chicago, 76, 77
University of Michigan, 77
University of Missouri, 25
University of Wisconsin, 74, 77, 157

Vanderbilt, Cornelius, 57
van der Linden, Cort, 83
Vander Meer, Philip, 125
van Wulffton, Mevrouw, 82
Vardaman, James K., 47, 171
Vatican, The, 85
Vera Cruz, 9
Verdun (battle), 33
Vernon County (Missouri), 25
Versailles Conference, 141, 152
Vienna, 84
Viereck, George Sylvester, 36
Vietnam War, 1, 141
Vigilancia (steamship), 45
Villard, Fanny Garrison, 73
Villard, Oswald Garrison, 101, 123
Viviani, Premier, France, 86
Vladivostok, 141

Wake Forest College, 112
Wald, Lillian, 75, 91, 137
Waldorf-Astoria Hotel, 78
Wales, Julia Grace, 74, 77, 81, 83, 86, 89, 90, 101, 148, 179
Wallenberg, Swedish Foreign Minister, 87
Wall Street Journal, 122, 161
Wanamaker, John, 101
War Department, U.S., 116
War resolution, 46, 47, 66, 111, 124–127, 154, 155, 170–176
Ward's Island, 170
War of 1812, 2, 64

Index 219

Washington, D.C., 81, 145, 167
Washington, George, 40, 41, 180
Washington Post, 19
Watterson, Henry, 7, 23
Ways and Means Committee, U.S.H.R., 112, 115, 122
Webster, Daniel, 176
Wellesley College, 75, 94
Wells, H. G., 53, 130
Western Hemisphere, 66
Westfallen (German dreadnaught), 118
Wettin (German dreadnaught), 118
White, Edward D. 171
White, William Allen, 72
Whitman, Alden, 141
Williams, John, 175
Williams County, Ohio, 60
Williams County Gazette, 60
Wilson, Edith Bolling Galt, 22, 23, 29, 34, 87
Wilson, Ellen Axson, 7
Wilson (North Carolina) *Times,* 127
Wilson, Woodrow, 2–47, 50–57, 63–65, 68, 71–74, 76, 78, 81, 85–87, 89–93, 99–102, 105, 107–109, 112–117, 119–122, 124, 125, 129, 130, 132, 133, 136–141, 144, 149, 151–153, 155, 159–183
Wisconsin, 157–159, 164, 166, 169
Wittelsbach (German dreadnaught), 118
Woman's Lawyer Association, 77
Woman's Medical School, 77
Woman's Peace Party, 73–76, 78, 81, 92
Works, John D., 38
World Court of Conciliation and Arbitration, 72
World Tomorrow, The, 139
World War I, 4
World War II, 4
Wright, Chester, 51

Yale University, 72
YMCA, 129, 135
Young People's Socialist League, 156
Ypres (battle), 80

Zahle, Danish Prime Minister, 86
Zahringen (German dreadnaught), 118
Zoological Gardens, The Hague, 79